'The past is never dead. It's not even past.'
— William Faulkner, *Requiem for a Nun*, 1950

Published by Melbourne Books
Level 9, 100 Collins Street,
Melbourne, VIC 3000
Australia
www.melbournebooks.com.au
info@melbournebooks.com.au

National Library of Australia
Cataloguing-in-Publication entry
Creator: Steve Harris
Title: Solomon's Noose: The True Story of
Her Majesty's Hangman of Hobart
ISBN: 9781922129741 (paperback)
Notes: Includes bibliographical references.
Subjects: Blay, Solomon, 1810-1894.
Executions and executioners--Tasmania.
Tasmania--Social life and
customs--1803-1900.
Tasmania--Social conditions--1803-1900.
Tasmania--History--1803-1900.
Dewey Number: 364.6609946

SOLOMON'S NOOSE

The True Story of Her Majesty's
Hangman of Hobart

STEVE HARRIS

M
MELBOURNE BOOKS

AUTHOR'S NOTE

This book describes actual people and events. There are no fictional characters. To the maximum extent possible information is taken from contemporary records, such as newspapers, government archives, documents, memoirs and correspondence. I have eschewed footnotes and references so as not to disrupt the flow of a narrative story, and because the information is readily accessible and verifiable from the quoted sources and bibliography. Any direct thoughts of Solomon Blay are based on his own comments and correspondence, and suggested thoughts are interpretatively drawn from the memoirs and observations of other hangmen.

Dedicated to family past and present.

CONTENTS

INTRODUCTION

O f all the faraway places of the British Empire of the 19th century, nowhere was further than Van Diemen's Land. This was where the Empire banished its unwanted, as far away as possible, out of sight across the horizon to an isolated island at the very bottom of all the maps of the known world.

Seventy thousand men and women, many of whom had barely ventured outside their own village or town, were despatched across 20,000 kilometres of seas they had never seen to an island Bastille with walls of wilderness and wild southern oceans, its arrowhead shape seeming to point ominously towards even deeper unknowns. It was a land first discovered in honourable deeds of exploration, but its identity quickly became one of damnation as the mightiest empire's adopted hell on earth.

The home of a peaceful indigenous civilisation for thousands of years became a hellish prison colony for an advanced civilisation's human waste, those thousands who had challenged or transgressed an empire's authority and law in England, Ireland, Scotland, Africa, America, Canada, West Indies, Italy and even Iceland. Survival and wellbeing would depend on the personal choices of those in positions of, or subject to, authority. The former could arbitrarily decide whether to free or gaol, forgive or punish, save or hang; the latter could individually resolve whether to obey or challenge the law, endure or resist punishment, accept or escape.

There was often little differentiation between those clothed in bewigged finery and red army uniforms and those in rough convict cloth, whether their days were spent amid polished wood and chandeliers, or irons and stone cells. The line of authority did not always differentiate between those who were just, civil, fair, learned, honourable or progressive, and those who were despotic, cruel, illiterate, greedy, drunk, incorrigible and inhumane.

But all of their lives, one way or another, were defined and connected by a vice-regal stamp, judicial gavel, bureaucratic quill, whip, manacle, cell-key and gallows.

Remarkably, in the swirl of damnation and despair there were among the exiled, and those watching from afar or drawn to visit, seeds of ideas, theories and beliefs about law and order, punishment, democracy, religion, education, medicine, welfare, women's rights, race, sexuality, biology, and the environment. Designed as a dumping ground at the end of the earth, the penal island drew the fertile minds of Charles Darwin, Anthony Trollope, Charles Dickens, Mark Twain, William Booth and James Backhouse, as well as various kings, princes and bishops. These were people intellectually engaged, one way or another, in the contest between Paradise and Hell, the hand of God and Man, the balance of hope and hopelessness.

But for tens of thousands of banished individuals, theirs was a more personal, more life and death interest. The challenges of survival were common, but of all the 70,000 convicts sent to Van Diemen's Land, one man's choices made his story unique.

He was born Solomon Bleay, but became better known as Blay. He sought to overcome his impoverished childhood in England by stealing and making fake coin, and when he was caught he was banished to Van Diemen's Land. His chains would be unshackled, and he would eventually become a free man by law, but by his own hand he was condemned to a life without true freedom or peace.

Blay chose to overcome his imperilled life in Van Diemen's Land by making the fateful decision to deal in the currency of death. He chose to carry out the last sentence of the law as the final and ultimate hand of an empire's judgement — the man who would put a rope around the neck of men and women and hang them until they were dead.

Solomon Blay would be Her Majesty's public executioner.

He became the embodiment of an empire's iron fist in its most distant exile, the Empire's youngest hangman, its longest serving executioner. He became its most feared man — one who, some newspapers speculated, put to death more people than perhaps any other man in the world.

But his choice of escaping punishment by becoming a hangman was its own life sentence. Every time the bells tolled to foretell a hanging, they also tolled for Blay. Every time he dropped another soul into eternity, he retreated into his own cell of self, living with his own noose of personal demons and public damnation.

Blay was the last man to look into the eyes of more than 200 men and women, some as young as 16 and others as old as 76. He was the final witness to the struggle between law and order, good and evil, humankind and Mother Nature, hope and fear.

This is the story of Solomon Blay, a unique man in a unique time in a unique place: Van Diemen's Land.

1

AN OXFORD GRADUATE

The great town of Oxford offered rich lessons in life for young boys like Solomon Blay, with its trinity of university (the oldest in the English-speaking world), church (established in the 1500s) and castle (dating back to William the Conqueror).

But Solomon's lessons didn't come from educated men, in what had been a *universitas* since 1232 under the patronage of kings and popes. Its motto *dominus illuminatio mea*, the Lord is my light, meant nothing to him. The earnest prayers and hymns in Christ Church, where King Charles I lived during the English Civil War, weren't for his ears.

Blay wasn't of this Oxford's history and traditions. His was a world without patronage. The Lord's light had not shone on him or his family. The Oxford of fine robes and fine words about curriculum, church and commerce was not their world. Those of little learning and income spent their time in the shadowy fringes of university and church, trying to stay clothed, fed and warm, to survive as best they could.

Young Solomon was never going to enter the world of the learned, but his keen eyes readily read the play, the two sides of the Oxford coin: on one side, those who made rules, imposed judgments and punishment and reaped rewards, and on the other, those who lived by harsh laws, provided cheap labour, suffered impoverishment and severe punishment. This was brought home on a grassy mound just outside the walls of HM Oxford Prison, William the Conqueror's former castle tower. Here hundreds, sometimes thousands, of men and women, many carrying babies and with young children skylarking around their feet, could see the lottery of life played out for one of their own, one who had poached or robbed in order to survive, only to be caught and found guilty by men of learning and affluence, now condemned to hang by the neck until they were dead.

These were men like William James and Henry Pittaway, who were on the scaffold early on a summer Monday morning in 1824, when young Solomon was just eight years old. Hangings were intended to impart a lesson to others. For hundreds of families like the Blays, it made little impact on the reality of a constant life on the edge, and a hanging such as this was widely seen as a form of entertainment, such that the term 'gala day' would emerge from the word 'gallows day'. What might the condemned say at the last minute? Would they confess or reveal something to gossip about? Would they collapse sobbing or remain defiant? How well might they 'dance' the last dance at the end of a rope?

Pittaway was 25 years old, nominally a labourer but familiar with poaching as a means of supporting his wife and two children, with a third due any day. James was a 48-year-old labourer who married his first cousin and had six children, two of whom were described as 'cripples and idiots'. He had completed an apprenticeship as a slater and plasterer, but found stealing deer an easier way to feed his family.

They now stood beside each other on the gallows atop the tower at Oxford Prison, found guilty despite their consistent protests of innocence to charges of fatally wounding a gamekeeper to Lord Churchill in the Forest of Wychwood.

They were taken from their cell into the prison chapel a little before 7am, where the chaplain, who had given them their first sacrament the previous day, now did his best to prepare the men. At 9am, the boisterous crowd outside could finally see what they had been waiting for: two condemned men, flanked by prison officials and the chaplain, ascending the scaffold platform.

The men continued to protest their innocence, but the crowd, especially excitable boys like Solomon Blay, were more fascinated to see a real-life performance by a living 'Jack' Ketch. John Ketch was the infamous and feared English executioner of the 1600s under King Charles II, more infamous after he took four agonising blows with the axe to execute Lord William Russell, who had plotted to assassinate the king. Now his name had become symbolic of terror, synonymous with every hangman and with Satan, and parents invoked his name to cow their children into good behaviour. But children like Solomon were more likely to relate to the Ketch character in popular Punch and Judy skits: people of all ages enjoyed the skit where Ketch, who arrives to 'see that you [Punch] pay for your crimes ... you are to be hanged by the neck until you are dead, dead, dead!' is instead tricked into showing how to put one's head into the noose, and is thus hanged by his intended victim.

Pittaway and James reckoned they too would escape the noose, although James, who had been in prison twice for poaching, understood the odds when first arrested: 'My neck is but short now. Perhaps it may be longer at midsummer.' He and Pittaway maintained their innocence and refused to finger the other, thinking a court couldn't find them both guilty when only one gun was fired, and it was largely circumstantial evidence that pointed to either of them as the guilty party. But they thought wrong, and were both found guilty by a jury after just 15 minutes' consideration.

Having poached together, they now prayed together with the chaplain. The crowd finally hushed, and silence fell as the hangman put a rope around the necks of the two men. James grimly continued to make light of his situation: 'The rope is tight enough for me already but I suppose it will soon be tighter.' He supposed correctly, and before he knew it the drop fell and his world of Oxford faded to nothing.

The bodies hung for several hours, as was the custom, before, as further punishment, they were cut down to be dissected and anatomised by Oxford scholars and students, who callously fought over the latest 'prize' for their own 'education'.

For youngsters like Solomon Blay, this was one of the lessons of Oxford: if you are born on the wrong side of the street and break the law to survive, then know the odds, know that you're playing with your life, know that you could easily end up on the wrong end of the rope.

As an eight-year-old, Solomon had seen enough to sense that life could be hard and cheap, but he couldn't fully grasp the reality of life and death, or be aware his young life in Oxford would become so life-changing, or imagine the extent to which he would grasp the reality of a hangman's rope.

Eight years earlier, he had been named Solomon after his father. The name meant 'peace', and King Solomon was known for his wisdom and wealth. But neither father nor son was to know peace, wisdom or wealth. What they would share was a destiny of being banished forever from the shadow of the seat of knowledge to the unknown side of the known world.

Solomon Sr was born in 1777 in Iffley, the first village downstream from central Oxford on a site thought safe from the Thames' floods.

The village history went as far back as 941 AD in the chronicles of Abingdon Abbey, and Blay's family name might have originated from the French 'Bleye', 'Bleau' or 'Bloise', or perhaps from 'le Blay' — farmers who had been around Oxford as far back as the 1200s. But the Solomon of the late 18th century was of distinctly English impoverishment, one of many thousands whose expectations and horizons didn't extend beyond their next meal and their own village or town.

The most exciting thing to occur in Solomon Sr's life was when, as a seven-year-old, he gathered with hundreds of people at Christ Church meadow to see James Sadler become the first Englishman to make an ascent in a balloon. Sadler rose 3000 metres and landed 10 kilometres away, further than many villagers ventured in their lifetime.

While Iffley's prominent watermill had been producing malt, barley, corn and other cereals since the 12th century, as an unskilled labourer Solomon Sr had to find work where possible around the Oxfordshire villages, in the fields and stables of the gentry, churches and colleges.

In neighbouring St Ebbes village he met and married Mary, and then went to St Aldate's alongside the Thames, or the Isis, as it was called in its stretch through the heart of Oxford. Mary was still a teenager when she had her first child, also named Mary after Solomon's mother, and then another 11 children: Solomon, David, William, Frederick, George, Joseph, Sarah, Kezia (2), John and James.

Solomon Jr was born at St Aldate's on 20 January 1816 into a family caught up in England's rising tide of impoverished people. Long working hours, meagre incomes, social injustice, harsh and dirty living conditions and rising crime were the birth-pains of the Industrial Revolution, and the by-products of a rapidly rising population.

Solomon Sr could barely afford to support his expanding family, and young Solomon was just three when his father was charged with stealing a brass pot, and at nine his parents were forced to seek parish relief. Under the law, fathers had to return to their parish of birth to receive any support, so the family was sent back to Iffley with five shillings to buy bread.

The Industrial Revolution was reshaping England, but many towns and villages still lived in pre-industrial conditions. With the struggle to feed and clothe large families, crime became widespread. Most items were still made by hand, so even basic goods made of metal and cloth, such as kitchen utensils and clothing, were of value, easily stolen and sold for cash.

Poverty hurt children, too. Poor, orphaned or abandoned children as young as 10 turned to petty crime, living the life of the characters in Charles Dickens' *Oliver Twist*. Pickpocket character Jack Dawkins, the Artful Dodger, and his young gang stole handkerchiefs because a simple cotton handkerchief could be easily stolen and resold for sixpence, while a silk one, costing fashionable gentlemen as much as six or seven shillings to dust snuff from their clothing, might fetch enough to provide hot food for several days.

The rising crime rate — one Frenchman visiting London in the late 1700s noted that 'from sunset to dawn the environs of London became the patrimony of brigands for twenty miles around' — led to more repressive punishment, so much so that around the time Captain James Cook was seeking the great southern land, more than 200 crimes carried the death penalty.

Reformers like Sir Samuel Romilly complained that there was 'probably no other country in the world in which so many and so great a variety of human actions are punishable with the loss of life as in England'. When reformist MP William Meredith walked into a House of Parliament committee room, he heard a clerk working through a list of names and frequently uttering 'shall suffer death'. Asked by Meredith what the crimes were, a fellow MP replied: 'Why sir, we country gentlemen have suffered much by the deprivation of our turnips … we have at length determined to put an end to this practice and my good friend the Minister has been so obliging as to make it death.' Dickens, who had spent some of his own childhood in debtors' prison with his father, drew on the great crime of turnip thievery through his *Great Expectations* character Abel Magwitch — 'how dare you steal turnips to survive as a homeless, orphaned little boy' — and his ultimate deportation to Australia for life.

It was an easy temptation to steal handkerchiefs or turnips, but under the Bloody Code it was also an easy path to the gallows, or, as later became more likely, transportation. Crimes that could be severely punished included: any theft above the value of one shilling; multiple thefts under the value of one shilling; receiving stolen goods, jewels or plates; stealing lead, iron or copper; stealing from black lead mines; stealing from furnished lodgings; stealing from naval stores; setting fire to underwood; stealing letters; assault with the intent to rob; stealing fish from a pond or river; poaching with a 'blackened' face; stealing roots, trees or plants; cutting down a tree; stealing from a rabbit warren; bigamy; clandestine marriage; assault; cutting or burning clothes; counterfeiting coin; stealing a shroud from a grave; and carrying too many passengers on the Thames.

Solomon Sr knew any crime carried serious risk. After being fined five shillings for being 'drunk and riotous in the streets', now in his mid-fifties he was again before the court, in April 1833, this time for stealing a gun worth 40 shillings and a jacket worth two shillings. He was fortunate to be sentenced to just a month's imprisonment. Joseph Blay, possibly the older brother of Solomon Jr, was charged the same day with receiving, but was discharged.

The next year, Solomon Sr was caught stealing again. This time it was for stealing two coats, and was to have life-changing consequences for Solomon the father and the son.

In Oxford court on Monday 13 October 1834, Mrs Mary Gee, who lived near the turnpike on old Abingdon Road, testified she had cleaned a great coat belonging to her son Charles and hung it on a bush in the garden to dry in the afternoon sun, only to notice it missing within an hour. A near neighbour, Eliza Hall, saw Solomon Sr carrying a bundle and informed police constable George Bossom. The constable found Solomon with the coat, vowing he had bought it from a ragman, and took him into custody.

Solomon was sentenced to be transported for seven years.

But this wasn't the end of it. Later the same day, he was back before the bench for stealing another coat from John Gee. It may have been part of the robbery on the same day at the same Gee household, but he was again found guilty and sentenced to another seven years.

Two coats, perhaps one for himself as the cold months approached and another to sell, cost him 14 years transportation. At the end of this sentence he would be 71, if he survived that long.

While his father had been stealing coats, the younger Solomon Blay, just 16, was stealing food. His first offence was for stealing onions. The magistrate sought to persuade yet another young man before him to avoid a path of crime:

> Young man, you have been found guilty of a crime, for which in years gone by your life might have been forfeited; and even now, there are many who are passing their lives in hopeless servitude, for smaller offences. It is, I hope, your first departure you have made from the path of honesty, and in the trust that your escape may make you in future a worthier member of society, I pass upon you the nominal punishment of four months' imprisonment.

But a 'nominal' four months in gaol, and the magistrate's counsel, was not enough to keep young Solomon on the 'path of honesty'. Aged 17 and with the help of John Dupe, 18, he was seen stealing three or four bushels of potatoes from a field in 1833. Soon after, Blay was seen in the market at St Aldate's where 'he was with his mother who sells cherries', and was followed home by James Gardner, the

City Marshall, who 'found there the sack and potatoes' and took him into custody.

The jury found both teenagers guilty. Dupe was sentenced to seven years transport, Blay 'the younger' was given 12 months gaol with hard labour. And just to reinforce the message the magistrate ordered Blay to 'be in solitary for three fortnights at equal intervals during the time'.

In gaol Blay became more solitary, not just in an isolation cell; he hadn't seen his father for some time, and would never see him again. His father was being moved to the prison hulk *Ganymede*, a former French frigate captured by the English and now a prison hulk on the Thames at Woolwich, east of Greenwich, to wait with 219 other convicts for transport on the *Westmoreland* to Sydney Town.

Young Blay's father was banished and gone, his mother was nearing 50 with 11 surviving children, including four younger than he, eking out a living selling cherries at St Aldate's, and he had a criminal past and no viable future.

His world was one with a history of poverty, sweat and stench around the Thames. His birthplace of St Aldate's was centred on Jewry Street, its name reflecting its primary identity since medieval times. Here, close to 100 people of Jewish heritage operated pawn shops, money-lending and university student accommodation, even though Jewish people themselves were prohibited from attending Oxford until they became baptised Christians. Blay scrapped his way around nearby Preacher Lane, Brewer Street, Fisher Row, Cattle Street, and even Gropecunt Lane.

The physical heart of St Aldate's was Christ Church, with its imposing 17th century tower designed by Christopher Wren, and its bell, Great Tom. Opposite Christ Church was a sweet shop, frequented by Alice Liddell, daughter of the Dean of Christ Church College and inspiration for *Alice's Adventures in Wonderland* and *Through the Looking-Glass and What Alice Found There*, written in 1871 by Oxford Professor Charles Dodgson, better known as Lewis Carroll.

But young Solomon Blay's life was worlds away from the sweet shops, churches and colleges in the 'city of dreaming spires', as poet Matthew Arnold described Oxford. His life was not of learning or dreaming, but survival. He earned a few pennies a day when he could on the Oxford Canal link to the Thames, a national highway between London and the midlands for ferrying coal, stone, textiles, paper, pottery and food products. On its banks were brewing, leather, fishing and cleaning industries that fed off and into the river, where thousands of young men lacking formal education sought whatever work they could as boatmen, bargemen, fishermen, watermen, factory hands and laundrymen, lucky if they could make a shilling a day.

Blay's choices were limited. He had no skills, work on the water was giving way to the iron horse after the newly opened Liverpool and Manchester railways fired the Railway Age and, on the land, manual labour in weaving houses and factories was giving way to machines. His parents couldn't be the answer. He was on his own and had to find his own means of surviving. But he also knew work was getting harder and harder to find, and while he could steal the necessities of food and clothing, this was high-risk and had landed his father, friends and himself in prison.

What was he to do? This question surely filled Solomon Blay's mind while he was in HM Oxford Prison, in the heart of the centre of learning, as he served his 12-month sentence for stealing potatoes. Here he sat in on a master class on crime in 19th-century Britain, with pickpockets, burglars, thieves, highway robbers, muggers and fraudsters giving him much to think about. And with six weeks in solitary confinement he had plenty of time to think.

Just as Dickens' Artful Dodger graduated from silk handkerchiefs to silverware (a stolen silver snuff box led to his presumed transportation to a penal colony in Australia), so Blay left prison in

March 1836 with a resolve that he had no choice but to take the risk of becoming more artful himself.

As winter slowly gave up its grip, he teamed up with two young friends, Henry Roberts and William Quartermaine, to find a more 'artful' way of sustaining themselves, something more rewarding than stealing onions and potatoes.

They resolved that a better way to make money was to literally make money.

They weren't alone. Coining or counterfeiting was on the rise, so much so that by the mid-1800s about 20 percent of all trials in England were to do with forgery and coining. At the start of the American Civil War in 1861, it was estimated that half the banknotes in circulation there were forgeries.

And it wasn't money without risk. Until just a few years before, counterfeiting was a crime of 'treason' carrying the death penalty — between 1797 and 1829 about 600 people were hanged in Britain for note forgeries alone — and was seen as so serious it once required something more than a swift execution. Counterfeiters in medieval England were hung, drawn and quartered, while out of deference to female nudity being an unacceptable indignity, a woman was not drawn and quartered but 'burned with fire till she was dead'. Counterfeiters in Russia had molten lead poured down their throats, Germans were burned alive in oil.

Counterfeiting began the day after coins were first circulated, and the basic techniques hadn't changed much since forgeries of the earliest Greek coins were made by covering a base metal core with a layer of more precious metal. Blay and his two friends knew the most sophisticated technique of 'multiplying the coin' was to make a mould of a genuine shilling, and fill it with a diluted mix of a base metal, such as copper, and silver which could be clipped or melted from coins of smaller denomination, such as a threepence or sixpence.

The threesome headed 34 kilometres north-west along the

Oxford Canal to the market town of Banbury, not inspired by the nursery rhyme to 'ride a cock-horse to Banbury Cross, to see a fine lady ride on a white horse', but to rent a small flat to see about riding their luck. To create their fake coins they first bought some gypsum, commonly known as plaster of Paris after the discovery of a large gypsum deposit at Montmartre. Next day, they bought more plaster of Paris and a pewter spoon. Pewter was a malleable dull silvery metal alloy composed mostly of tin, but also copper, lead and sometimes silver. With their plaster, pewter, a fire and some basic tools, the young men were ready to make money.

Unfortunately, the purchase of plaster of Paris on consecutive days by roughly dressed strangers aroused some local suspicion, reinforced when they sought a silver-coloured spoon. Tipped off, Banbury's newly installed Police Superintendent, William Thompson, followed the men and surprised them at their 'obscure house in Calthorpe Lane'. He saw Blay quickly seize something from the fireplace and throw a plaster of Paris mould onto the floor, and discovered part of a pewter spoon and metal corresponding to the pewter in an iron spoon on the hob in the fireplace. He searched Blay and found what looked like six shillings.

For these newly cast shillings, the three were now cast in serious trouble.

Superintendent Thompson took the 'gang of coiners' to be examined by Reverend William Lloyd, who praised Thompson 'for his vigilance on this occasion'. On 17 March 1836, Lloyd signed the warrant stating Blay had in his possession 'six pieces of false counterfeit silver coin' and also 'a certain die or mould'.

The young men were committed to Oxford Gaol to await trial. Four months later, on 15 July 1836 in the Michaelmas (autumn) session of Oxford Assizes, Blay was found guilty of making base coin, or counterfeiting. The court wasn't impressed by Blay's apparent inability to stay on the path of honesty; he already had sentences of four months for stealing onions and 12 months for stealing potatoes.

The court asked about the whereabouts of his father. 'Don't know where … believe he was transported about three years ago,' Blay answered.

In fact, his father had been transported just a year before. It didn't give the court any confidence that this young man's life could be turned around with more imprisonment or parental discipline. Blay, 20, was sentenced to 14 years transport, as was Roberts, 22. Quartermaine, 23, was found guilty of aiding and abetting, and received two years gaol.

Blay was again in Oxford prison, this time awaiting transportation for 14 years and in the company of syphilis. The prison surgeon, Mr Wood, issued a bill for 13 quarts (15 litres) of sarsaparilla, at 5s 6d a quart, for 'treatment of Bleay' for his sexually transmitted disease, known as the Great Pox, which left open sores, especially on the genitals. Sarsaparilla was commonly mixed with potassium iodide, a new therapy that reduced doses of traditional mercury, whose toxic effects, including blackened teeth, outweighed its benefits.

Perhaps due to the discomfort of imprisonment and syphilis, or the inadequacies of a diet of oatmeal gruel, bread and potatoes, the gaol report for Blay described him as 'bad', although this was a badge easily earned. After four months and copious amounts of sarsaparilla, on 26 July 1836 he was loaded into a prison wagon for a 150-kilometre trek south to a prison hulk in Portsmouth Harbour.

Here, he joined prisoners also brought overland from all points of England, Scotland, Ireland, or shipped in from North and South America to a floating prison, to await his banishment. Queen Elizabeth had introduced exile so that 'dangerous rogues … may lawfully … be banished out of the realm, and all dominions thereof, and to such parts beyond the seas', and be permanently branded with an 'R' for rogue. The threat of exile was as great as a walk to the gallows.

Now, following the American Revolution and rising criminality at home, Britain was using transportation on an industrial scale to deter criminality. The 'dregs drained', as one writer described the approach.

Tens of thousands of its people, like Solomon Blay, were being sent for seven years, 10 years, 14 years, or life. First they were put onto a prison hulk, one of a fleet of 50 ships deemed insufficiently seaworthy but able to be used as floating prisons, to help Britain cope with its overflowing gaols. Each housed as many as 650 convicts. Blay's floating prison *Leviathan* was more than 40 years old and a veteran of the Battle of Trafalgar, its name associated with sea monsters.

The British Parliament initially intended to use hulks like *Leviathan* as a temporary measure after the American Revolution ended the export of 60,000 prisoners across the Atlantic. The first parliamentary authorisation, in 1776, was limited to two years, providing that

> for the more severe and effectual punishment of atrocious and daring offenders, be it further enacted, That, from and after the First Day of July ... where any Male Person ... shall be lawfully convicted of Grand Larceny, or any other Crime, except Petty Larceny, for which he shall be liable by Law to be transported to any Parts beyond the Seas, it shall and may be lawful for the Court ... to order and adjudge that such Person ... shall be punished by being kept on Board Ships or Vessels properly accommodated for the Security, Employment, and Health of the Persons to be confined therein, and by being employed in Hard Labour in the raising Sand, Soil, and Gravel from, and cleansing, the River Thames, or any other River Navigable for Ships of Burthen.

But rising crime fuelled an appetite to get the criminal lower classes out of overcrowded gaols and out of sight, so the 'temporary' authorisations continued for 80 years. The hulks took on more and more prisoners, despite being condemned as stinking cesspools full of vermin and disease. Between 1776 and 1795, nearly 2000 hulk prisoners died, and when transportation to Australia started with the First Fleet in 1788, following Captain Cook's recommendation of Botany Bay as an ideal site, many convicts took typhoid and cholera with them.

Blay was on the *Leviathan* for four months, off the ship only for 'Hard Labour in the raising Sand, Soil, and Gravel'. Prisoner James Hardy Vaux, who contributed Australia's first dictionary and autobiography, described hulk conditions:

> There were confined in this floating dungeon nearly 600 men, most of them double ironed; and the reader may conceive the horrible effects arising from the continual rattling of chains, the filth and vermin naturally produced by such a crowd of miserable inhabitants, the oaths and execrations constantly heard amongst them …
>
> On arriving on board, we were all immediately stripped and washed in two large tubs of water, then, after putting on each a suit of coarse slop clothing, we were ironed and sent below.

Another prisoner wrote:

> We were stripped to the skin and scrubbed with a hard scrubbing brush, something like a stiff birch broom, and plenty of soft soap, while the hair was clipped from our ears as close as scissors would go.
>
> Our next experience was being marched off to the blacksmith who riveted our ankles, rings of iron connected by eight links to a ring in the centre, to which was fastened an up-and-down strap or cord reaching to the waist belt.

Blay's chained sleep was disturbed around three each morning when the cooks started boiling breakfast for the hundreds of prisoners. It was usually ox-cheek, boiled or made into soup, or occasionally a sloppy porridge, or a piece of often mouldy bread or biscuit.

At 5.30am he was woken again as all *Leviathan* ship hands were noisily called up. Fifteen minutes later, he and the other prisoners were mustered and served breakfast. At 6.45am the prisoners stowed away their hammocks before going onshore to their assigned labour, while the three decks were washed.

For the first two weeks Blay had to walk the quarter deck every morning with his cap off, so officers and guards could become familiar with every new prisoners' features and gait in case of any attempted disguise to effect an escape. He was also searched and mustered each morning to make sure nothing was being concealed or stolen.

At noon he returned for lunch and was locked up until 1.20pm, before resuming hard labour until 5.45pm, followed by basic reading and writing classes. He had the option of prayer in the chapel at 7.30pm, but after a final muster and search he was locked up for the night in cramped, foul berths.

Saturday nights was wash night, when every prisoner 'washes his person thoroughly before he is allowed to go below', to be confirmed on Sundays when everyone was inspected to ensure they were clean and their clothing in proper repair, after which the chaplain performed divine service.

The Superintendent of the convict hulks, Mr John Capper, made sure everything was recorded in detail, the first stage of what would become a convict's lifetime of surveillance. Perhaps Blay decided there was no point displaying anger or insolence; his behaviour on the hulk was simply noted as 'good'.

Now, after four long months being 'good' in a bad place, Blay was about to be tranferred from the *Leviathan* to another ship, one that would take him on a journey across seas he had never seen, to a place of exile with the ominous-sounding name of Van Diemen's Land.

2

VOYAGE TO EXILE

The morning of Sunday 13 November 1836 broke uneasily over Portsmouth Harbour. Under thick grey clouds, everyone could sense that winds out in the Atlantic were mustering their angry energy into what would soon become a gale. Lowering his eyes from the growing threat overhead, Blay's gaze met those of soldiers. Holding their muskets, they unloaded *Leviathan*'s convicts into long boats to be rowed across the harbour to HM Convict Ship *Sarah*.

Like most convict ships, *Sarah*, a 488-ton brig originally built in London, had been converted from commercial to criminal trade, but conversion couldn't address their narrow construction. Such boats weren't suited for long voyages, prone to rolling wildly on heavy seas. But at least *Sarah* was relatively new. It had been caulked up, fumigated and fitted out at Deptford, the British Navy's depot on the

Thames. Then, loaded with provisions and medical stores, it sailed the 200 nautical miles to Portsmouth to pick up its human cargo.

Sarah marked the halfway point of the 327 convict ships to make the journey to Van Diemen's Land between the first, *Indefatigable* in 1812, and the last, *St Vincent* in 1853. On the surface its cargo of more than 250 was typical: all-male (as two-thirds of convict ship lists were), and all ages, from the youngest, like Blay, to the oldest at 50. Most were single but nearly 90 of the men were married, 60 of whom had families of up to eight children, and 155 children would never again see their banished father.

But *Sarah* wasn't just another ship on another convict voyage. It had some unique passengers, and those in charge had more than the usual concerns.

James McTernan was surgeon-superintendent, responsible for delivering the convicts to Van Diemen's Land. He was a medical officer with considerable experience, including as surgeon on the *Dragon* during important naval operations in the Chesapeake and sea battles with the French. And he had taken convicts across the world six times, his first and only trip to Van Diemen's Land on *Sir Charles Forbes* in 1827, and to New South Wales: *Ocean* in 1823, *Asia* in 1828, *Eliza* in 1829, *Lady Harewood* in 1831 and *John Barry* in 1836.

Dr McTernan was familiar with the likes of Solomon Blay: the counterfeiters, muggers, pickpockets, thieves and vagabonds of Dickensian England, the poor criminal underbelly being eradicated out of sight and providing the collateral benefit of cheap labour for new defensive posts in Australia. Dr McTernan calculated the average sentence was nine years, with nearly 40 percent being sent for life.

But they weren't all from England and Scotland. As the winds whipped up Portsmouth Harbour, so Dr McTernan could see that political storms had been blowing across the British Empire's colonial outposts.

The spirit of revolution and freedom was beginning to rattle the Empire's chained fist of convictism and slavery, and he noted the names of more than 50 men from places like Ireland, Nova Scotia, Quebec, Ontario, Newfoundland, Gibraltar, Montserrat, Barbados, Trinidad, Grenada and Jamaica. One way or another, they had got on the wrong side of an empire and been convicted, rightly or wrongly, of theft and rape, but also political activism, disobedience, insolence and desertion.

Twenty-two had names like 'Blue Boy' and 'Hamlet'. Listed as servants or grooms, they were former slaves denied freedom at the end of the West Indies slave trade. As the prospect of abolition neared, nervous local authorities feared bloody uprisings and insurrection behind every coloured face and every misdemeanour, and between 1831 and 1848 some 140 black felons were despatched under Royal orders to England's floating prisons, and then onto convict ships like *Sarah* to Australia.

Dr McTernan was concerned enough about the potentially volatile mix of blacks and whites, all resentful of authority and punishment, despairing of homes and families they would never see again, fearful of what lay waiting for them at journey's end, and unhappy about a diet absent of sex and liquor, but not poor food and weevils. He also knew the ship was in the hands of sailors who themselves were often not much beyond felon status, more than capable of violence and rebellion.

And now, as *Sarah* sat waiting for the wild seas to abate, Dr McTernan had more cause to worry as four new convicts were brought aboard, and they came with an official warning.

James Porter, Charles Lyon, William Cheshire and William Shiers had already been to Van Diemen's Land as convicts. They were among a group of 10 convicts who in 1834 seized the *Frederick* at the penal settlement of Sarah Island inside the 'Hell's Gates' of Macquarie Harbour on the west coast, and after six weeks made it to the southern Chilean port of Valdivia.

In Valdivia, where they stayed two years, their story was known to many, including Charles Darwin, who was in port and had not long before been in Hobarton/Hobart Town in early 1836 on his *Beagle* voyage and heard of the piracy. Most of the convict pirates escaped on other ships to America and Jamaica, some after marrying Chilean girls. Local authorities initially tolerated the remaining four, but they were eventually handed over to a British naval ship for shipment to London, and re-shipment to Van Diemen's Land.

Colonial Secretary Lord Glenelg made sure Dr McTernan was aware of the risk the pirates posed, possibly equating the convicts to Alexander Pearce, the first escapee from Sarah Island to reach settlements on the east coast, but only after killing his fellow escapees and eating their flesh in order to survive.

Dr McTernan wrote in his journal that the *Frederick* capture came under 'under circumstances of great atrocity'. In reality, the pirates had left their overseers unharmed on a beach with half the ship's supplies, but more remarkably they succeeded where many had failed: there had been more than 150 escape attempts from Sarah Island, with more than half the escapees dying in the mountain wilderness and the rest recaptured.

Dr McTernan knew the Diemen Four faced certain capital punishment if he was to deliver them to Hobart Town, and knew the risk of another piracy plot was real, as mutiny attempts occurred on convict ships almost every year.

He didn't want to make the mistake of the captain and surgeon of the *Chapman* in 1817, when the anxiety and nervousness of their first voyage had led to severe repression and rising tension. Men were kept in irons for the whole journey, shackled on a long cable chain and denied fresh air and food. At one point the captain ordered his men to fire down the hatchways below for at least 30 minutes, dozens of men were flogged, had pickling brine rubbed into their wounds, were chained naked and keel hauled (dragged underwater below the ship's keel). By the time the ship arrived, 14 convicts had been shot dead.

On his own first convict voyage in 1823, Dr McTernan was only five days out of Portsmouth when convict informers on the *Ocean* named five others as ringleaders of a mutiny plan. He drew on his experience in Navy discipline and quickly ordered the five to be flogged, and other suspects kept in irons. But despite his experience, it seemed ominous that pirates who seized a vessel at Sarah Island were now aboard *Sarah*, and he feared they would have little trouble attracting support and help from other convicts or crewmen.

Dr McTernan's experience and personal habits informed his approach: maintain tight discipline but keep men with as much fresh air, food and daily exercise as was viable. Despite the best of intentions, however, even before leaving Portsmouth there was a queue for his sickbed, above the convict quarters and below the main deck, and he was quickly working '18 of my 24 hours … superintending cleanliness, visitation, education and cheering the desponding'.

While *Sarah* fared better than many with scurvy, typhus and cholera, it had its share of seasickness, dysentery and diarrhoea. But Dr McTernan's major concern was that weeks of foul weather led to a severe outbreak of *erysipelas*, a streptococcal bacteria that thrived in the drenched bedding and ate into the skin, causing a raw, red skin infection, a painful burning sensation, fevers, hallucinations, muscle spasms and seizures. Known as St Anthony's fire since medieval times, the outbreak hit 68 convicts, or more than a quarter, and would cause the death of seven on the voyage.

Dr McTernan had to be vigilant of 254 men, especially the Diemen Four, as well as deal with a major bacterial outbreak. He was both relieved and anxious when on 24 November, *Sarah* was finally fully loaded and sailed.

But within two days, the gale force winds raging in from the Atlantic forced Captain Whiteside to return, minus an anchor, to a crammed Portsmouth Harbour. The harbour was somewhat sheltered by a five-kilometre sandbank called the Spit, but still for the next month 'the elements formed league against us', Dr

McTernan wrote, and convicts and soldiers unused to the sea were drenched and ill. But Captain Whiteside, on his first convict ship, wasn't going to risk another premature departure and have to return with a damaged or unseaworthy vessel.

A month of waiting in the cold and wet put everyone under strain. Dr McTernan was personally frustrated he could not undertake his routine of early morning exercise, as the decks were simply too wet, often white with salt. And he was concerned about the emotions below deck, knowing the misery and delay would only aggravate 'the usual predisposing mental condition of creatures about to be expatriated'.

During the enforced wait, Solomon Blay and the other convicts learned of the Diemen Four pirates and their remarkable escape across the oceans of the world. Many eyes watched their every movement.

One of the pirates, James Porter, stood out. He was blind in the left eye and referred to by fellow convicts as 'a man with seven sides' (a right side, left side, foreside, back side, outside, inside and blind side). With several scars on his face and two bare-fisted boxers tattooed on his left arm, he was a self-confident, brash schemer, unafraid to let anything, or anyone, get in the way of a self-serving story or plot.

Porter volunteered to help Dr McTernan's efforts to curb the *erysipelas* outbreak by scraping and swabbing men's sores with lime, herbs, hot vinegar, sulphur, quinine and camphor. Despite Porter later writing that he received 'great praise from the Doctors and Officers on board', Dr McTernan wrote that while he enlisted anyone, even Porter, to assist him, the conduct of the Diemen Four 'justified the necessity of great caution'. He was convinced the Four had no interest in helpfully and happily voyaging to Van Diemen's Land to be greeted by a noose around their necks. Having been pirates once, he thought it 'natural they would [have] a similar design ... and bring many to their views'.

Many on *Sarah* suspected the same, and Blay was among those watching and wondering about conversations the pirates could be seen having with other convicts. One was with John Perez de Castanos, who had been caught stealing gold seals from jewellers in London's West End. He had a pocketbook of business cards from numerous silversmiths and pawnbroker tickets for jewellery, and in his rented room in Leicester Square were numerous silver and gold pencil cases, spectacles and watch guards, and 17 gold seals hidden in the lining of a large Spanish cloak.

Castanos, of Spanish origin, and his Italian accomplice Piedro Caligani were referred to in *The Times* of 6 October 1836 as 'dashing Foreign thieves', and the sergeant at the bar described Castanos as the most 'finished swindler' he had ever encountered. They were sentenced to transportation for life, reduced to 14 years on appeal.

Others talking to the pirates included John, Abel and Francis Blades. The young brothers were being transported after being caught poaching pheasant in Lincolnshire and attacking the gamekeepers in a bid to escape. Their village of Stamford was sympathetic, signing a petition to the King seeking mitigation, and the local jury was reluctant to support the capital charge of assault. But the magistrate demanded the jury comply and the brothers were given life transportation.

The poachers, the dashing foreign thieves, and some Canadian patriots were receptive to the Diemen Four's plotting of a mutiny, with the promise of some inside assistance from one of Captain Whiteside's men, a French-born sailor called Wilson. They decided New Year's Eve offered their best prospect, and waited for the ship to resume its journey.

Finally, on the night of 22 December 1836, after a month's delay in a fierce English winter, HM Convict Ship *Sarah*, with 254 convicts on board, once more drew anchor and heaved out from Portsmouth. In the Channel and into the Atlantic, heavy seas washed over the ship and through the hatchways, washing some convicts out of their bunks, and drenching prisoners and crew for a week. The ship rolled wildly, and below deck the crammed convicts, some at sea for the first time, were violently ill. As the icy water washed over and through the ship, flooded bilges spread a sickening slime across the decks.

Blay had been a 'boatman' on the Thames, but this was beyond comprehension. Raging storms and gales pushed and pitched the ship every which way, and many times convicts thought their demise at sea would precede whatever fate lay in store at Van Diemen's Land.

Rough as the crew were, Blay could only admire these sailors as they responded to the sound of a whistle and orders to 'shorten', 'reef topsails', 'bout ship' or 'shake out the reefs'. In raging squalls, they would 'mount the shrouds and trip up the ratlines to perform their often hazardous duty', as Joseph Syme recalled on a journey earlier the same year.

The bare-masted *Sarah* groaned in protest against nature's violent assault, and foundering often seemed inevitable, but the storms eventually abated and *Sarah's* convicts were cheered by the reassuring order of 'steerage-way', while the sailors joyously consumed their 'allowance' of grog.

The storms gone, the way now seemed clear for the New Year's Eve mutiny. Just a day before, however, it was thwarted when a number of convicts, seeking to curry favour for themselves, alerted Dr McTernan and Captain Whiteside.

The informers included Henry Pointon who, with his brother and fellow pigeon-stealer Frederick, might have been anxious to protect £14 they had in safe keeping with Dr McTernan. Early on 31 December, more convicts revealed the plot in a note to Dr McTernan, and the French sailor on the inside, Wilson, had to tell the conspirators their scheme had been discovered.

Dr McTernan and Captain Whiteside weren't entirely sure who had been ringleaders or who to believe, but they were sure that decisive and symbolic punishment was needed. At 8am they stopped the ship and called for all hands on deck, where the captain read out 60 names provided by various informers.

Convicts might have been assumed to share some kindred spirit, but it was invariably a case of every man for himself. James Hardy Vaux, a convict transported to Australia no less than three times, described the attitude among convicts: 'Many of my old … acquaintances were all eager to offer me their friendship and services, that is, with a view to rob me of what little I had; for in this place there is no other motive or subject for ingenuity. All former friendships are dissolved, and a man will rob his best benefactor, or even messmate, of an article worth one halfpenny.'

Even the Diemen Four, despite their shared escape to Chile, had long been suspicious of, and antagonistic to, each other. While Porter protested his innocence, Lyon and Cheshire confessed, and claimed the mutiny plan had been for Porter and Shires to lead a dozen Canadian convicts to the quarterdeck and seize control and 'put to death [all] with the exception of those who fought for their Liberty'.

Protests of innocence were largely ignored, and for three hours the decks turned red. Blay and the other convicts winced with each lash of the 'cat', a line of rope knots, and the cries of the victims. Some had 48 lashes before being carried below deck, where their feet were chained and hands tied behind them while they bled and seethed for several weeks, before being allowed back on deck for some warmth and washing.

Dr McTernan was convinced this 'timely infliction of punishment in the active members of the plot' had saved the day, but the continuing havoc of the bacterial infection was mitigating, as 'its effects were awe-inspiring, even on the boldest mutineers'.

It had been almost impossible to prevent the spread of St Anthony's fire. Dr McTernan wrote of waves washing through the lower decks, soaking all the bedding, which had to be brought up on deck to dry as and when weather permitted or, as he wrote, 'ordered on deck to incur the hazard, I might say the certainty, of receiving additional [but a fresh supply] of wet'.

Dr McTernan had few opportunities to get the convicts on deck for some fresh air and exercise, but approaching the equatorial heat he was afforded more opportunity. This still remained risky, as one French Canadian found when a half-ton cask broke loose on deck and smashed his leg, causing tetanus and the voyage's first death. And while heat allowed the quarters below deck to slowly lose the worst of the foul-smelling air and slime, the pitch used for caulking leaks in the timber also melted and dripped onto those below.

Captain Whiteside was relieved *Sarah* did not lose much time at 'The Doldrums', an area near the equator where north and south currents converged and ships often became becalmed for weeks. Having been initially turned back at Portsmouth and forced to wait a month before the worst of the weather cleared, he was now making good progress and not in the mood for any delays. He rejected stopping at Rio de Janeiro for some respite and fresh supplies, a common practice despite the Admiralty's disapproval because too many crewmen used the opportunity to trade goods for private benefit.

Fearful of another attempted mutiny, the captain kept his eye firmly on charts showing the most direct line south-east toward Cape Town, before he needed to head east to Hobart Town.

In a letter written on board to the ship's owners, the captain explained:

The ship sails remarkable well, which you will easily imagine by the quickness of our passage so far. We have certainly been a good deal favoured by the winds since we sailed, and which I hope we shall continue to be, so that we may get over this unpleasant trip as soon as possible.

For it has not only been rendered unpleasant but rather dangerous from a most formidable conspiracy which we have discovered among the convicts, aided by one of our sailors, named Wilson, a Frenchman by birth.

They had got everything regularly planned, and the attempt was to have been made on the 31st of December, and if they had succeeded, they were to have murdered us all, made the best of their way to South America, which if they reached, they intended to scuttle the ship and land in the boats.

It appears that the principal instigators were four escaped convicts, a Spaniard named Castanos, Wilson the sailor, and two or three other desperate characters.

Beyond the mooted mutiny and whipping of any convict deemed to be insolent, any distraction or 'entertainment' was welcome. Convicts gaped at the longest wingspan of any bird, as the albatross used 11 feet (3.4 metres) of wing to ride the currents and glide for hours, alert to any rubbish thrown overboard.

Some sailors amused themselves by affixing a red cloth to a hook on a line, which the albatross readily gulped at. But any convict looking for the albatross to provide fresh food was sorely disappointed, Joseph Syme noting that 'their flesh is almost uneatable, for even sailors refuse to cook or use them, however desirous of fresh meat or substitute for salt beef or pork'.

Sailors tried harder to spear one of the dolphins playing around the Sarah's bows, but they remained elusive. The greatest delight was 'the appearance of a whale … the immediate cause of the greatest surprise and exaltation … its appearance is announced with shouts and exclamations calculated … to alarm those who are not aware of the cause, and who had not … witnessed the first appearance of this monster of the deep'.

In the calmer seas beyond the equator, storm petrels, known by the sailors as Mother Carey's chickens because they seemed to walk on water while feeding, were abundant, while cape hens and gulls indicated a shoreline wasn't far away. Blay was amazed some mornings to see flying fish lying on deck, attracted overnight by a ship's lamp.

Sailors and convicts spent time puncturing their hands, arms and chests and marking them with gunpowder, creating tattoo-like images of hearts, ships and the names of loved ones, but also unknowingly making it easier to be identified at the penal destination.

Rounding the Cape, *Sarah* was sped along by the Roaring Forties, the trade winds found between 40 and 50 degrees latitude, pushing seas uninterrupted for more than 10,000 kilometres. When Captain Whiteside reached the Great Southern Ocean, just before hitting Bass Strait he shifted course a few degrees southward, away from the route taken by ships heading to Port Jackson, Sydney. His course was toward Port Davey, an inlet on the south-west coast of Van Diemen's Land. It had been identified on maps since navigator Marion du Fresne recorded it in 1772 as part of the French incursion onto *Terre de Diemen*, the first Europeans to invade its isolated silence since Dutch seafarer Abel Tasman some 130 years before.

Finally, on Tuesday 28 March 1837, almost four months since first boarding *Sarah*, and 96 days after leaving Portsmouth and sailing through violent storms, illness and death, Solomon Blay and the other surviving 253 convicts heard the cry: 'Land! Land ahoy! Land ahoy!'

Through the salty spray, he could gradually make out the emerging south-west coastline of this most southern land, a land born from a violent Mother Nature smashing the former super-continent of Gondwana, cleaving it from Antarctica, New Zealand and Patagonia, and shoving it away from the equator.

This land of unforgiving basalt and granite had existed for 1270 million years. Blay couldn't know this, but on this small ship in massive oceans he must have sensed the enormity of coming to a land that was a world away from the only world he had known. He had been wrenched from the cradle of the Empire and was about to be dumped 20,000 kilometres away into a penal grave.

Captain Whiteside and Dr McTernan were among the few on board to have some sense of how old and how new this land was. They knew it wasn't so long ago that the theories of Pythagoras, Plato and Aristotle about a great southern land having to exist to 'balance' the known lands of the northern hemisphere had been proven. Their English charts had only recently substituted *Terra Australis* for what was once *Terra Incognita* (land unknown) and *Australis Incognita* (the unknown land of the south), what the French knew as *La Grande Isle de Java* (the great island of Java), the Spanish as *La Australia del Espirity Santo* (the southern land of the Holy Spirit), and others, including the Chinese in 1602 as *Magellanica* (the land of Magellan). They knew this was a destination which, since its first sighting by Abel Tasman in 1642, was the ultimate symbol of isolation, variously described as 'beyond the seas' and 'the end of the world'.

It was the stuff of imagination. Irish writer and clergyman Jonathan Swift in 1728 placed his imaginary land of Lilliput, inhabited by pygmies and giants, to 'the north-west of Van Diemen's Land', this being the place of greatest imaginable isolation with unimaginable inhabitants, in *Travels into Several Remote Nations of the World. In Four Parts. By Lemuel Gulliver, First a Surgeon, and then a Captain of Several Ships*, better known as *Gulliver's Travels*.

Now Solomon Blay was heading to this greatest imaginable isolation of Van Diemen's Land, or Vandemonia, and the spectre of unimaginable inhabitants known as Vandemonians forming what previous arrivals described as an 'infernal country of torments'.

He could have no grasp of how an accidentally discovered small island on the other side of the earth came to assume a strategic import for great nations of Europe as Empirical force and revolution reshaped the world, and set in motion the forces which now led him toward its shore. He only understood his own history: he had been caught up in his country's desire to drive out its unwanted and criminal underclass, banished to be a slave in exile for 14 years, to help resource a remote island Bastille.

Blay might have thought Van Diemen's Land was named because it was full of demons, either those in its wilderness or among the Empire's damned. He had no reason to know the island had been named Van Diemenslaandt, in honour of Anthoonij van Diemen, a former merchant who became bankrupt before heading the Dutch East India Company and becoming Dutch colonial governor in Batavia, now Jakarta. In August 1642, van Diemen sent Abel Tasman in search of the Great South Land. Tasman missed the south coast of their 'Nieuw Holland' continent, but after sighting land on the west coast of what he didn't realise was an island, he named it in honour of his patron.

He planted a tricolour Dutch flag on what is now Tasman Peninsula so that 'those who shall come after us may become aware that we have been here, and have taken possession of the said land as our lawful property', all the time watched silently from a distance by descendants of ancient Aboriginal occupiers. They couldn't know what was to come, and Tasman was unaware this Van Diemen's Land would be his high point: he eventually died in disgrace after drunkenly trying to hang two disobedient sailors.

Blay could see this new land of cliffs and blue gum forest coming into focus, but he couldn't be sure how to feel about it, torn between relief of a journey ended, but also anxiety about the destination, the southern-most point of the known world, this final exclamation point under the axis of 'balance' of *Terra Australis*.

Steering *Sarah* eastward under the tip of the arrow-headed island, Captain Whiteside knew if he followed the arrow's direction he would find the route from the Indian Ocean, taken for the first time just six years previously by English sealer John Biscoe, to the ice of Antarctica 2100 kilometres away, not much further than Portsmouth to Rome.

Instead, the captain approached a channel named after Antoine Bruni d'Entrecasteaux, a French naval officer who explored much of the coast of Australia and spent 50 days on Van Diemen's Land in two visits from 1792 to 1793 while searching for the La Perouse expedition. He discovered that the western end of Storm Bay was in fact the mouth of a river he named Rivière du Nord, and with the help of Felix de la Haie, later head gardener to Empress Josephine, left in the soil some vegetables for future expeditions, as well as the first buried European.

Captain Whiteside was momentarily tempted to steer his ship through the narrow channel separating mainland Van Diemen's Land and Bruny Island, but as keen as he was to end the journey he knew the risks. Two years previously, the captain of the *George*, having endured a difficult journey with a fire and scurvy outbreak, opted to make a run through the channel only to smash into rocks at night. Panic ensued, and guards fired guns to keep male convicts below deck while women and children were helped. In total, 133 lives, of whom 128 were convicts, were lost in one of Australia's worst maritime disasters.

Captain Whiteside resisted the shortcut temptation, and steered around the island toward Hobart Town and the mouth of a river wider than anything Blay had seen. The great Thames artery was less than 80 metres wide at Oxford and calm, but this Derwent River was four kilometres across, with white caps and whales.

On Wednesday 29 March 1837, Captain Whiteside rested his compass and sextant on his charts for the last time, with some satisfaction. *Sarah* had reached 42 degrees south, 147 degrees east, the cove of Hobart Town, in 97 days, beating by two days a record set 16 years prior.

The captain ordered the hoisting of a white flag with a red cross, proclaiming it to be a friendly British ship on His Majesty's service, and a red flag indicating a cargo of male convicts. The flag messages were relayed to Battery Point and the township well before Captain Whiteside made his final call to 'reef' the sails, and the ship's bell tolled its arrival.

The cable chain rattled out of the hawse-hole and the anchor dropped nearly 20 metres to the bottom of Sullivan's Cove. Soon after, shouts of 'Rouse out! Turn out! Rouse out! Turn out! Huzzah for the shore!' rang out as 245 surviving convicts mustered on deck.

Nine had not survived the voyage: one due to tetanus, one from pneumonia, and seven from the St Anthony's fire outbreak.

Solomon Blay had survived. He now caught the eye of the only person on board he knew, Henry Roberts, his Oxford counterfeiting accomplice. They silently acknowledged relief the voyage was over, but their eyes could not hide their anxiety about facing other uncharted waters.

3

ARRIVAL AT THE END
OF THE WORLD

Solomon Blay turned 21 on the voyage, although he probably wasn't aware of it. His 'coming of age' came midway between the end points of the British Empire, his birthplace and his designated hell of a New World.

As *Sarah* finally anchored on 29 March 1837 in the cove of Hobart Town, Blay couldn't know what to think. How had it come to this? What does being a convict mean? Does this mean being in chains for the next 14 years? Can anyone survive this? What sort of demons and cruelty lie ahead? Is England never to be seen again? What is one's fate?

Blay's senses swirled. Relief to still be alive at the end of a tough journey on an ocean prison. Loss that all that was familiar to him from his life in Oxford, however hard and troubled it had been for him and his family, was now gone forever. Distrust of almost everyone around him, ready to do or say anything or sacrifice anyone for personal gain. Anxiety about what convictism would be like, and what sort of cruelty he might face amid chains, irons, bars and lashings. Foreboding about this prison whose only walls were a wilderness of fierce and strange tigers, devils, snakes, natives, even cannibals, all surrounded by wild oceans of whales, sharks and treachery.

Blay didn't see himself as anything unique among the latest boatload of convicts. Like so many, he had rolled the dice in his impoverished life when there seemed no other choice, taking to crime in order to survive, and had been caught and banished. Blay certainly didn't think that before too long he would need to roll the dice again, and this time it would be a choice that would stand him as unique among all the 70,000 convicts sent to Van Diemen's Land.

Right now he was taking in his new surrounds as *Sarah* waited for row boats to come and take the convicts onto Hunter Island, a small island linked by causeway to the township. The new arrivals sensed an anticipatory mood as people gathered dockside. Some hoped to sight an old friend or relative, or get news of family on the other side of the world. Some came in search of a convict assignee as a cheap maid or labourer, others to barter with sailors for food, alcohol or sex.

But beyond this was a broader anticipation, as the colony gave an extended welcome to His Majesty's new governor, Arctic explorer John Franklin, and a welcome good riddance to George Arthur. Arthur had been an autocratic ruler of Van Diemen's Land, with an eye to please his British masters and God, and his legacy was the world that Blay was about to enter.

While only 39 when he arrived, Arthur had already accumulated a long CV since joining the British Army in 1804. Admitting 'promotion … being my idol', he rose through the ranks in service in Calabria, Sicily, Egypt, Jersey and Jamaica before landing the role of superintendent and commandant of Honduras, a position he held for eight years before arriving at the hardship post of Van Diemen's Land with the Godly conviction that some 'enlightened rigor' was needed to eradicate the colony's shambolic ways. He believed the heart of every man was 'desperately wicked' unless the Gospel tidings had their way and that 'you cannot make straight that which God hath made crooked'. Convicts in particular were in a form of 'mental delirium', and this 'infirmity' could be removed only through 'firm and determined' supervision.

Arthur was not one of His Majesty's governors who arrived drunk, like Thomas 'Mad Tom' Davey, or left his wife and six children behind in London while taking up with the wife of another officer, like William Sorrell. This new ruler arrived in the rum society of Van Diemen's Land a teetotaller, bringing a prim wife, family Bible, organ and a firm resolve as God's policeman. Arthur had an administrator's passion for reform and detail, and a tyrant's appreciation of information, punishment and cronyism. His modus operandi was an elaborate system of convictism — a pathway of seven convict classes through which a convict could move, from chain gangs to domestic service to a ticket-of-leave, pardon and eventual freedom — overseen by a despised chief police magistrate, Matthew Forster, who was blind in one eye and had greed in the other. He was married to Arthur's niece, and reported to Colonial Secretary John Montagu, also married to one of Arthur's nieces, and their frontline troops were personally appointed police magistrates, senior constables and flagellators.

The Arthurite view was that the island colony was primarily a gaol for convicts, and there was no room for debate about justice, fairness, rehabilitation or the concerns of early settlers. And his front-liners could interpret the rules to suit: one magistrate who was challenged over masters breaching the rules on the use of convicts said, 'The regulations are all damned nonsense, only written for people in England to read.'

Arthur had a deep hatred of criticism, especially from those favouring civil liberties, and disdain of freedom of the press. The *Colonial Times*, founded by Andrew Bent, a burglar-convict who became a pioneering printer-editor, said Arthur 'hated truth' and 'had he dared every type in the colony would be melted into bullets to destroy those who were opposed to his tyrannical rule'.

Frederick Innes, a Scottish journalist who arrived in Hobart Town the same year as Blay to join the *Hobart Town Courier*, described the police office as an 'established tyranny, which penetrates a man's politics, presumes to investigate his character, exposes him to spies, has him enrolled as a favourite or a marked man'.

With a magistrate and chief constable in charge of seven police zones, and a constable for every 90 people, Blay was entering one of the most intensely policed societies in the world. But the Colonial Office was still concerned that too many convicts were conveying the message that convict life in Van Diemen's Land was better than impoverishment in Britain, and transportation wasn't to be dreaded, so Arthur set out to ensure that on his watch transportation was seen as intended: severe punishment and deterrence.

The chain gangs, previously focused on public works, became a means of punishment with convicts, in Arthur's words, 'kept rigidly at the spade and pick-axe and wheel-barrow … from morning till night, although the immediate toil of the convicts be the only beneficial result of their labour'.

Arthur believed every man was afforded opportunity 'in a great measure [of] retrieving his character and becoming useful in society, while the resolutely and irrecoverably depraved are doomed to live apart from it for the remainder of their lives', but also later acknowledged that assigned convicts were no different to the slaves of North America or the West Indies: 'Deprived of his liberty, exposed to all the caprices of the family in whose service he may happen to be assigned, subject to the most summary laws, [the convict was] in no way different to that of a slave.'

Arthur contended his slavery didn't have to be a life sentence, but it was not quite what Arthur Phillip had in mind in his first decree in 1788 as governor of 'a plantation', New South Wales, that 'there can be no slavery in a free land, and hence no slaves'. Arthur also maintained that a convict could not be flogged by his master and had the right to complain, but masters easily found compliant magistrates willing to order a flogging for any real or perceived 'crime', and complaints could lead to arbitrary extensions of punishment. The reality was underscored just a few years later when the *London Quarterly Review* said Captain Alexander Maconochie, private secretary of Arthur's successor, complained that 'physical coercion [flogging etc.] is resorted to upon every little breach of regulation etc; in short, he says in so many words that the settlers who have convicts assigned to them are slave-holders and the assignees slaves'.

Arthur also had little time for the colony's remaining 1000 Aboriginal people, who had watched with rising dismay and anger as white footprints stamped over their ancient land, and the consequences when they retaliated by spearing and taking livestock, and when they attacked some settlers. The governor initially endeavoured to mollify the original inhabitants, when in 1824 William Tibbs, the first man to appear before the country's first Supreme Court, was charged with fatally shooting 'a black man'. But he was convicted of manslaughter, not murder, and transported for only three years, while the following year Arthur hanged 'Musquito' and 'Black Jack', and the next year 'Jack' and 'Dick' to set 'an example'. Despite official proclamations of equality in law, the Aboriginal people weren't to see Arthur set an example by hanging a white man for killing one of their own.

Conflict escalated in what became known as the 'Black War', during which Arthur imposed martial law, ordering the capture of leaders and declaring hostile natives 'open enemies' and banning 'a most treacherous race' from entering settled districts. Convinced that any 'reconciliation cannot be reasonably entertained', in October 1830 Arthur left his wife in childbirth to oversee 5000 men endeavouring to drive Aboriginal people into the Tasman Peninsula. But his 'Black Line' caught just two of them at a cost of about £15,000 each.

The next year, as a last resort, he sent George Robinson, so-called protector of the Aboriginal people, on a mission to persuade the 'hostile tribes' to 'settle' in certain areas, such as Bruny Island, and to learn the English way of life, work and become Christians. The scheme failed and the atrocities didn't cease, Aboriginal people's numbers continuing to decline and offenders, when captured, were readily removed and sent to Gun Carriage Island, a small 800-hectare island in eastern Bass Strait between Flinders and Cape Barren Islands, and later to Flinders Island. Here they were given a catechist and left.

While endeavouring to please his Lords in London and his Lord above, Arthur was not shy about pursuing his own self-interest, becoming one of the biggest and wealthiest landowners in the colony and one of the most usurious lenders. His accumulated assets caused additional resentment, but Arthur resisted any criticism of tyranny and patronage, opposed civil liberties and trial by jury, and prosecuted critical newspaper editors.

But as the settler population grew in number, so did its confidence and influence in London amid emerging debates about transportation and convictism. After several petitions seeking an end to convictism were ignored, Thomas Horne, an anti-Arthurite lawyer and later a judge, warned the Home Government in 1834 it risked 'a dissatisfied and turbulent people, ready to use their power, and assert their rights, if necessary, by force of arms'.

London couldn't risk such a local uprising and was concerned with the rising costs of a police state, so resolved it was time to move Arthur on. His recall after 12 years was a bitter blow, but he was mollified by his London masters rewarding him with a knighthood, concluding his term 'placed on a yet firmer basis his claims to the approbation of the King and to the gratitude of His Majesty's subjects'.

But as pleased as Arthur was with the King's approbation, so were His Majesty's subjects in Van Diemen's Land with his departure. Amid the usual 'wanted' posters for bushrangers, the colony now saw posters proclaiming Arthur as unwanted: 'Is Ordered home! Tomorrow ought to be a day of general Thanksgiving! Deliverance from an iron hand and acts of abomination. Rejoice! For the Day of Retribution has Arrived!' The *Colonial Times* said 'the obnoxious Colonel Arthur' was dutifully saluted off the Hobart Town dock in late October 1836 by government officials, but 'the governor was about as desirous of being seen as a fox when the hounds are skirting his cover'.

The delight was heightened with the news that polar explorer John Franklin, who had been unable to raise enough finance for a third attempt to find the north passage in the Arctic, would now be moving close to the Antarctic as the new governor. Franklin had left Portsmouth just four months before Blay, bringing to Van Diemen's Land the hope of a more fair-minded administration. Weeks of celebratory banquets and balls marked Franklin's tour of the colony, 34 years after he had first visited as a companion of Matthew Flinders. In Launceston, he was escorted by 300 horsemen and 70 carriages, and locals warmed to his candor in contrast to the coldness of his predecessor.

Franklin got the message that while Vandemonians wanted security against bushrangers, re-offending convicts and settlers breaking the law, many felt the police powers were abusive and subject to corruption. In the larger settlements of Hobart Town, and especially Launceston, he heard people beginning to argue for individual liberty, freedom of the press and a representative parliament.

The cheer for a vice-regal exit and arrival converged on the day of Blay's arrival, a red-letter day in the 'uncivilised' colony with the opening of the country's first theatre, the Royal, featuring five-act comedy *Speed the Plough*, a staple of British Theatre since it opened 40 years previously at London's Covent Garden.

But Solomon Blay wasn't in a position to know of vice-regal or artistic performances any more than he was aware of the island's natural or geo-political history. He was only concerned with what was to become of him. It was now almost a year since he was first caught and sentenced in Oxford, a year of being shackled and shipped from prison in Oxford to a harrowing three months on a convict hulk, a month on *Sarah* in Portsmouth harbour and then three months of treacherous seas, sickness, death and floggings.

And Blay hadn't merely been witness to floggings. A note in the ship's journal said he had been whipped for 'insolence', accompanied by a notation of being 'as bad as can be'. The charge of convict insolence was very much in the eye of the beholder, and could be as trivial as cursing or verbally challenging authority.

An insolent attitude might have been expected given his life had been one of constant struggle. Blay had seen a deficit of justice and fairness, and a surplus of greed, venality and abuse on both sides of the law, and had the mental and physical scars to show for it. The lesson of life seemed to be one of having to be prepared to do anything to satisfy desire, or just survive.

He was at least fortunate in one respect. *Sarah*'s voyage of 97 days set a record — among the fastest in the 40 years of convict trade. Some ships took as long as 188 days, and some ships didn't make it at all: *George 111*, which grounded on rock near Bruny Island with the loss of 134 lives; *Neva*, which smashed into a reef near King Island with only 15 survivors out of the 240 Irish convicts on board, including 150 women and 33 children; and *Cataraqui*, wrecked off King Island with only nine survivors among 400 people, including 73 children, in Australia's worst civil maritime disaster.

Dr James McTernan was well pleased to have arrived safely, not least because he would receive a half-guinea fee for each of the 245 prisoners who made it to Hobart Town.

On the other side of the convict coin, Blay's arrival had him thinking less about what he had endured to date and more about facing this next and ultimate test of his ability to survive. Then his attention went to raised voices: one of the precious mail bags from London had fallen into the river. Blay jumped into the water and grabbed the bag before it sank.

Perhaps he reacted instinctively as he might have done with cargo on the Oxford canal, or perhaps he opportunistically saw a chance to gain favour. Either way, his 'good conduct' was recorded and the new lieutenant governor, keen to signal a more compassionate vice-regal attitude and relieved his mail was saved, was later 'pleased to grant a remission of two years of the regulated time for this'.

For Blay this was an unexpected dividend in the lottery of an empire's law and order, one which very much depended on the mood of the day of a magistrate, judge or governor. Convicts understood that in this lottery only those in the King's house would hold the winning hand, even if they could often see little to differentiate between law-breakers and law-makers, captured in convict verses such as:

> The law locks up the man or woman
> Who steals the goose from the common
> But leaves the greater villain loose
> Who steals the common from the goose.

And:

> He bade the judge good morning
> And he told him to beware,
> That he'd never rob a needy man
> Or one who acted square,
> But a judge who'd rob a mother
> Of her one and only joy
> Sure, he must be a worse outlaw than
> The wild colonial boy.

As for many a colonial boy, life would continue to be a lottery for Blay. Behind him, London was starting to engage in long debates that would eventually end penal transportation. But it would be another 18 years before the last convict ship arrived in Van Diemen's Land, and Blay would spend the rest of his life in exile, in more ways than one.

4

DESTINATION
HOBART TOWN

Ninety-seven days and an eternity from Oxford, Solomon Blay cast his eyes about the cove. Around *Sarah* he could see a fleet of merchant ships, fishing boats, whalers, punts and barges, each with its own posse of seagulls chasing any rubbish thrown overboard.

On the eastern side he could see a small island where scarlet-clad soldiers with muskets flanked colonial officials waiting to process the latest convict arrivals. Black swans and ducks glided beside a muddy convict-built causeway linking the island to Hobart Town, and in the distance, beyond the Derwent, heavily treed hills led to the Meehan Range.

On the western shore, former wetlands were being transformed into Salamanca Place, named after the Duke of Wellington's victory in 1812 in the Spanish province of Salamanca. A line of sandstone warehouses was emerging to store whale oil, wool, fruit and grain, and imported goods from around the world, interspersed with numerous stables and inns. One warehouse was owned by Askin Morrison, an enterprising merchant who shipped a cargo of tea from China, reputedly making a profit of £10,000, another by Richard Willis, who imported the niceties of pianos, wines and silverware.

Blay could see the terrain rise steeply behind Salamanca. Up a pathway of huge sandstone blocks cut and carried by convicts was Battery Point, with its gun battery, part of the Royal Navy's defences against the French. There was also a flag signal station, windmill, and St George's Anglican church tower under construction. Beyond Battery Point, gullies rose to lap the foot of a 1271-metre sentinel of cold, hard dolerite pushed up from the seabed in the Jurassic Period 170 million years ago. The local people had long called it Kunanyi, then it was christened Table Mountain by Matthew Flinders because of a similarity to Cape Town's mountain. It was now Mount Wellington, in honour of the Duke of Wellington's defeat of Napoleon.

Hobart Town was already remarkably different to how it appeared 30 years before, when it first became part of the British Empire's strategy against any French ambitions in the South Pacific. The original waterside area of Wapping, a low-lying flood-prone area polluted by human and commercial waste, had been redeveloped. Blay could see a concentrated township of sandstone and timber buildings, including military barracks, a government store, a gaol, powder magazine, inns, stores and cottages, interspersed with garden plots. Now, Hobart Town's 14,000 inhabitants could utilise five banks, numerous newspapers, churches and chapels for every denomination, a library, breweries, tanneries, timber and flour mills, and a soap and candle factory.

Blay was seeing just what Charles Darwin had seen a year

earlier. The English naturalist arrived on 5 February 1836 on the HMS *Beagle* expedition, describing Hobart Town and the Derwent estuary in his *Voyage of the Beagle*:

> We entered the mouth of Storm Bay: the weather justified its awful name …
>
> … The lower parts of the hills which skirt the bay are cleared; and the bright yellow fields of corn, and dark green ones of potatoes, appear very luxuriant … I was chiefly struck with the comparative fewness of the large houses, either built or building.
>
> The streets are fine and broad, but the houses rather scattered, the shops appear good.
>
> Hobart Town, from the census of 1835, contained 13,826 inhabitants, and the whole of Tasmania 36,505. If I was obliged to emigrate I certainly should prefer this place: the climate & aspect of the country almost alone would determine me.

Darwin had been disappointed by what he saw earlier in Sydney, especially the conflict between settlers and convicts, lack of intellectual life and immorality. Nothing but 'sheer necessity would compel me to emigrate' there.

While Hobart Town was somewhat less than what he expected — 'in London [where] I saw a panorama of Hobart Town; the scenery was very magnificent but unfortunately there is no resemblance of it in nature' — societal and intellectual life was more agreeable than Sydney. On the day the *Beagle* arrived, a local newspaper applauded the fact that 'science, the natural associate but long alienated helpmate of literature, is gradually coming by the voice of common sense in all our most approved places of instruction into closer alliance'.

Darwin, in the company of Surveyor-General George Frankland, had 'the most agreeable evening since leaving home' to help celebrate his 27th birthday, and the following night the attorney-general, Alfred Stephen, hosted him, his 'house large, beautifully furnished, dinner most elegant … an excellent concert of rare Italian music'. On hearing Stephens' home had recently entertained 100 guests in fancy dress costume, he asked, 'Is not this astonishing in so remote a part of the world?'

More significantly, he spent his birthday collecting 130 specimens, including dung-beetles, snakes, flatworms and insects, and was struck by the similarity of plants he found in Van Diemen's Land and places as far away as Patagonia and Tierra del Fuego. Darwin's discoveries informed his then 'very presumptuous' thinking. Aided by other visiting naturalists, including Quaker James Backhouse, and locals such as Ronald Gunn of Launceston, who collected botany for the director of Kew Gardens in London, William Hooker and his son Joseph, a close friend of Darwin, the presumptions would emerge as revolutionary theories about evolution.

The evolution of the colony was remarkable in itself. In the 33 years since two small boats carrying 24 convicts and a handful of soldiers first 'settled', Van Diemen's Land had grown to more than 50,000. Hobart Town was growing much faster than Sydney, and would remain the continent's second biggest settlement until the 1850s.

Darwin felt the efforts to transform vagabonds into active citizens 'has succeeded to a degree perhaps unparalleled in history', but European settlement was just a small part of a bigger story. The area around Hobart Town had been occupied for at least 8000 years, possibly as many as 35,000, by the semi-nomadic Mouheneener tribe, a sub-group of the Nuenonne, or south-east tribe. Somewhere between 5000 and 10,000 members of eight tribes hunted and gathered across the island, moving between basic bark huts and campfires since the last Ice Age physically separated the island from a mainland which had once adjoined Patagonia.

The most southerly people in the world had their own language and an understanding of their environment and the seasons, enabling them to harvest a variety of foods. They used fire to control the growth of grasslands, which supported an abundance of wallaby and kangaroo, and bark canoes to reach outer islands to capture mutton-birds and seals.

Captain Cook, on his visit to the Derwent River in 1777, wrote of the Nuenonne welcoming the visiting Europeans as being 'of middling stature, slender and naked. On different parts of their bodies were ridges, both straight and curved, raised in the skin: the hair of the head and beard was smeared with red ointment'.

Small groups of eight to 10 Nuenonne men were generally welcoming of early French, Dutch and English explorers, with friendly shouts and gesticulations, happy to exchange food and water for trinkets. At first the Aboriginal people thought the Europeans were spirits who arrived on the backs of great birds, believing their ship sails looked like seagull wings. They initially had no cause for concern, as the 'spirits' stayed briefly and sailed off. They watched, bemused, as early French explorers planted vegetables alongside the 'Riviere du Nord' for use by future expeditions.

There were occasional tensions — the French were the first to fire muskets at the Nuenonne on the east coast — but these escalated when the first Englishmen set up camp at Risdon Cove, firing fatal shots at 300 Aboriginal people, including women and children who were herding a mob of kangaroo. There was more tension when permanent buildings emerged on the Nuenonne's traditional hunting grounds and their access to the fresh water flowing in a rivulet down from Mt Wellington was denied.

Now there was no Aboriginal welcome for convict ships like Blay's *Sarah*. Their goodwill and numbers had rapidly diminished, with only 200 Aboriginal people left in the colony. Rapid growth of pastoral interests in the hinterland between Hobart Town and Launceston — by 1830 some 700,000 sheep were in the Midlands — caused clashes and reprisal killings, and those who the 50-year Black War and bullets didn't kill fell to imported European diseases such as smallpox, influenza and pneumonia. Some rural settlers even boasted how 'prussic acid', or cyanide, had been administered at one station 'where they died about the place like rats'.

Darwin observed in his diary of 1836 that 'the Aboriginal blacks are all removed and kept, in reality as prisoners, in a promontory, the neck of which is guarded'. The decimation of the original people had been caused by the misconduct of whites, but Darwin felt it impossible to have avoided 'this cruel step'.

A few years later, preparing his famous Journal, he wrote: 'When two races of men meet, they act precisely like two species of animals — they fight, eat each other, bring diseases to the other etc, but then comes the most deadly struggle, namely which have the best fitted organisation, or instincts (ie intellect in man) to gain the day. In man chiefly intellect, in animals chiefly organisation.' While he had seen 'organisation' favour the indigenous peoples of Africa and the West Indies, in Australia he believed it favoured the settlers, 'and in Van Diemen's Land they have been exterminated on principles strictly applicable to the universe'. Darwin was convinced these universal forces, beyond good and evil, had sealed their fate. As cruel as it was, Van Diemen's Land was 'rewarded' with 'the great advantage of being free from a native population', and he was not aware of 'a more striking instance of the comparative rate of increase of a civilised over savage people'.

His view of this striking 'reward' was not shared by fellow naturalist and missionary James Backhouse and his Quaker colleague George Washington Walker, who would become known as the 'conscience of the colony'. The Quakers were plain of dress, but provided a clarity of thinking and plain speaking that eluded many in the colony.

They didn't accept the notion that Aboriginal people were intellectually inferior. 'They exceeded the Europeans in skill, in those things to which their attention had been directed in childhood,' Walker wrote, 'just as much as the Europeans exceeded them in points to which the attention of the former had been turned in the culture of civilisation.'

Backhouse said, 'We cannot help but deprecate the short-sighted policy by which the lands of the aboriginal inhabitants have been wrested from them, with little or no regard for their natural and indefeasible rights,' and that as whites took possession of their land and depleted their food supply by destroying kangaroos and emus, and through over-grazing, 'heavy responsibility lies on the British nation and colonial government to make restitution'.

The Quakers argued in reports to governors Arthur and Franklin, and the Colonial Office, that the Aboriginal people were the just possessors of the land, a view embraced succinctly by Lady Jane Franklin: 'This priority of claim must be admitted by anyone who wants equity and common justice.'

The devastation of this ancient civilisation — which English writer H. G. Wells said in the preface to *The War of the Worlds* 'were entirely swept out of existence in a war of extermination' — came from the empirical ambitions of men on the 'civilised' side of the world.

The British and French had competitive designs on the great south lands. They literally bumped into each other in 1788 when Captain Arthur Phillip, despatched to plant a British flag, was startled to see two French ships just outside Botany Bay. After some friendly contact between the British and French officers, the scientific ships of Jean-Francois de La Perouse sailed off, later found wrecked with almost total loss of life near the New Hebrides, now Vanuatu.

But upon hearing news of the fresh outbreak of the Napoleonic Wars in 1803, the governor in Sydney, Philip King, felt he had to move quickly to avoid the risk of France establishing a naval base in the south, especially in Van Diemen's Land, only confirmed as an island five years previously by George Bass and Matthew Flinders.

King wrote to London seeking support, but while waiting for an official response he ordered 23-year-old Lieutenant John Bowen to take a surgeon, storekeeper, 21 male and three female convicts, a

lance corporal and seven privates on a whaler and supply ship from
Port Jackson to establish a colony on Van Diemen's Land. He told him
that should 'any French ships ... attempt to form an establishment
anywhere in the neighbourhood of where you are settled ... you will
endeavour to prevent them'. While Bowen was endeavouring to fly
the flag at Risdon Cove on the Derwent River, London responded
to King's entreaty by despatching David Collins, a colonel who had
been part of the First Fleet 15 years earlier, to set up a protective
settlement on Port Phillip at Sullivan Bay, near current Sorrento.
But Collins wasn't happy with the Victorian location, and secured
King's support to relocate to the more sensitive Van Diemen's Land.

Collins arrived on 16 February 1804, along with a boatload
of convicts sentenced for seven or 14 years transportation, and
others for life for stealing horses, sheep, ribbons or uttering forged
promissory notes. He took command from the young Bowen and
set about looking for a better site than Risdon, or Restdown, as it
had a poor supply of fresh water and was susceptible to changing
tides. After five days and three reconnaissance trips to the western
side of the Derwent, he relocated the settlement eight kilometres
downriver, at Sullivans Cove, and named it after Lord Hobart, his
Secretary of State for War and the Colonies.

Governor King was still anxious about the French, and in
October despatched Lieutenant-Colonel William Paterson from
Port Jackson to establish a second colony on the northern coast
of Van Diemen's Land. Paterson initially landed at the mouth of
the Tamar River, near current George Town, but after only a few
weeks weather and water issues forced him to move 50 kilometres
south to found Australia's third white settlement, initially called
Patersonia, but later changed to honour Governor King who was
born in Launceston, Cornwall.

In addition to dulling any French ambitions, the island's
isolation soon appealed as a secondary penal colony. The convicts
who arrived with Bowen were soon joined by many more from

Botany Bay, and then from England. And as if Hobart Town and Launceston weren't isolated enough, more remote places, like Sarah Island on the west coast and Maria Island on the east coast, were available to shut away repeat offenders.

Hobart Town was isolated enough for Blay. He and other wide-eyed convicts listened to crewmen talk salaciously of the devils, tigers, snakes, 'wild natives' and dangerous outlaws to be found in the bush surrounding the township, and whales and sharks in the cove itself. Onshore he could see glimpses of unimaginable wildlife: two-metre tall birds with huge brown feathers, and animals with short forelegs, bounding on two hind legs. Some were kept in a private zoo established beside the governor's mansion.

There was some familiarity: blackbirds, imported by settlers but now cursed as pests best dealt with by periodic shooting culls and egg bounties; rabbits, which first came out on the First Fleet; the red uniforms of soldiers and the style of their barracks; the sandstone buildings. And a prevalence of English names: inns named the Cornish, Rose and Crown, Coach and Horse; the Derwent after a river in Cumbria; and Hobart after the Colonial Secretary.

Like Darwin the year before, Blay was in a place both familiar and unfamiliar. There was some comfort in the familiar, and more comfort again when he realised that while he was a prisoner he wasn't to be kept under lock and key; his prison walls would not be of stone but wilderness and ocean. Only six percent of convicts were kept confined in gaols, the majority being used in government work gangs, or as assignees to free settlers.

Signs of punishment were still painfully obvious. As Liverpool settler Joseph Syme wrote on his arrival just a few months prior, a newcomer couldn't but 'be struck with wonder' at seeing six or seven men drawing along a cart on two wheels, with a leading pole for steering; men manacled with a strong ring riveted around their ankles and linked by chain; prisoners wearing 'somewhat grotesque' clothing made up of patches of black and yellow cloth, with black leather caps, which 'tends to remind you of the appearance of a merry clown'.

This was a place where, Quaker James Backhouse lamented, administrators literally flogged the 'radically erroneous' supposition that 'severity towards a convicted offender has a reformatory tendency'.

And this was a place where a *Sarah* crewman jovially pointed out that in the good old days convicts were hanged and gibbeted right there at Hunter Island, but now 'if you coves play up there's a rope there for you over the wall at that there gaol'. Blay winced, but followed the sailor's outstretched arm and made out the gaol in Murray Street, built six years earlier for convict re-offenders and settlers committing crimes. And, he heard, in the bush up beside the rivulet leading into town, a former rum distillery was now a gaol for women, known as the Cascades Female Factory.

As he waited to step none too bravely into this new world, Blay had no sense how familiar he would become with gaol, rum and rope.

5

TERRA VAN DIEMEN

With *Sarah* firmly anchored, the ship's crew rushed off to sate their thirst for rum and sex in one of the dozens of inns and brothels before even contemplating a return voyage to England. Dr McTernan and Captain Whiteside looked forward to marking their successful convict delivery with some good food and wine before returning to the bosom of the Mother Country.

But for the convicts there were no such pleasures and no return ticket.

On board, they were reviewed by the Principal Superintendent of Convicts, Josiah Spode, grandson of the founder of the famous Staffordshire pottery, and Muster Master William Champ, a former British soldier who would go on to run Port Arthur and then Tasmania as its first Premier.

They watched as clerks with measuring tapes worked through the lines of prisoners stripped to the waist, calling out their heights: five two, five six, four nine. Full physical descriptions, including any scars or tattoos, were recorded in 'the books', large leather bound volumes designed to impress on the convicts that everything about them was known.

They identified who could read and write, what trades, skills and specialisations were on offer. A tailor or boot maker might be more adept at men's, women's or children's wear. Farm labourers might have different abilities to sow, harrow, plough, mow, milk, thatch, shear or castrate.

Blay was listed as a 'boatman' with basic reading and writing skills. He was not suitable for public service assignment as a clerk and didn't have the valued skills of a blacksmith, mason, carpenter or bricklayer. But neither was he so unskilled, illiterate or insolent to be despatched to a government work gang, nor was he a 'cripple', 'vacant' or 'ill'.

The Superintendent looked hard at this man in front of him, and what the book showed:

Solomon Blay. Convict No. 2598.
Trade: Boatman.
Height (without shoes): 5ft 8 3/4. [175 centimetres]
Age: 20.
Complexion: Sallow.
Head: large, long.
Hair: dark brown.
Whiskers: same.
Visage: long.
Forehead: medium.
Eyebrows: brown.
Eyes: blue.
Nose: M length.
Mouth: rather wide.
Chin: medium length.
Remarks: deeply pock-pitted, small lump under right eye.

This and the brief outline of his convictions for theft and counterfeiting, his gaol record ('bad'), his hulk record ('good') and his ship record ('as bad as can be'), was all that Van Diemen's Land knew of convict #2598. The Superintendent put Blay among the 151 convicts to be assigned to settlers. The rest were assigned to public projects, roadworks and clerical work, while four were cited as 'cripples', nine as 'vacant', 12 as 'sick', and the four Sarah Island pirates as 'absentees returned'.

The clerical process over, the convicts were finally shuffled off *Sarah* to be rowed onto Hunter Island. Here they formed a long line to walk into town along a causeway built by earlier convicts, to the prison barracks, also convict-built, to await the start of the rest of their lives. They were escorted by red-coated British soldiers with muskets, and eyed by other soldiers guarding sandstone buildings. Others watched from behind wheelbarrows and carts, or from the windows of shops, inns and brothels.

At the barracks, Blay was issued his convict clothing, described by one:

> The convict's suit consisted of trouser and jacket, made of a grey kind of cloth, coarser and rougher even than common carpeting, and which permitted the wind to circulate through the interstices almost as freely as through a sieve ... a striped cotton shirt whose fabric was correspondingly as coarse ... and a skull cap, made of stiff sole leather closely fitting the head and projecting in four points from the four sides ... and a pair of thick, clumsy shoes without socks. These, with an extra shirt for change, constituted our whole wardrobe, every article of which was branded with the broad R.

The 'broad R', or arrow, was used by British military to signify government ownership, its origins dating back to the mid-1500s, and a mark still used to identify Australian Defence-owned property.

Blay was quietly relieved to be advised his 'boatman' background had seen his name inked beside that of ferryman James Murdoch. His new master was a settler who operated a ferry and public house further upstream on the Derwent at Green Point, where the river narrowed and reverted to fresh water, and had become a crossing point for travellers between Hobart Town and the chain of villages through the Midlands to Launceston in the north.

James Murdoch had come to the colony with his brother Peter to help set up Governor Arthur's penal settlement on Maria Island, and they became part of the police magistracy, receiving numerous land grants and running the Green Point business with their third brother, Robert, until Peter returned to Scotland in 1836.

Just a week before Blay's arrival, James and Robert had advertised for 'two good boatmen', with the requirement of being 'acquainted with the navigation of the river and be of sober character', so they must have been pleased to be able to pick up a free but experienced convict boatman, albeit with no Derwent knowledge and of unknown sobriety.

Under the assignment system which ran until 1840, free settlers could seek convict labourers in return for feeding, clothing and housing them. The premise of the system was that convicts would be reformed under the proper moral guidance of their masters, and eventually be given a ticket-of-leave, a form of parole providing some freedoms with conditions, and then eventually a pardon and freedom. In the process, the settlers could develop the colony with cheap labour, and the government would avoid considerable convict maintenance costs.

Some masters embraced the philosophy, even allowing convicts the freedom to grow their own vegetables, or eke out additional income in their own time. But many were unambiguously focused on the benefits, and resorted to reporting any convict misdemeanour or misbehaviour in order to hold their cheap labour beyond the agreed period.

After Murdoch collected Blay from the barracks, they rode almost 20 kilometres upstream to his public house and ferry operation. On the ride out, Blay could see the west bank of the Derwent being cleared for farming. He passed the small settlement of New Town, where he later learned his counterfeit partner, Henry Roberts, had been assigned as a labourer.

In the public houses of staging points like Black Snake and Green Point, there was much talk about the return and fate of the convict pirates and their attempted mutiny on *Sarah*. The Blades brothers and the dashing foreign thieves had been immediately despatched to Port Arthur, where Castanos, the 'most finished swindler', later became one of many convicts to become a constable overseeing other convicts. So too did Pointon, the poacher who had helped foil the mutiny. He had a note in his conduct record: 'in his favour for his highly praiseworthy conduct upon the occasion of an attempt at Mutiny on board the Convict Ship "Sarah" when upon his passage from England, in giving information and maintaining the discipline of the ship, by which the attempt was happily frustrated'.

The Diemen Four and the French-born sailor, Wilson, were taken under close guard to face trial before Chief Justice John Pedder and a military jury, Wilson for 'endeavouring to create a revolt' and the Diemen Four for 'piracy and felony on the high seas'. Porter, Shiers, Cheshire and Lyon were indicted for 'piratically and feloniously carrying away on 30 January 1834, the brig Frederick ... belonging to our Sovereign Lord the King, and of the estimated value of £1200 from the high seas, to wit, Macquarie Harbour on the Coast of Van Diemen's Land.'

The jury took only 30 minutes to produce an 'all guilty' finding. The Diemen Four appealed, arguing ingeniously that the ship they seized was not registered, there was doubt whether Macquarie Harbour constituted the 'high seas', and because they were not qualified sailors they should only face the lesser charge of stealing 'a bundle of materials in the form of a ship'.

The appeal was unsuccessful, and the four then languished in Hobart Town Gaol for two years awaiting their fate. Chief Justice Pedder, who had arrived to a 13-gun salute as the island's first judicial supremo aged just 31, had some doubts about the conviction, and he was not known as a man for quick decisions. Governor Arthur once remarked: 'Though a man of great talents and unbending integrity, of the purest intentions and a very safe adviser, he is so tedious and so minute that life is much too short to wait for his opinions and decision'.

After much paper shuffling between Hobart Town and London, Pedder resolved the Diemen Four should not hang but instead be sent out on the seas again, this time to Norfolk Island for life. While this was a fate many regarded as worse than death, the slippery Porter soon had his sentence reduced to 14 years, and then to seven for twice helping rescue Norfolk Island officers when their boats capsized.

He later admitted Dr McTernan had been right to be suspicious of him on *Sarah*'s voyage, despite his eloquent protests that he was a minor player in the *Frederick* piracy and falsely accused over the *Sarah* mutiny plot. He wrote that he had to protest his innocence because if he confirmed anything 'they would have looked sharper after me and prevented my making an escape, for it was my intention as soon as we made the headland of Hobart Town to endeavour to make my escape, as I knew every creek and corner of it'.

Blay, like the whole colony, followed the fate of his fellow *Sarah* passengers with interest, and picked up plenty of chatter among travellers on the punt and in the public house.

In 1838 an enterprising William Elliston, who had run the Royal Theatre in Drury Lane in London's West End before realising the potential of a liquor business in a thirsty colony, ploughed some of his profits into acquiring the *Hobart Courier* for £12,000. He published Porter's hand-written version of events at Macquarie Harbour. Datelined 'Gaol Hobart, 1 November 1837', the mutineer had sent his version to Sir John Franklin in the hope it might be passed on to London for favourable consideration. Elliston published the essay as 'A narrative of the sufferings and adventures of certain of the convicts who piratically seized the Frederick at Macquarie Harbour in Van Diemen's Land, as related by one of the pirates, whilst under sentence of death at Hobart Gaol'. Knowing he was on to a good thing, he reprinted the material the following year in 13 episodes.

Blay was glad he was on the Green Point ferry and not with Porter and the others behind the walls of Hobart Town Gaol or the Prisoners' Barracks Penitentiary. He had seen and heard enough of life at 'The Tench', where convicts, or 'government men' as officials preferred, were taken out on daily work parties for government road and building construction. Those with bad records spent the day on the treadmill grinding wheat, or breaking large rocks into small stones for roadworks.

And he wasn't wearing the irons and arrow-branded convict clothing of the chain gangs. Male prisoners in assigned service were entitled to an annual issue of two 'strong' jackets and trousers, three shirts, three pairs of half-boots, two waistcoats, one hat or cap and some handkerchiefs. He still felt the chill of the Derwent Valley, often submerged under a cold blanket of thick fog, or 'jerry' as convicts called it, and the winters could be icy. But he had lived through freezing snow in Oxford, and a lean-to at the back of Murdoch's public house was preferable to a stone cell.

And he was doing something familiar, helping load chain gangs, settlers, animals and stage coaches onto the punt across the Derwent. Punts were needed, as 200 convicts had not yet completed a kilometre-long causeway called Bridgewater, despite years hand-shifting and wheel-barrowing two million tonnes of soil, clay and stone, some of which sank 15 metres into the riverbed before a solid base was found.

Blay vowed he would not become a member of a chain gang, one of those shackled, exhausted and harshly treated convicts clearing land, building roads, heaving rocks and sandstone blocks under the hard hand of soldiers.

He also vowed to avoid the fate of a hanging. Only two months after his arrival he heard passengers returning from Launceston talk in horror of seeing a convicted man's body hanging by chains.

One of the passengers was Martin Cash, an Irish farm boy transported for house-breaking in 1827, who went on to achieve fame as a bushranger and someone whose path Blay would cross more than once. In his life story, Cash told of 'crossing in the punt' and seeing constables from Hobart Town escorting a cart with a coffin in it: 'We afterwards seen the body hanging about one mile from Perth ... in a few weeks however it became so offensive that the inhabitants petitioned to have it removed, averring that the large flies, after leaving the body, flew into their dwellings and let upon their provisions, and that the thing had become a dangerous and disgusting nuisance.'

The body was that of John McKay, who along with John Lamb was convicted of shooting and fatally bashing a man on the road between Perth and Launceston. Chief Justice Pedder sentenced the men to hang 'and when dead, their bodies to be hanged in chains'. The under-sheriff in Launceston duly received instructions to 'cause the body of the malefactor [McKay] to be gibbeted, as near to the spot at which he committed the murder as possible'.

This was in line with England's Murder Act 1751, stipulating that 'in no case whatsoever shall the body of any murderer be suffered to be buried'. The body had to be publicly dissected or left 'hanging in chains'.

Blay heard how the under-sheriff, watched by spectators, had erected a gibbet of 20 feet (6 metres) from the branch of a she-oak on the main route into Launceston, from which the body was securely chained. Here the rotting corpse hung for four months, ravaged by birds, flies, ants and animals, at one point accompanied by two of McKay's friends drowning their sorrows in liquor.

This roadside 'advertising' was to warn anyone considering the attractions of highway robbery or bushranging. Consistent with justice in Van Diemen's Land often lagging years behind decisions made in London, McKay's body was 'hanged in chains' five years after the practice ceased in Britain. He was believed to be the last person in the British Empire to endure gibbeting.

Blay wanted nothing to do with gibbets, hangings or chain gangs, so he did his best at Green Point to stay on the right side of the law. This generally meant resisting the temptations of liquor, but this wasn't easy; in this isolated life, the warm embrace of liquor was seductive.

Less than a year after his arrival, Blay was so seduced, and charged in January 1838 with being drunk and delivering a female, also drunk, to the Cascades Female Factory. He was sentenced to 14 days in prison on bread and water.

Blay may have been enjoying a rum libation as he watched visiting and local ships race on the Derwent, in the country's first regatta courtesy of the new governor, Sir John Franklin, and Lady Jane Franklin. There were numerous toasts to young Queen Victoria, who had just ascended to the throne after the death of King William IV, her uncle, a man who had 10 illegitimate children with an actress but no surviving legitimate heirs. Just 18, Victoria became the first monarch to live in Buckingham Palace and soon be the first to have her image on England's stamps.

Blay was more interested in securing a ticket-of-leave stamp, a form of parole and internal passport entitling convicts to certain freedoms within a given district. This was on the proviso they remain of good behaviour, participate in regular musters and attend church on Sunday. Despite his alcoholic frolic, Blay received his stamp on 13 February 1838, tickets-of-leave being offered as an incentive for convicts to become constables.

It seemed unimaginable that a prisoner could be a policeman, but then again Blay had never imagined anything like Van Diemen's Land. The police state demanded large numbers, but the low pay was unattractive to free men, one magistrate feeling 'no intelligent able bodied man' would enlist. So officials looked to convicts.

The one shilling and nine pence a day was sufficiently attractive to Blay. Three months after receiving his tick-of-leave stamp, he was still a convict but now also a police constable at Brighton. For a period this was supplemented with a daily ration of 1 pound (450 grams) of flour, after the district magistrate successfully argued this would help convicts survive and their pay less likely to be 'misapplied'.

Pay was easily 'misapplied'. Alcohol was a major part of the lifeblood of Van Diemen's Land. On Blay's arrival, there were almost 300 public houses, inns or taverns in the colony, many not much more than small houses in alleyways behind shopfronts. For the convict half of the 57,000 inhabitants, such public houses were the only place where they could congregate in any number and forget their plight or share their thoughts, without the close watch of soldiers and masters. Settlers and officials also used public houses to relax and hold meetings to organise sports, unions and rallies, and stage inquests.

Rum had been the fuel of the Empire's Navy, often mixed with water or beer to make 'grog'. It flowed to Botany Bay with the 'rum corps', and then flowed easily to Van Diemen's Land. With no official currency in its early life — one traveller to Hobart Town in the 1830s wrote that 'in receiving change for a pound note or a sovereign it is difficult to ascertain with any degree of certainty whether you have obtained the right change. Our first change for a pound consisted of two dumps [an old Spanish dollar with the centre cut out], two holey dollars [the outer ring of the Spanish dollar], one Spanish dollar, one French coin, one half crown, one shilling and one sixpence' — convicts and soldiers alike were rewarded or paid with the favoured currency of rum or grog.

Consumption was reckoned to be three times the rate in England, as sailors, settlers, convicts and police constables joined in alcoholic union, a union that once ran all the way to Government House. When Thomas Davey came ashore as the second lieutenant governor he was drunk, perhaps still frustrated at failing to sail before his wife boarded. 'Mad Tom' became known for his invention of the cocktail 'Blow my Skull' — 3/4 cup demerara sugar, about six limes, a heavy dose of both porter and navy-style rum (57 percent alcohol), and strong domestic brandy.

Governor or convict, it could be a severe battle to keep one's head in this land of rum and rope.

6

CHAINS AND IRONS

In the unique world of Van Diemen's Land, convict Solomon Blay was now also Constable Solomon Blay, one of 400 new members of the police state created by former Governor George Arthur. He was initially based at Brighton, about 26 kilometres north of Hobart Town. It offered the welcome benefits of a little income and some freedom of movement, and from time to time he could live in the houses of anyone under prosecution. He was also able to supplement his income through selling 'second-hand' any goods that might come his way, however surreptitiously. It was a useful little sideline, although he wasn't to know it would become an authorised part of the life he would soon be leading.

Rum and women were also very welcome, though risky for someone on the blurred line of convictism and constabulary. In

November 1839, barely six months after joining the force, and less than a year since he had dined on prison bread and water for 14 days for being drunk with a woman, he was now charged with gross misconduct and again for taking a woman into the female factory while drunk. The magistrate had no time for a convict spurning his opportunity, dismissing him from the force and sentencing him to six months labour on the Campbell Town chain gang.

Chain gangs were seen to be effective in punishing re-offenders and those deemed insolent toward authority. Standing orders issued to supervising soldiers outlined punishments of hard labour, solitude and whipping 'not exceeding 36 lashes' for crimes of drunkenness, absence, disobedience, idleness, neglect, indecent language, profanity, insolence 'or any other misconduct'.

One soldier wrote to his mother in England: 'Never were men better worked, better flogged and better managed than they were in the gang.' He said he watched over them 'with a stick in my hand' and that he was 'obliged to be very severe with them, for neglect they get 25 to 50 lashes'.

To his horror, Blay now faced what he had vowed to avoid, the life his fellow *Sarah* convict and pirate, James Porter, described in his memoirs:

> They were locked overnight in rough huts, lying down on bare boards, with space so tight that in some instances do not allow more than 18 inches [0.45 metres] in width for each individual to lie down ... at 5.30 each morning, which could be bitterly cold in the Midlands, they were called to muster and marched to the quarries for 3 hours of stone work ... before being given a pint of skilly or gruel, a hasty pudding composed of flour, water and salt and a slice of bread. After more hours of stone work, lunch might be mutton and potatoes, then more hours of work, then finally back to camp and more 'skilly'. At night, the soldiers had no interest in what happened amongst men already degraded and incorrigible, and deprived of women for years.

In quarries men were ironed and chained to a ship cable, forced to break rocks all day, or put into teams of four or six to pull cartloads of quarried stones weighing up to a tonne. In fields, 20 to 30 prisoners were driven by guards using long whips and ropes with a spiked ball at the end, convict verse referring to them being 'yoked up to the plough, my boys, to plough Van Diemen's Land'. In 1836, four-man teams of convicts powered the first railway in Australia, carrying supplies in a seven-kilometre line uphill from the beach at Taranna to Port Arthur.

Convict verses in newspapers read:

They chain us up two by two, and whip and lash along,
They cut off our provisions if we do the least thing wrong,
They march us in the burning sun, until our feet are sore,
So hard's our lot now we are got upon Van Diemen's shore.
We labour hard from morn to night, until our bones do ache,
Then every one, they must obey, their mouldy beds must make,
We often wish when we lay down, we ne'er may rise no more,
To meet our savage governors upon Van Diemen's shore.
Every night when I lay down, I wash my straw with tears,
While wind upon that horrid shore do whistle in our ears,
Those dreadful beasts upon that land around our cots do roar,
Most dismal is our doom upon Van Diemen's shore.

Blay was a bigger man than most at 5 feet 8 3/4 inches (173 centimetres). But he had already suffered one whipping on *Sarah*, and the thought of being in chains for six months breaking rocks and fields all day, and avoiding sexual advances at night, was too much.

Within a month, in December 1839, he was charged with misconduct in 'ovalling', the flattening out of leg irons so they could be slipped off at night or to enable escape. He received an additional two months of hard labour. Desperate a few weeks later, he again tried to slip an iron. He was again unsuccessful and given another four months hard labour in addition to his existing six and two month sentences, and ordered to be moved to the Jerusalem chain gang.

The origin of Biblical inspiration to name Jerusalem, halfway between Richmond and Oatlands, and nearby Baghdad, Jericho, Lake Tiberius and the River Nile, was unclear. Some cited Private Hugh Germain, a well-educated soldier-explorer. Others credited Jorgen Jorgenson, a Dane whose lifetime of adventure included a reign as self-proclaimed King of Iceland before becoming a convict constable in Van Diemen's Land.

But there was nothing divine about the road to Jerusalem. Manacled to another prisoner and carrying his few possessions in a swag, it took Blay close to a week to walk the 70 kilometres to Jerusalem. Here a new probation station housed convicts who built a courthouse and gaol, and laboured in coalmines and quarries, watched over by a garrison of 'lobsters', as they called the red-coated soldiers.

Fellow convicts at Jerusalem included Martin Cash, who wrote in his memoirs of meeting Blay, 'a Jew [*sic*] who had been transported for making counterfeit coins', and how 'this Jerusalem was no Holy City, but a citadel of despair, suffering, cruelty, terror and treachery'.

Cash was placed in solitary confinement in mid-winter for three days for feigning illness as part of an escape plan, three days where there was no sense of the passing of time, all light and sound shut out except for a few moments each day. This was when a shutter was opened and a face peered in to make sure he was still alive before delivering 1 pound (450 grams) of black bread and a can of water. Immediately on his release from solitary into an exercise yard, Cash waited until he was the only man in the yard, up-ended two wooden 'night tubs' against the four-metre stockade wall, clambered over and ran. He wasn't to know he would be all too close for comfort to Blay in their lives after Jerusalem.

Blay was fortunate compared with Cash and others. Rather than having to walk several kilometres every day to break rocks, he was given relatively light duties as a washerman. But he still chafed under the rough yellow and black gang clothing, chains and irons — they could weigh as much as 28 kilograms — and the dark nights were full of fear. 'Sodomy' was preached and practised in Jerusalem, as men sought sexual satisfaction as and when they could find it. For British administrators, sodomy was the ultimate sin. Naval authorities charged men with 'mutiny' as code for the offence, and it was a fact of life in barracks, prisons, female factories and chain gangs. Ernest Slade, superintendent of the convict barracks at Hyde Park, Sydney, asserted Australia was the most homosexual society on earth, telling an 1838 parliamentary committee in London that it was at least 100 times more prevalent than in England.

After visiting Van Diemen's Land and Norfolk Island, the Roman Catholic Vicar-General in Sydney, William Ullathorne, wrote: 'Fifty thousand souls are festering in bondage ... we have made it a cesspool ... we are building with them a nation of crime to be ... a curse and a plague ... crimes that dare I describe them would make your blood to freeze, and your hair to rise erect in horror upon the pale flesh.'

In Hobart Town, Bishop Francis Nixon warned that sodomy was so common it risked ensuring 'the moral degradation of the colony [and] draw down divine vengeance upon it', claiming convicts escaped to the bush to 'commit their foul acts, some even did so in the chapel itself'.

English author Alexander Harris more obliquely wrote that, especially in the bush, 'habits of mutual helpfulness arise and these elicit gratitude that leads on to regard. In fact it is a universal feeling that a man ought to be able to trust his mate in anything'.

But out in the bush of Jerusalem, Blay couldn't trust anyone, not the 'lobster' soldiers, not fellow convicts. He just wanted to escape any undesirable punishment or sexual advances.

He could become a 'bolter', or bushranger, like Cash, but he knew this would inevitably have an unhappy ending, either at the hands of angered Aboriginal people, cannibals, soldiers, police or a hangman.

Or, given his boatman experience, he could escape the colony altogether. He knew of convicts, like those on *Sarah*, who had stolen or taken control of small boats, or made their own makeshift craft, and successfully escaped across Bass Strait to the mainland, New Zealand, Pacific Islands and Indonesia, and some even as far as South America, Japan and China. But these would be voyages into wild unknown seas, full of whales and sharks.

The easiest way for a convict to escape was to stow away or volunteer his labour to one of the whalers in the Derwent in return for a secret passage to North America, South America or Europe. So many convicts from Van Diemen's Land and Sydney took this route to San Francisco that an explosion of crime in the 1850s elicited warnings from the *Sacramento Daily Union* that they should go elsewhere to pursue their 'rascality' if they wanted to avoid summary punishment, with vigilante groups lynching eight men.

Governor Arthur hated the idea that men could escape him so readily. He ordered ships coming into Hobart Town to take their sails and rudders ashore to reduce the prospect of a convict hijacking, and demanded 24-hour watches and sulphuric fumigation to force out any stowaways hiding below deck. If a ship was found with a convict on board, Arthur fined every member of the crew a month's wages, to be paid before they were free to sail.

The whalers were watched closely, as they were crewed by hard men with little respect for the laws of Washington or London, let alone Hobart Town. They were fond of fierce hand-made liquor, and some were known to keep Aboriginal women chained to remote coastal huts for personal enjoyment.

And there were a lot of whalers because there were a lot of whales, particularly southern right whales (*Eubalaena australis*) in the bays and inlets along the coast during their annual migration north from Antarctica. A whale-rush had been underway since a crewman with the first lieutenant governor, David Collins, counted 60 whales in the Derwent River in a three-month period and wrote of 'so many whales that it was dangerous for the boat to go up the river unless you kept very near the shore'. By the time Blay arrived, Hobart Town was a global whaling centre, with an estimated 3000 whales caught in the preceding decade, their oil used for street-lighting, their bone for stiffening women's corsets and parasols in Britain and America. Newspapers enthused about the promise of the great fortune 'this Colony is likely to possess for a century to come', but bloody exploitation soon killed off the 'century of fortune'.

Blay was struggling. He was now enduring three separate sentences totalling 12 months in a hated chain gang, further away from completing his original 14-year sentence. He didn't have the bravura to become a pirate or risk stowing away on a visiting whaler for another long voyage. He had no skills to survive in the wild bush as a bushranger, or defend himself against the tigers and wolves he had heard about, or avoid cannibal convicts who were the talk of London, such that a London newspaper hoped its next report on a new Bishop in the colony would not 'bring word that he has been eaten up'.

His experiences as a river boatman didn't count for much in these wild waters, he had already been dismissed from the police force, he had no other skills, and more and more convicts were competing for fewer jobs as the local economy slipped into depression. And even if he could find a job he risked being assigned to a cruel and capricious master. Blay could see his choices were limited, but couldn't see how to 'escape'. He needed a lucky break in the lottery of life on Van Diemen's Land.

It came in the late winter of 1840, when the government advertised for 'a sheriff's operator'. A hangman.

The notice was brief, but Blay didn't miss it. He had no taste for physical violence, let alone hanging people. He couldn't even be certain he had the nerve to do a single hanging, let alone do it over and over. He knew a hangman was despised by almost everyone. But still he looked at the notice, wondering if he could bear the weight of such a role. At least there shouldn't be too much competition for the job, and it was clearly a 'steady' source of income as convicts were continuing to pour into the colony and judges were showing no sign of abandoning their black caps.

Weighing it all up, Solomon Blay came to a conclusion. He couldn't see any better choices. He had nothing to lose. Somebody had to do it. He could do it as well as anyone else. It might be his one chance in life, his rising 'tide' in the affairs of men.

So he decided to roll the dice.

7

BECOMING A HANGMAN

Solomon Blay filed his application and waited. He kept telling himself he had done the right thing because he didn't have many choices. It was a hard choice, but the other options seemed worse, and perhaps no one else would want such an abhorrent task. If he could secure this job it was the least risky option to stay alive, the best way to avoid chains and whippings, the best option to find some income.

Life in a house of death was not as unattractive as Blay might have thought, with 19 applications sent to Under-Sheriff Thomas Crouch. The under-sheriff weeded out anyone he sensed might be too much of a 'brute', knowing some men got joy from smashing a skull or plunging a knife, and he didn't want that blood thirst on his gallows watch. Nor did he want anyone with an excessive thirst for alcohol. He also didn't want a man who might not have the nerve to complete the task. He wanted someone literate enough to read government orders, strong enough to handle any difficult prisoner, and strong-willed enough to kill someone and live with it.

Blay's record wasn't exemplary, but if Crouch ruled out any convict who had been insolent, drunk or attempted escape, there would be no man left standing. Perhaps his application was the least bad, or he was still of a young age and might respond well to Crouch's instruction and temperance principles. Or perhaps it was because Crouch knew the governor had rewarded this man who had saved his mail in the Derwent, or it reminded Crouch that on his own arrival in 1825 he had also entered the water, falling in while trying to help secure the boat.

Either way, on 3 August 1840 Lieutenant Governor Franklin accepted Crouch's recommendation and that 'in consequence of his undertaking to perform the duty of operations', as it was recorded in Blay's convict conduct record, he quietly approved 'this man to be employed as Hangman at Hobart Town'. He would still be kept in prison with hard labour for four years, but Blay was now Her Majesty's hangman, with a salary of £7 1s 7d a month. The salary was about what a labourer could earn, and less than what a stone mason or cabinet maker could make per day, but he did not have any skills in demand and it carried a remission on the remaining three months of his chain gang sentences.

It was an immense relief to win this prize, to secure this 'escape', but there was a price to be paid, the price of becoming the grim reaper, the agent of death. Blay knew that as 'the man butcher', as hangmen were most commonly called, he was now the most despised and feared public servant in the colony.

Hangmen and flagellators were seen as symbolic of the worst of convictism, at risk of attack and revenge from fellow convicts. But Blay must have thought he could live with this more than he could live with the alternatives. He was big enough to handle himself, and surely the Sheriff and other officials would offer more protection for their 'operator' than any other convict. And while he was still to complete his original 14-year sentence of exile, this new occupation might be a fast-track to freedom.

Crouch was under the jurisdiction of the sheriff, Peter Fraser, who had only been in the role for six months, and he had no experience in the art and science of hanging. Fraser was definitely interested in art — he was an enthusiastic landscape painter, and within five years of his arrival organised the first ever exhibition in Australia — but in his official role the Scottish-born clerk was more comfortable with the recovery of money, seizure of property and sale of debtor's property than the despatching of the condemned. The early sheriffs of Van Diemen's Land were clerks, artists, adventurers and usurers, but they weren't hangmen. While their role as executive officer was to oversee the death penalty, and do their best to ensure the process was orderly, properly recorded, quick and painless, the real work was deferred to under-sheriffs like Crouch, who would be Blay's superior for his whole life.

The hierarchy of punishment, all the way from colonial officials in London to Hobart Town, was exacting, but their ultimate punishment of hanging was not an exact science. Such knowledge as there was came only from those who had hanged before, and there were no regulations or manuals that Crouch, a former barrister, could pass on. He was able to show Blay through the inside of Murray Street gaol, near the corner of Macquarie Street. Blay had seen it when he arrived three years prior, a small two-storey gaol built on English lines with separate cells for convicts and settlers, including women and children, and those awaiting execution. Originally on the edge of the township it was now at its heart, but in poor condition, the price of inferior bricks, damp ground and overcrowding. But it remained the town gaol and scene of all executions from 1825 to 1857.

The under-sheriff showed Blay around his new workplace. Here the cell where the condemned were held, there the scaffold, the trapdoor, the bolt. The scaffold was a sight to see, one that the colony chaplain, Dr William 'Holy Willie' Bedford had inspected and declared: 'They will be hanged in comfort if there are nine of them, but ten will be crowded.' Blay could barely imagine having nine or 10 men to hang in unison.

Crouch unlocked a heavy wooden box and showed him his tools of trade: a rope, calico cap and soap. The rope was brown, and clearly not new: 'Oh yes it's been used, the government can't afford a new rope for every hanging.'

Crouch outlined the mechanics of hanging: pinion the prisoner, get them to the scaffold, put a soaped noose around the neck, place the hooded cap over the head, step back and stand clear lest you fall with the prisoner, wait for my signal, and pull the bolt.

It sounded straightforward and simple, but Blay sensed it would not be thus. Especially when Crouch talked about the task.

We don't want to make it any harder for the condemned, Crouch said. You've got to get it done as quickly as possible, and we don't want any trouble. The decision that a man's life is to end has been made under Her Majesty's authority and it is my duty to ensure that it is done. My job is to make sure you do your job well and deliver what others have judged: hang a condemned prisoner by the neck until they are dead.

Crouch, a Methodist lay reader and temperance advocate, also told his new young operator to stay 'low', keep your position quiet, avoid attracting attention as you go to or from a gaol, understand that your conduct and behaviour must be respectable and discreet, not only at the place and time of execution but before and subsequently, and do not give any person any particulars on the subject of your duty. He should dress suitably, suggesting a black suit and a practical broad-brimmed hat would be appropriate.

Crouch's final word to Blay was to stay sober, young man, and wait for me to call you.

A call, Blay understood well enough, that would change his

life. Hanging another by rope in full public view was the task transported from England and inaugurated within a month of the First Fleet's arrival, when Thomas Barrett, 30, was accused of robbing or conspiring to rob the government stores. He was hastily deemed guilty by six military officers and doomed to be hanged at sunset the same day. As no hangman had come with the First Fleet, it is likely John Freeman, a co-accused, was persuaded to escape punishment by turning King's evidence and becoming Australia's first executioner. He hanged his fellow convict from the 'arm of the large tree' with a large party of Marines 'drawn up opposite … in case an insurrection should take place … & all the Convicts were summon'd to see the deserved end of their Companion'.

The first man hanged in the newest outpost of Van Diemen's Land was a man called England: Thomas England, of the infamous New South Wales Corps, formed in 1789 as a permanent regiment to relieve the Royal Marines who had accompanied the First Fleet. He was hanged in 1806 for 'feloniously breaking into 3 casks of provisions of His Majesty at Port Dalrymple' and with two other soldiers stealing 35 pounds (15.8 kilograms) of pork.

The English had enjoyed a strong taste for hanging since Anglo-Saxon times. Many hundreds were executed for dozens of crimes, including murder, sheep-stealing, robbery, forgery, counterfeiting, rape and sodomy, but also for more minor offences. Most offenders were men, but women and even children were not spared: five 'criminals' under the age of 14, including one just eight years old, were hanged at the Old Bailey as late as 1814.

As transportation to Australia became England's answer to crime, so hanging was also transported, and nowhere did the noose swing more heartily than in Van Diemen's Land. Queen Victoria presided over about 1100 hangings in England in her 64-year reign, during which time close to 1500 were executed in Australia, with Van Diemen's Land accounting for about a third.

As a young boy, Blay had joined hundreds of others to watch men swing in William the Conqueror's Oxford castle tower, but there only a few men each year entered 'the sheriff's picture frame'. In Hobart Town, Blay had seen much more of 'the tree that bears fruit all year round'. Sometimes as many as 12 men were hanged simultaneously. They took place along the wall of his new workplace, the Murray Street gaol, clearly visible and generally attracting a crowd, sometimes up to 1000, of men, women and children.

The local newspapers also conspicuously reported executions from England, America, India and France, including stories of victims struggling and taking long periods to die, some having to be re-hanged because trapdoors didn't open or the rope wasn't long enough, and even of the occasional decapitation.

But there was no official 'how to' manual, and Blay's predecessors weren't much help. The position had become vacant because the last hangman, William Thompson, had been charged with stealing blankets and clothing. He had his convict sentence extended by two years and been sent to Port Arthur. An earlier hangman was well on his way to drinking himself to death. Another, refused lodgings in Hobart Town, responded by cutting the throat of an innocent old woman and been hanged himself, alongside Thomas Jeffries, a former hangman in Edinburgh who was transported and became a bushranger, killer and cannibal.

Blay had seen, read and heard enough to know he would need to tread carefully. He knew things could go awfully wrong, and not just for the condemned. Hangmen risked the same hatred and fate as the stories about flagellators. One convict's memoirs recalled one 'tortured by bushrangers in … the colony of Victoria … torn limb from limb, horses being fastened by traces to his legs and then driven different ways'. Another convict confessed on the scaffold that he deserved to die 'on account of roasting to death a man who was a flagellator in Van Diemen's Land'. And George Grover, who reportedly whipped a chain gang dragging heavy carts of stone to build a bridge at Richmond, was vengefully murdered and tossed from the same bridge.

Flagellators were as despised as their deeds were common. In the seven years leading up to Blay's arrival in Hobart Town, more than 650 convicts had been flogged and given 22,533 lashes, an average of 34 each. One convict received 3000 lashes in his lifetime. Around the time of his appointment, heavy flogging was beginning to diminish, though the Supreme Court still ordered a private whipping of a 'lad' for stealing a wooden chair, and an 1846 report stated that 'only' 516 convicts had been flogged.

Like most convicts, Blay, who had a whipping on *Sarah*, feared the lash of the 'cat', or cat o' nine tails, nine knotted ropes thrashed against bare backs. Convicts prided themselves on not crying out in pain, thus becoming known as a 'pebble', taking the lash silently as a stone. Those who cried out as their skin shredded were known as a 'sandstone' or a 'crawler'.

Bushranger Martin Cash, in his memoirs, recalled one flagellator standing ready with his 'cat' in hand while a prisoner was stripping, asking him to name the highest mountain in the colony. 'The prisoner said Ben Lomond was considered the highest. When he was at the triangle, the flagellator said: "Well, I'll make you believe in less than five minutes that you had Ben Lomond on your back."'

Knowing hangmen were equally despised, and waiting for the call, Blay tried to prepare himself for his first public performance.

He fingered the rope he would soon be asked to put around someone's neck, a rope about as thick as his thumb. He could feel the natural twist of the manila hemp, long favoured by hangmen and mariners because of its durability and flexibility.

He practised making a noose. Initially he laid the rope, sent down from Sydney, on the floor. He started with a simple 'c' shape, then formed an 's' shape and wrapped a series of loops, before poking one end through the loop and tightening it into a form of slipknot. Some hangmen wanted 13 coils in their noose as an extra foreboding for the condemned, but each coil added friction and made the noose harder to pull closed, so seven or eight coils was more common. Blay had tethered boats in Oxford, so was soon able to create a hang knot while standing upright.

He greased the noose. Under-Sheriff Crouch warned him not to forget to maintain a supply of local yellow soap, made from boiled tallow, to rub inside the noose to reduce friction as it tightened, giving rise to the convict term of wearing 'a greased cravat'.

He rehearsed hanging with a heavy sack to represent a victim, rehearsed pulling the trapdoor bolt.

He imagined the whole process: getting the call from Crouch, walking to the condemned cell, opening the door of the doomed, pinioning the prisoner, escorting him to the scaffold, putting a noose around his neck and a cap over his head, listening to the ministrations of clergy, waiting for the signal and pulling the trapdoor bolt.

Blay rehearsed and imagined, but nothing could fully prepare him for the 'live' flesh-and-bone deliverance of his line of death.

He could feel the pressure building in his head, living with the dark secret of his new occupation and waiting to be summonsed for his first job. Captured and gripped by his fears, doubts and anxieties, he waited.

It was a long five months before, in January 1841, the call from Crouch finally came. Blay was required to travel to Launceston for his first hanging. Crouch told him he would need 'rope, soap and calico for two'.

8

THE FIRST HANGING

Christmas 1840 was, as ever, a fine time for the ruling class of Van Diemen's Land. Inside their convict-built sandstone buildings, replete with chandeliers, fine polished furniture, and convict maids and servants, they clinked crystal glasses to all that gave them a satisfying semblance of respectability in, and separation from, this land of reprobates.

They toasted conspicuously. To Her Majesty, the glorious Queen of the motherland and the Empire. To Charles Darwin, for his recently published glowing references to grand costume balls, fine dining and Italian music in Hobart Town. To the art world in London and its introduction to the unique Australian landscapes of John Glover. To the governor and his wife, Lady Jane Franklin, for making Hobart Town the intellectual centre of all the Australian colonies, founding a scientific society that would lead to the first Royal Society for the advancement of science outside Britain. To the governor's cousin, Lieutenant Joseph Kay, who was heading up a new observatory linking Hobart Town with Toronto, St Helena and Cape Town in a global 'magnetic union'. To the success of Captain James Ross, who had just left Hobart Town on his Antarctic expedition with HMS *Terror* and *Erebus*.

Lady Franklin's projects were the subject of much discussion. She had bought 53 hectares of land for a botanical garden, a museum of natural history and a replica Greek temple she used to store apples, the cultivation of which was one of her interests. She corresponded with English Quaker Elizabeth Fry, 'the angel of prisons', about the welfare of women and orphans, and initiated efforts to help reform female prisoners, drove the foundation of a state college, and pushed for a university and art gallery.

More controversially, she adopted a young Aboriginal girl, a victim of Arthur's Black War. She arrived at Government House with a kangaroo skin, a rush basket, shell necklaces and a pet possum. In the vice-regal domain she was renamed Mathinna, and she later wrote: 'I am a good little girl. I have pen and ink because I am a good little girl. I have got a red frock like my father. I have got sore feet and shoes and stockings and I am very glad.'

But the majority of inhabitants this Christmas were not so much interested in the predilections of vice-regal rulers or intellectual discovery, but the cost of living with the realities of the colony's raison d'etre. Simple and more mundane matters of survival and security remained their focus.

Bushrangers, or 'bolters' as they were also known, had been a feature of the colony since the settlement's earliest days, when some convicts were sent into the bush to hunt for desperately needed food and not all returned, preferring to live by stealing from, or trading with, settlers in remote villages and properties. Martial law, executions and offers of amnesty had somewhat contained the spread of bushranging, but there were always convicts willing to chance escaping into the bush, either alone or by joining a gang, with up to 100 on the loose at any one time.

For Solomon Blay, who had chosen his own 'escape' by becoming a hangman, his Christmas was one of nervously awaiting the first call to do his duty in the name of law and order.

His nerves tightened just after Christmas, when the chief justice, Sir John Pedder, commenced a historic hearing, the first time in the colony that a criminal case would be heard by a jury of 12 civilians following the abolition of military juries. Two bushrangers, Patrick Wallace and William Watson, were on trial for robbing the house of John Holding, at Ashby in the north of the colony, putting him 'in bodily fear'.

The first civilian jury found the men guilty of the capital offence of burglary, impressing the *Launceston Courier* which noted

> the increased interest which they evidently displayed, when compared with military juries, and the diligence with which they cross-examined some of the witnesses, when opposed to the old silent system of the military jurors, would be a convincing proof of the superiority of the former to the latter ... the greatest evil of military juries is ... that they are apt to look too lightly upon life and liberty.

Two days later, the chief justice took his seat at 9am, and the two bushrangers were brought up for judgment. The chief justice outlined how the charges flowing from an armed burglary against them had been fully borne out by the evidence, and nobody could doubt their guilt. The Legislative Council thought it right, having regard to the protection of the settlers, that such men should be liable to capital punishment. He saw nothing in the case that could induce him to hold out any hopes of mercy.

His Honour then put a black cap atop his whitish horsehair wig to pass the sentence of death upon each of the two prisoners: 'You will be taken hence to the prison in which you were last confined and from there to a place of execution where you will be hanged by the neck until you are dead and thereafter your body buried within the precincts of the prison and may the Lord have mercy upon your soul.'

While the chief justice was in no doubt about the pair's guilt, there was some lobbying of the lieutenant governor to show mercy. The *Cornwall Chronicle* commented that 'it was not proven in evidence on their trial that they were guilty of violence to any persons who fell into their hands when engaged in the prosecution of their unlawful practices, and were not, therefore, according to the liberal notions of the age, deserving of death'.

But the men had form, including the theft of silk handkerchiefs in Sydney, for which they were sent for three years to Van Diemen's Land. Here they broke into a shop in Ross to demand tea and sugar, stealing clothing and cash, and putting the household in 'bodily fear'.

The *Chronicle* acknowledged they were

> characters who for years had put the laws at defiance, and had carried on a system of plunder upon the inhabitants which might have been attended with bloodshed. Patrick Wallace was a party in the murder of Dr Waddle in Sydney some years back — he turned King's evidence — gave up his accomplices to justice who were convicted on his evidence, and expiated their crime on the gallows.
>
> For this service Wallace received a free pardon and was shortly afterwards, for some crime committed by him, transported for life and sent to this colony. His conduct ever since has been atrocious.

The historic case had been heard, the sentence passed, clemency rejected. Now the execution process could begin.

Blay received his orders from Under-Sheriff Crouch: be in Launceston three days prior to the nominated time of execution, 8am on Saturday 30 January, and have rope for two.

The newly appointed 'finisher' packed his tools of office into a small bag: two ropes, two cloth caps, a tin of soap and a knife, and boarded a coach to take him through the heart of the colony. He tried to stop his heart from racing as fast as the galloping horses, wondering what his fellow passengers would think if they knew what was in his bag and why he was heading north. He stayed silent and avoided eye contact. He checked and re-checked that the bag stayed securely under his feet, but his heaviest baggage was anxiety.

The under-sheriff required him to stay in a small room inside the Paterson Street gaol, so he could be sure the new hangman's nerves would not succumb, or he sought too much alcoholic comfort, and be unable to perform his duty or seek to flee. He knew the first hanging would be hard for anyone, let alone someone so young. The temperance man would have preferred that if Blay 'can't do it without rum, don't do it at all', but traditional gaol regulations allowed Blay the choice of a pint of malt liquor or a quarter-pint of spirit with his dinner and supper.

Blay gratefully downed the spirit, but his own spirits had to be on edge as he sat in what felt like his own condemned cell, feeling as much a prisoner as the two men awaiting their fate. He found it hard to eat, and harder still to find answers to the questions gnawing at his mind like rats: What if he lost his nerve? What if the prisoners resisted or attacked him? What if the prisoner grabbed at the rope? What if the noose came off? What if the rope broke? What if the trapdoor didn't work? What if the prisoners bled, or there was a rush of shit or piss? What if they dropped but didn't die? What if he had to hang them twice? And what if anyone found out he hadn't hanged anyone before? It didn't help Blay that he had not long ago read of the first hanging in the new colony of South Australia, and how a novice hangman had botched the noose and the pinioning ropes. The condemned man was 'hanging in the air, uttering the most excruciating cries of oh God! Oh Christ! Save me!' and was able to free his hands and reach up to the rope above his head to prevent his choking. Blay remembered the awful description of how the condemned man twisted and turned around 'like a joint of meat before the fire', how women fainted and others called on the marines to shoot the man and put him out of his misery. The hangman was forced back to the scaffold, where he 'made a fiendish leap upon the dying man', hanging on the legs of the dying culprit for at least 13 minutes, until finally 'his agonising cries were heard no more'. Blay must have wondered what the consequences would be if this happened to him on his first job.

While Blay searched for answers to the unanswerable one of the condemned, Patrick Wallace, was in his cell nearby, calmly writing a lengthy and eloquent letter to Thomas Hemor, 'an accomplice of mine in crime' because 'my inward monitor urges me to do so'.

The *Launceston Courier* said if the letter 'was his original compilation, without any assistance whatever', as it had been assured, then it was 'an extraordinary production, and the accuracy of the spelling, together with the correct distribution of capitals, would seem to imply that Wallace was a man of more extended education than is usually found amongst his class'.

Wallace said that, as a dying man, he wanted his friend Hemor to cast himself on the anchor of hope, Jesus, before 'a ground surf rises and carries you into the depth of the waters from whence there is no recovery'. He described how 'on Wednesday night Jesus Christ appeared in the form of man at the foot of my bed'. He had then prayed, extolled the virtues of faith, forgiveness and salvation, and urged his accomplice: 'if you value your soul and eternal welfare, you will mend your ways'.

Blay didn't need to be woken on the Saturday morning, as he had barely slept. 'One eye shut and the other open, thinking and fancying things that never will be and which is impossible', as English hangman James Berry later recalled of his own first hanging. Blay didn't have the stomach for breakfast, and didn't want to hear the bells tolling. But shortly before 8am, the gaol governor quietly but firmly told him, 'It's time.' The time to do what he had signed up for, to 'hang until dead' these two men, and do so without showing his nerves, without making any mistakes.

He had rehearsed in his mind over and over again for months, and privately practised with ropes and sandbags. But this was now very real, very public, very personal.

He might have been uncertain about whether he felt more dead or alive, but had gone too far to retreat now. He walked to the condemned cells to join the gaol party to escort Wallace and Watson to the gallows. He managed to pinion each man without too much fumbling of the ropes. He was dreading what was to come as much as the condemned. He joined the processional walk to the wooden scaffold with the under-sheriff, some constables known as 'javelin men' because of the ancient tradition of guarding prisoners with a spear, Reverend Dr William Browne for Watson, and the Reverend James Cotham, Launceston's first Catholic priest.

Wallace had chosen Father Cotham despite his Protestant upbringing. Blay would come to see many prisoners convert to, or adopt, Catholicism in their final days because Catholic clergy sought to persuade condemned men to confess their earthly sins, promoting a doctrine of purgatory and the belief that earthly sufferings atoned for future punishment.

Some prisoners were told the truly penitent could expect a heavenly welcome from 10,000 angels and the chance of becoming 'a trophy of sovereign grace', and Catholic bishops sometimes personally appeared on the scaffold to read Psalm 51, the Miserere, known by convicts as 'the neck verse'. It was a plea by the condemned for God to 'have mercy on me ... in your compassion blot out my offence ... blot out all my guilt ... cleanse me from my sin' and not spurn 'a humble, contrite heart'.

Some hangmen preferred hanging Catholics because they had been 'taught' to die with resignation and gave the least trouble. Blay was certainly conscious that the two condemned men appeared 'to pay deep attention to the religious consolation offered ... and from their manner [appeared] quite abstracted from what was passing around'.

Blay was relieved the two men passively played their role in the dance of death, seemingly not perturbed that they would be hanged by someone so young. He waited anxiously to see if Wallace and Watson were going to make any final remarks or confession, but they did not. He took a deep breath and walked to face the two men. Trying not to look into their eyes, and trying to keep his hands from shaking, he placed a soaped noose around their neck, one by one, and a cap over their heads.

He took a step back, making certain he was away from the trapdoor. He avoided looking at the two men, put his hand on the release bolt and waited for what the under-sheriff said would be his 'usual signal', a silent nod of the head.

The nod came, he pulled the bolt and the trapdoor dropped with a sharp bang. The two men dropped silently and the nooses tightened.

Blay held his breath. The trapdoor had opened and now the two men were hanging below, ropes still securely around their necks, their bodies twitching.

'The drop fell and the souls of the misguided men ascended to their maker to answer for the deeds committed in the flesh', the *Cornwall Chronicle* reported.

The souls didn't ascend immediately because death was not immediate. Blay's task was to hang them 'until dead', and the next few minutes seemed to take a lifetime before he felt a surge of relief on seeing the bodies become inert. Only when the two men had clearly drawn their last breath did Solomon Blay breathe more easily. He had just become a hangman, one of the few people in the Empire in the unique position of being paid to personally and legally take the life of another. It was just two weeks after he turned 25.

The historic civil jury had judged, the chief justice ruled, and the novice hangman delivered. The life and liberty of two more Vandemonians had been despatched into eternity. Blay's life would never be the same again.

While life-ending for the bushrangers and life-changing for Blay, it was just another hanging day in the colony, as the *Chronicle* perfunctorily described: 'This morning the utmost penalty of the law was carried into effect at the usual place of execution upon Patrick Wallace and John Watson, the two bushrangers, convicted during the last sittings of the Supreme Court, of a robbery with firearms at Ashby, and putting in bodily fear ... after hanging the usual time, the bodies were cut down and consigned to the tomb.'

The double hanging merited no more space or significance in the newspapers than other colonial affairs of that day: the capture of a 'notorious sly grog seller', the impending arrival of a schooner with a batch of female prisoners for assignment, a house fire, a fisherman abandoning his master's boat and expending £23 of his money, a constable sent to work in a mill for 30 days after stealing money from a woman he had arrested, a settler prosecuting another for the theft of a goose, horses in the coach from Hobart Town being forced to run through bushfires beside the road, a new magistrate arriving at Circular Head, new rates and fares for licensed carriers and boatmen, and the death of Jorgen Jorgensen, the former King of Iceland turned convict constable.

Blay was immensely relieved; he had held his nerve enough to perform his grisly duty, the task was over, and his name was not in the newspapers.

He had been through a lot in his short life: impoverishment, imprisonment, syphilis, banishment, piracy, whipping and chain gangs. But this was something else. With his own bare hands he had just put two living souls to death. He now had to live with his choice of the lonely life of a death merchant, a personal choice but one that would not remain private for long. He had been seen by a crowd watching from outside the gaol wall, and not one he could easily walk away from because it would be almost impossible for a hangman to find any alternate means of income.

Inside the walls of his own mind, Blay was in need of some comfort. Not the religious comfort sought by the condemned, but a different spirit.

9

ROPE AND RUM

There was no going back. After months of doubt and anxiety waiting for his first execution, Solomon Blay now had the weight of living with the reality that he had put a noose around two men in tandem. Blay was now the man everyone despised and feared, and the one they would call 'the agent of death', the man who carried out 'the last sentence of the law' by 'turning them off', dispensing 'hempen fever', conferring 'the order of the halter', serving a 'hearty choke for breakfast', allowing them to 'dance with a stranger' and 'dance upon nothing' in a 'greased cravat' before being sent into 'the long sleep'.

The hangman was the subject of many conversations, but Blay had no one he could talk to about what it was like to have just become the 'man butcher', no one to provide any comfort or advice about how to keep the mental demons at bay, no one who knew what it was like to be uncertain of when the next 'job' would be, no one who could guide him as to how he might live while delivering death.

In a quiet corner of one of the red-curtained inns of Hobart Town, he found a rum friend. Some preferred the company of a dark Bengal, which found its way from India and Indonesia, others the sweeter and less potent Jamaican, which came with whalers from North America. Some preferred the mix of rum and water or beer, known as 'grog'.

But if the rum was beginning to quieten some of his inner demons, it was diluted a few weeks later when the local papers reported that another young sheriff's operator, on the scaffold in England for the first time, had fainted on seeing blood spurt from a condemned man's neck. 'When restored to animation he was found to have lost his reason, and has ever since been confined in a madhouse, where no hopes of his recovery are entertained.'

The torment of hanging, and wondering whether the rope would lead to his own death or a madhouse, led to Blay's first hanging year being one where his hands alternated from rope to rum, treading a precarious line within himself and with the under-sheriff and the judiciary.

Blay's nerves were soon challenged again when he faced the prospect of having to hang five men, with their fate, and Blay's anxiety, swinging in unison for more than a week. The five men sitting in Hobart Gaol were three bushrangers condemned for absconding and robbery 'without any hope of a reprieve', and Joseph Broom and Patrick Minehan for stealing clothing from a Campbell Town landholder and putting one of his convict servants in bodily fear.

The *Colonial Times* argued for mercy for the three bushrangers on the grounds their efforts to escape 'a state of abject slavery' was human nature and there was little violence involved. Furthermore, it said, a death penalty would only encourage all bushrangers to more violence and bloodshed, with a view that 'as every man's hand is against them their hand will be against every man'.

A week passed and still the men, and Blay, waited. He had to ready himself with five ropes, but the under-sheriff hadn't received his official orders to proceed. Preparations were made and checked, nerves were steeled and frayed. Finally, the *Colonial Times* reported that 'mercy has been graciously extended' to the three bushrangers, and then to Minehan, although he would meet Blay soon enough.

A five-fold hanging was a fearsome prospect for Blay, but then again a full hand would have meant five hanging fees of £5 and the right to five sets of clothing for his second-hand sideline. But now he needed just one rope for the only man not reprieved. Joseph Broom declared his innocence to the last, asserting the servant had given false testimony, and according to the *Courier* it appeared 'he died the most hardened that ever came under the notice of authorities here'.

While the *Colonial Times* had argued that the colony was not so overrun by bushrangers as to make 'an awful example' of three of the five condemned, a reward of 50 sovereigns and a pardon was now on offer for the capture of the bushrangers who murdered two shepherds at Great Lake, near Bothwell, just after Christmas. The government said if the murders were committed by three men it had been pursuing for more than six months, an additional 100 sovereigns was on offer.

The government was wrong about the three it suspected, but two other bushrangers, William Hill and James McKay, were captured, the latter confessing to a constable that one of the shepherds had recently 'got him flogged, a fustian jacket he called it'. The men were condemned and despatched in May, the *Colonial Times* saying they 'died reckless and obdurate'.

It had only been six months, but Blay's tally now already included two double-hangings, and he'd almost been called on to despatch five in unison. In the winter of his disconcert, Blay was again in the company of rum, and charged with being drunk and disorderly. He was sentenced to three days in solitary.

But even as he was drying out, the Supreme Court was readying his next job. After being among the five Blay thought he would have to hang just a few months ago, Patrick Minehan had been sent to a 15-man chain gang breaking stones at Port Arthur, where he joined a group wanting to escape using a stolen file to cut their irons. But the plot was revealed and the would-be escapees suspected James Travis, described in court as a 'lad'.

'On the morning of the day when the lad was struck,' the court was told, 'the prisoner had used several threats against him, saying he had got something for him … he asked the lad how long he had to serve, and on being answered about two years, the prisoner said he would be in Little Island long before that', referencing the place where prisoners were buried.

According to the evidence, when the men were unlocked from their chain, Minehan went to Travis and smashed him down with a stone hammer. An overseer told him, 'Paddy, you should not have done that', to which Minehan replied, 'There lies one bloody dog, stiff enough.' But the lad wasn't yet stiff, able to make a compelling deposition about who had attacked him before dying three weeks later.

Minehan explained he was tired of his life and that the deceased deserved it for depriving him of liberty. At his trial, Minehan sought supporting evidence from other chain gang members. But they were described as 'repulsive specimens of humanity', and he was found guilty.

It was not even six months since the chief justice had passed a death sentence on Minehan, only for it to be commuted. 'This is the return you make for the clemency', the judge said. 'Your savage disposition, for savage it was, was still untamed and as a cowardly ruffian you took away the life of a poor boy when he had no means of resistance. You showed no mercy to him, and you can expect no mercy here.'

While he had put little value on his own life, he had no right with little or no provocation to deprive the life of another. The judge put on his black cap and passed the death sentence, and ordered Minehan's body to be 'anatomised and dissected', to which Minehan loudly exclaimed: 'Thanks be to God! You cannot dissect my soul, although you can my body!'

For the second time in six months Blay prepared to hang Minehan, while the condemned man, with the help of Catholic clergy, prepared his last declaration, confessing to the murder and apologising for denying his guilt and speaking disrespectfully in court. But he was more sorry for having 'frequently offended the great judge of the living and the dead, at whose dread tribunal I am now about to appear'.

Minehan said he was 'more desirous to die than to live, in the hope that this shameful death may contribute to expiate my offence'. His wish to die rather than live was granted by Blay on 18 June.

The hangman's next finishing was also on a man twice condemned. Edward Allen was convicted of murdering another Launceston man over a small debt. But after the judge was said to have omitted 'a portion of the usual form of words' in his passing sentence, he recalled the prisoner the next day to ensure there was no doubt about the words and the message: prepare for the eternity before you, be taken to the place from whence you came, thence to the place of execution, to be hanged by the neck until dead and your body afterwards to be given over for dissection.

Now Allen, who the Launceston *Courier* said had been of 'total indifference' during the trial, realised his fate. The prisoner 'changed to a most death-like hue, and for the first time appeared to feel the peril of his awful situation'.

Blay knew the job was imminent. But he always had to wait and see if the governor would grant clemency, and then wait while the execution warrant was signed and delivered.

In the same month he prepared for another multiple hanging, after three bushrangers escaped from his old Jericho chain gang and, armed with muskets, robbed a man at Macquarie River near Oatlands, before threatening a constable, saying they 'would blow a hole through him'.

At the death knock, reprieves meant only one noose was required. In early August, Thomas Dooner, who the *Colonial Times* said 'seemed perfectly resigned to his fate', appeared alone on the scaffold at about 8.15am, where the 'drop fell and put a period to his existence'.

The term 'resigned to his fate' had quickly become familiar to Blay. It was ascribed to men who had been so often punished and degraded that punishment held diminished fear and life held diminished hope. Blay's victims were frequently reported as being 'more desirous to die than to live', 'quite abstracted' and 'reckless and obdurate'.

Blay wanted to live but was less resigned to his own fate, and again tried to find comfort in rum. Three weeks after Dooner's hanging, the sheriff had to reprimand Blay for being 'disorderly'.

While he was being 'disorderly', James Broomfield and two other men were found guilty of armed robbery at a house on the Mersey River, on the north-west coast. The owner, Henry Bonney, pleaded with the men not to shoot him as he had nine children. But Broomfield said 'none of your cant' because Bonney had been a 'terror' to him and it was time to settle the ledger. He pulled the trigger, but it didn't fire. In late October, Blay pulled the bolt on Broomfield, and it worked.

After storing away his rope, Blay found it hard to restore his nerves. Just a few days after Christmas Day he was again reprimanded for being 'drunk and disorderly'.

Meanwhile, James Williamson was on trial for murdering a storekeeper at Swan Port on the east coast, along with George Bailey as an accessory. Williamson told Bailey he shot the man because 'a dead cock never crows', and that as he had done 'all the dirty work, you must do the clean', and forced Bailey to set fire to the body if he didn't want to suffer the same fate.

After being taken into custody, the court was told, Bailey said to Williamson in the presence of two soldiers, 'We'll both be hung, as round as a robin.' Williamson said, 'It won't be as bad as you might think,' but Bailey was sure: 'Jack Ketch and the rope will do it.'

The *Courier* studied Williamson in the dock. He was 35, born in Scotland of Irish parents, and said to be regarded at school as the king of dunces. Reflecting interest in the laws of phrenology, the posterior regions of his cranium were strongly developed, his eyes were small and deeply set with 'an expression of prying curiosity, mixed with cunning, which was considerably heightened by a sarcastic curl of the upper lip'. The paper said that with a deep scar on his face and a small neck, he conveyed 'ferocity'.

Bailey, from Wiltshire, was only 45 but with the appearance of being 60, perhaps reflecting his life as one of 'an uninterrupted tissue of crimes of every hue'. These included being transported from Gloucester for life for burglary, conspiring the death of his master, making a canoe in an attempt to escape and being convicted of 'an unnatural crime'. He evidenced a 'nervous stupidity', 'insurmountable dread' and 'an earnestness almost painful to behold', frequently perspiring, his handkerchief constantly wiping away tears from his bloodshot eyes, and dropping in the dock whenever the term 'capital punishment' was mentioned.

Williamson's sangfroid during the trial changed dramatically when the jury found him guilty, and 'a tear rolled down his cheek which … suddenly became pale, his lip quivered and his eye lost its fire'.

The two men shared the condemned cell, but Bailey refused to read to the illiterate Williamson, just as Williamson refused Bailey's entreaties to say he had nothing to do with the murder.

On January 4, the bells of St David's sounded the death knell. Bailey had to be carried up the scaffold ladder and was supported by two sheriff's men as Blay put the rope around his neck, while Williamson was pale and agitated, his knees shaking.

Williamson shook hands with his co-condemned before Blay drew caps over their faces, but even before the cap was secure on Bailey, the *Courier* said, 'his hands ... seemed to denote that he had fallen into a swoon, indeed we feel convinced that long before the drop fell sensibility in him was extinct'. The hangman withdrew the fatal bolt and they were consigned to 'whence no traveller returns'.

But Solomon Blay's inaugural *annus horribilis carnificem* wasn't over yet.

Barely a week after despatching Williamson and Bailey came the news that an 18-year-old convict at Port Arthur, Henry Belfield, had killed his 17-year-old 'companion' by stabbing him in the neck 'after the manner which butchers term pithing'. The young victim had told the chief constable at Port Arthur in the few days before he died of his wounds that Belfield had 'ill-used him', while Belfield claimed the victim was the cause of his being sent to Port Arthur.

Belfield's early life might have resonated with Blay. The illegitimate son of a Cheshire doctor who stopped providing even a scanty pittance for his support, young Belfield was left without friends, family or protection. Forced into burglary, he was convicted at age 15 and sentenced to 14 years transportation and 'from that moment until the hour of his death, his life has been an uninterrupted stream of misery'.

After arriving in the colony just a few years before Blay, Belfield was convicted of a second burglary, absconded four times and variously sentenced to 20 lashes, more than two years hard labour, solitary confinement for up to six months and two years in chains. It could easily have been Blay's story.

Now Belfield, barely 5 foot (1.5 metres) tall climbed the scaffold with 'fresh energy' and firm step, the *Courier* reported, his face holding the 'flush of youth', before he was covered in a cap and noiselessly 'loosened his hold of a world which had, from his cradle, reflected on him only misery and degradation'. Like the *Courier*, Blay could not have missed the mood of the spectators, who 'while they detested the horrible deed for which he thus prematurely and ignominiously died, felt a sympathy for the youth of the sufferer'. Others, the paper reported, had openly commented that 'he died game' and 'didn't he die a pebble?'

Hanging a man was one thing, but a small teenager was a special ordeal. Blay was reminded of it when he later read how James Berry felt when he hanged a boy of the same age:

> With trembling fingers, with tear-dimmed eyes, I know I shall find the task far beyond me … he was a child … poor little fellow … I can still see him, his tear-stained face as I went to pinion him. His eyes staring in dumb appeal, his lips moving convulsively.
>
> And it is the bitterest thought of my life that I was not man enough on that occasion to turn to the crowd in front of the scaffold and say — 'I refuse to do the duty you have brought me here to do'.
>
> What would have been the use? I could not have saved him from his fate, and it would only have been prolonging his agony. Some other hangman would have been called in to do the work.

In the week after despatching young Belfield, Blay was again trying to escape the noose that bound him, drinking and gambling in a public house. And he was again found guilty of misconduct, fortunate to escape with a reprimand.

Perhaps feeling a sense of hopelessness, he took a bigger gamble a month later, breaking and entering the house of William Nicholas in Warwick Street, and stealing two coats and a pair of trousers. Nicholas told the court he had gone to the races at New Town and returned home to find the house had been broken into. Mr Thomas Symmonds, the son of a lieutenant, said he saw Blay and John Phillips come out of the house and throw the clothing away before he apprehended them.

The court refused the prosecutor any expenses for leaving his house unprotected, which 'although a very common practice, is a very improper one', but found Blay guilty. Not just guilty, but this time he would not escape with a reprimand and a few days in solitary. He was sentenced to transportation for life.

Transportation for life meant Norfolk Island, but there was no life there. Everyone knew a lot of convicts found it hellishly worse than the gallows. And once they knew he'd been a hangman, they'd do their business with him. He was done for.

The sentence was heavy for Blay, but nothing unusual in the colony, being recorded only in a brief sentence in the *Colonial Times*. The newspaper, whose masthead featured English poet William Cowper's line 'What is it but a map of busy life — its fluctuations and its vast concerns', missed identifying Blay as a hangman. It had also missed the fluctuations of two Solomon Blays, father and son convicts now guilty of the same crime of stealing clothes.

Transported to Sydney for stealing coats in Oxford, Solomon Sr stole a pair of trousers from Hyde Park Barracks only a year after his arrival and was sentenced to a month on the treadmill. He was now 63 and quietly working out his sentence around the Windsor area, about to receive his ticket-of-leave.

In contrast the son, just 26, faced a second banishment, this time to Norfolk Island. Here some convicts, so despairing of hardship and debauchery, so deprived of real hope, deliberately committed crimes knowing the penalty would be execution.

Sir Francis Forbes, the chief justice of New South Wales, told a House of Commons select committee in 1838 that experience 'has proved that transportation is capable of being carried to an extreme of suffering such as to render death desirable, and to induce many prisoners to seek it'.

He cited cases of men at Norfolk Island who cut the heads off their fellow prisoners with a garden hoe, knowing the certainty of being detected and executed. 'They did this without malice, and when charged said it was better to be hung than to live in such a hell,' he said, and he himself would 'not hesitate to prefer death under any form' rather than endure what happened on the island.

Blay must have thought his number was well and truly up. Being banished from the banished, he would be ending his life deranged or dead on Norfolk Island. He'd had his chance to escape serious punishment and to make a life for himself as a hangman, and he'd strangled it. Like the hangman in Punch and Judy shows he'd seen in Oxford, he'd allowed himself to become the victim.

But in the lottery of life and death in the colony, Blay was presented with the unexpected: another chance to survive. Under-Sheriff Crouch didn't have another hangman on his books, and it wasn't a good look to have the courts condemn two of his hangmen consecutively. So while Crouch knew the young hangman had struggled with nerves and alcohol in his first year it was to be expected, especially in one so young, and ultimately Blay had in fact managed to hang everyone by the neck, as required, until they were dead.

And Crouch had another condemned man awaiting the noose. He decided to back his original judgement, and now asked Blay if he might choose to continue as executioner as 'this might work in your favour'.

What was Blay to do? He was damned whatever he chose. Live as a hangman in Van Diemen's Land or be banished to more danger at Norfolk Island? A life of killing people or risk being killed by the worst of the worst? Gamble on surviving as a hangman or surviving Norfolk?

It was a hellish choice, and there wasn't a lot of time to think about it. His first hanging year had been horrid and he wasn't entirely convinced he had the nerve to stay on the scaffold, but lifelong exile to Norfolk Island seemed even worse. He chose to think that some hope of freedom and life at the price of being a hangman was better than no hope on Norfolk Island.

Blay told Crouch he was indeed prepared to continue as executioner, and very much hoped it would work in his favour.

Both men were relieved when the governor quickly resolved in the affirmative, albeit that Blay 'in consequence of his undertaking to perform the duty of executioner, is to be kept in prison with hard labour for four years'. Officials resolved it would be better for all concerned if the sentence was served as a year at each of the four gaols, starting with Richmond.

As hard as Richmond Gaol was, and as tight as the cells could be — 8 feet 6 inches by 3 feet 6 inches (2.5 metres by 1 metre) — Blay comforted himself that it was sufferable compared to the Norfolk alternative. And unlike everyone else, he would be allowed to leave 'occasionally during the day, returning to the establishment at night', after the governor quietly approved him being able to travel outside the walls on Her Majesty's special service at Hobart Town, Launceston or Oatlands.

Hobart Town was now celebrating its confirmation as a city, and Blay was confirmed as the hangman. He had survived his first year as the Empire's youngest hangman, one in which he had despatched 12 men, including three double hangings. He had kept his job despite being punished or reprimanded four times, and had narrowly avoided transportation for life for stealing.

He now had to keep his head because there'd be no more chances. He wasn't the most popular resident inside Richmond Gaol, and the under-sheriff was watching him even more closely. This was a place of life and death chances, and Blay was in it up to his neck in more ways than one.

10

DOING THE BUSINESS

After his first dozen hangings, including three double-headers and despatching a teenager, and narrowly avoiding the hell of Norfolk Island, Blay waited inside Richmond Gaol for the first of his second-chance 'jobs'.

Within two weeks of the governor agreeing to his temporary release to perform his special duty, Blay walked beyond the gaol walls to despatch Thomas Turner who, after drinking at The Horse and Jockey, murdered his wife by punching, kicking and hitting her with a stick until it broke, then taking to her with an iron hoop, and finally throwing hot water over her. All watched by his 11-year-old son nursing a baby sister.

A single hanging seemed somewhat straightforward, but this one would be watched by a big crowd, unnerving for a hangman still becoming accustomed to the craft and not wanting to be recognised for his deeds. The *Courier* said Turner's hanging was watched by a 'thoughtless multitude' who witnessed 'a miserable fellow creature' without ever reflecting how soon, or by what unforeseen calamity, their own fate might lead them to the same undiscovered country of no return.

Blay was relieved there was no 'unforeseen calamity' on the scaffold, but he had barely stored his bag when two days later a warrant arrived in Launceston for the execution of a teenager, Elijah Ainsworth, convicted of what the *Cornwall Chronicle* described as 'an unnatural crime of a most repulsive description'.

While the details were deemed by authorities and newspapers as unfit for the public eye, Blay understood he would have to deal with numerous men who committed 'unnatural' crimes involving young girls and boys, other men and various animals. 'Unnatural' crimes and capital punishment were each seen by clergy and anti-transportationists as the two worst strands of convictism, adding a special dimension to Blay's task.

The teenager was charged with 'an unnatural offence' upon a five-year-old girl, Mary Jeffery. Young as she was, the girl appeared in court, giving her evidence 'with much clearness', the *Launceston Courier* said: 'We never recollect hearing a case wherein the majesty of truth and justice appeared in greater triumph; the simplicity of the child's statement; her very manner and expressions, were sufficient to carry conviction with every word she uttered; and the various links were rivetted by such strong circumstantial evidence that all doubt was necessarily excluded.'

The jury quickly returned a guilty verdict, and Chief Justice Pedder, in passing the sentence of death, was 'greatly agitated and affected; declaring to his God that he would not have believed such a case to be possible had he not heard the evidence'. The judge entreated the prisoner to banish all hope of mercy, as 'no government in the world dare spare the life of such a monster'.

Newspapers reported 'his voice was frequently broken, and tears were rolling profusely down his cheeks', while the attorney-general 'was also obliged to have recourse to his pocket handkerchief, and attempted in vain to subdue his feelings. The tears would come.'

The 18-year-old Ainsworth evinced no apparent anxiety or distress during his trial, but when he heard the judge's sentence he also burst into tears and left the dock protesting his innocence. He subsequently asked to see his former master and admitted the justice of the sentence, and asked him to tell the other convict servants to 'take a warning' by his fate. His fate, the *Cornwall Chronicle* reported, attracted 'a large number of females ... present at the disgusting spectacle which the execution afforded'.

Crime against young girls was a constant concern. When two convicts assigned as servants near Jericho were found guilty of taking liberties with a settler's young daughter, one newspaper commented that 'parents amid such a population as that with which we are surrounded, especially those who reside in remote parts, cannot be too cautious in the care of their female children (and we blush to say it) their age must not be an exception'.

Women and children in the hinterland could not be too cautious. Blay would separately hang men from just one village, Baghdad, for the rape of a woman, rape and murder of a six-year-old girl, and assault and strangulation of a 10-year-old girl. He also hanged a man for carnal knowledge and rape of a three-year-old at Triabunna, another for murdering a 15-year-old girl who had slighted him at Oyster Cove, and another for raping his step-daughter at Port Sorell.

Concern about the ugly side of convictism led to a Society for the Suppression of Vice, with the governor agreeing to become patron, presumably not expecting the society to seek an inquiry into the male and female gaols and factories, which it described as 'hells upon earth'.

'We learn that at Port Arthur upwards of 5000 men and boys are huddled together, in the female factories nearly 1000 females are shut up from intercourse with their species', the society said, and then after this 'probation' these 'wretches' were sent into the colony 'to improve the morals of the young and rising generation of Van Diemen's Land'. It said the governor should hold an inquiry into 'these modern Sodoms and Gomorrahs', and if he didn't think such isolation to be a mistake then the 'curse of heaven' would continue to be suspended over the colony.

In the lottery of life in the colony, some individuals took it upon themselves to seize what they thought ought to be theirs, and dispense their own justice, which was why Blay's second Christmas as a hangman was spent preparing for a double hanging.

Samuel Williams, described as 'a clownish looking lad', had escaped from Port Arthur but, still shackled in his leg irons, came across some goats and tried to kill one before being challenged by a frail old goat-herder. Williams struck the old man about 10 times with a pick-handle. It took a jury less than three minutes to return a verdict of guilty. The judge, in passing the death sentence, wondered why Williams, tired of his life, did not just take his own rather than deprive another of his.

Alongside him on the scaffold was James Littleton, convicted of 'cutting and stabbing, with malice aforethought and intent to kill' a fellow prisoner, Henry Seaton, who had called him a 'murdering thief'. Tired of such accusations, Littleton, who acted as barber to other prisoners, took to Seaton's scalp with an axe.

On the Christmas gallows, Littleton appeared, with prayer beads on his arm, telling the assembled crowd it was 'hard, very hard, for an innocent man to die', and, the *Courier* said, 'waved his pinioned arms in a token farewell'.

But Williams was not so co-operative, one of the hazards of the hanging trade which Blay always feared. The hanging process required something of a silent compact between the condemned and the hangman, whereby the victim stood still to allow the rope and cap to be put over his head, but the *Courier* said:

> Williams appeared in great trepidation and succeeded ... in extricating his arms from the rope which confined them. His first aim was to pull off the cap which had been drawn over his eyes, and when again bound, the apparently great length of his forearm enabled him to grasp the hood.
>
> The executioner, however, after several trials, managed to secure him more effectually, and immediately afterwards hurled into eternity two unhappy beings, whose depraved and reckless dispositions have, by their own avowal, for many years made them a burden to themselves and a disgrace to humanity.

Blay was relieved to be able to despatch the pair, and pleased to collect his usual fee and the condemned's clothes, and in this case some prayer beads, all welcome additions for his second-hand trade.

It wasn't long before Blay knew bushrangers would soon provide more clothing. A hunt was underway in May 1843 for two bushrangers who had killed a police constable in the Fingal district, leaving a family of orphans. Descriptions of the wanted men were distributed around the State, with a massive reward of 100 sovereigns, and a pardon and free passage from the colony. Blay sensed another double hanging if the men were captured alive, but before then he had to despatch another desperate man looking to find his own 'escape' from convict exile.

Henry Smith, transported for life in 1825 for horse stealing, had just had breakfast with his overseer, Henry Childs, at a Sandy Bay property. After their meal, Childs told Smith to 'go up and mend the fence, and take the hammer with you, and mind and bring it back'. Smith did not make it to the fence, but did bring the hammer back to the breakfast table, where he fatally smashed Childs over the head.

There was no evidence of previous quarrelling, and Smith had a conditional pardon for five years and was well on his way to full freedom. But, the coroner said, the prisoner had confessed, saying he had been unable to 'get rid of a disease, which had rendered his life burdensome to him, and had committed the murder for the sake of being put out of his misery'.

The jury took only a few minutes to return a guilty verdict. Smith protested that it was unfair to be sentenced to death when he was 'out of [his] mind when the murder was done'. But on the morning of 11 May, he faced death 'with an expression of vacant astonishment'.

Blay couldn't be astonished by the man in front of him. He might not relate to the grisliness of smashing another's head in with a hammer, but he could now relate to someone being so demonised by apparent hopelessness that they would want to be put out of their misery by killing in order to be killed themselves. Men living in a private hell, be it physical or mental, sometimes made desperate choices: to escape across unknown seas, 'bolt' from chain gangs into the bush or commit crimes to receive the ultimate punishment. In their own way Smith and Blay had sought an escape, and now one had to deliver for the other.

Blay didn't allow himself to dwell on Smith. He had come to understand that the more a hangman thought about an individual, the harder the task. It was easier to try to shut out any consciousness of living, breathing souls and any feeling for the consequences, and just focus on the mechanics. His sole focus, his job, was to escort, cap and drop them.

It wasn't for him to think about rights and wrongs, fairness or justice. He was merely the 'operator' at the end of a line of people sitting in judgment, a line that stretched from Her Majesty to the Colonial Secretary to governor to chief justice to sheriff to under-sheriff and then to him. It was a collective rope he held, and in the case of Smith he was giving the man what he had asked of him: to be put out of his misery.

Such desperation was not uncommon. One writer in the Hobart

Town *Almanack* said that 'the desperation to which some of these wretched men strive is truly appalling ... men committing the most barbarous of murders in open sight of their companions and supervisors, for no other intent than to be arrested, sent up to Hobart Town, tried, convicted and executed'.

One convict confessed that his motive for the attempted murder of another prisoner was that 'if found guilty, the parson would attend me and I would be sure of going to heaven'.

Catholic priest Dr William Ullathorne told of being tasked with telling a convict group who among them was to be executed. Those named 'one after another they dropped to their knees and thanked God that they were to be delivered from that horrible place, while the others remained standing mute and weeping. It was the most horrible scene I ever witnessed. Those who were condemned to death appeared to be rejoiced'.

Another convict moved a sentencing judge to tears when he said, 'Let a man be what he will be when he comes here, he is soon as bad as the rest; a man's heart is taken from him, and there is given to him the heart of a beast.'

Sometimes a man's heart had to break free, simply because the shackles of rule and authority were too much to bear. Convicts were known to 'bolt' even if they were close to receiving a ticket-of-leave, forfeiting any chance of freedom in the near future. Captain Alexander Maconochie said the 'monotony of their lives became insupportable, even in those cases where they were not cruelly treated'.

Blay knew desperation was the genesis of most of his jobs, and bushrangers were the most desperate. The colony was particularly outraged after two break-ins in the Fingal district over three days in May, during which two bushrangers had shot and killed a man who was a police constable, leaving a widow and 'seven orphans'. Riley Jeffs and John Conway were the subject of a major manhunt, excited by the reward of 100 sovereigns, a free pardon and free passage from the colony.

The *Hobart Courier* said the activities of the 'sanguinary ruffians' Jeffs and Conway 'greatly exceeded Cash's gang in the enormity of their conduct', and 'settlers in the interior are described as being in a great state of anxiety and alarm'.

Blay might have noted the reference to Martin Cash, his former chain gang colleague at Jerusalem, and in the same week another brief report about his recent conduct.

> THE BUSHRANGERS: Cash, Kavenagh, and Jones, after keeping their burrows for many days, presented themselves at Bashan Plains on Tuesday last, where they robbed the stock establishment of Mr. John Espie, and also Air Ring, the surveyor. The booty taken was so heavy as to induce the marauders to press a couple of horses to carry it for them. By their appearing in such an out of the way region, the bushrangers must evidently feel themselves hard pressed.

Blay would be crossing paths with Martin Cash again one day, but that was to come. For now the focus was on the two other bushrangers. Jeffs was just 22, a groom by trade, just 5 foot 1 inch (1.5 metres) tall; Conway was 23, a tailor, 6 foot (1.8 metres) tall, with two scars on each side of his neck and several initials tattooed on his arm. With the substantial reward and massive publicity, every settler was on high alert, and some sought local Aboriginal trackers to help find the men.

Over the next few weeks, suspicion fell on a remote shepherd's hut on the estate of James Youl, whose family had considerable pastoral interests around Symmons Plains, south of Launceston, and who would be remembered for introducing trout and salmon to Australia.

A party of seven constables from Campbell Town set out for the hut, anticipating a bloody showdown. But when they arrived the bushrangers were in the process of cleaning their firearms, and Jeffs was 'in a deplorable state' with a bullet wound after his firearm discharged while scaling a fence.

The Advertiser hailed the bloodless apprehension of these

'more than inhuman miscreants' as one that would bring delight throughout the colony and an anticipation of 'the dreadful vengeance of the law'. The newspaper opposed 'the abominable practice of capital punishment' — its owner John Pascoe Fawkner lamented valuing 'a man's life at less than a sheep' — but nevertheless 'if ever villains deserved, or crimes demanded, such an extreme infliction, the perpetrators of the late murder, stand amongst the foremost of the dreadful calendar'.

As long as the colony was 'the grand depot of British outcasts', it said, the government was obliged to provide protection against convict dangers.

On Monday 3 July 1843, a crowded courtroom in Launceston watched as Chief Justice Sir John Pedder and a jury heard the case and contemplated 'the dreadful vengeance of the law'.

On the first day the bushrangers, with Jeffs sitting in a chair due to his injury, faced the lesser charge of stealing a gun and other articles around Fingal, and were found guilty. On the next two days they faced the more serious charge of breaking into another property, shooting and killing the owner, district constable William Ward, leaving a widow and seven 'orphan' children.

A witness described how Jeffs had 'pointed a piece in and told us that if any of us moved he would blow all that was in the piece through those that did so'. There was a struggle with the district constable, who was fatally shot. After a short deliberation, the jury found the two guilty.

The following Monday, the chief justice asked Jeffs and Conway if they had anything to say as to why they should not be adjudged to die according to law. Both said, 'No.'

His Honour then addressed them, pointing out that the crime was atrocious, even for men in their situation; they were two to one and there was nobody to oppose them but a helpless old man and two women.

The jury sought mercy for Jeffs. The chief justice said he would take that recommendation to the authorities, but it would be wrong to hold out hope: 'There is mercy towards society to be shown, as well as mercy towards you.'

The *Cornwall Chronicle* said Judge Pedder was 'much affected' while addressing the prisoners. He was only three years into his law career in London when, just 31, he applied for and became chief justice, the only judge in the colony.

Shocked by the severity of the criminal code, Pedder had become well used to donning a black cap atop his white legal wig, a tradition dating back to the days, reported in the Scriptures and the classics, when it was a sign of mourning. He became so used to the black cap he was described in some newspapers as 'Australia's fastest hanging judge', who 'maintained the fodder supply to Hobart's gallows' and 'passed more death sentences than any other colonial judge'.

His reputation stemmed from the frequency of multiple hangings in his early days, including in June 1827 when 19 prisoners were led in to be sentenced for capital offences of sheep-stealing, cattle-stealing, house-breaking, theft, forgery, felonious shooting and highway robbery. Hard as he tried to find some circumstance to justify him refraining from passing sentence, he told all but one to resign themselves to their fate, and passed the sentence of death on 18 men.

As a devout Anglican, Pedder gave prisoners the benefit of every possible doubt, and would sigh with relief if he could avoid the black cap. His judgements and arguments to the Executive Council indicated his unease with the severity of the criminal code.

When one of his own assigned convict servants was sentenced to work on a road gang because of his 'disposition to dissipation', Pedder thought the man had some qualities and was unsuited to the hardship of a road gang so 'I will undertake to be his gaoler'.

But now as he faced the two bushrangers, the judge couldn't find any possible doubt about their guilt, and so passed the awful sentence of the law. Conway displayed the same 'hardened obstinacy', while Jeffs, whose case had excited some feeling of commiseration, shed tears.

As soon as Blay was advised the two men were to be 'hanged by the neck', he began to ready himself. A multiple hanging always increased the anxiety, but now the authorities also decided to make this the first public hanging away from the gaol in Launceston. A scaffold was erected in a park known as St John's Square (now Princes Square), originally a clay pit where convicts made bricks.

Just before 8am on a cold winter's morning, on 26 July 1843, Blay walked with Jeffs and Conway to the scaffold in the square to face more than 1000 men, women and children, many of whom had camped overnight to secure the best vantage points.

Jeffs, the newspapers reported, 'requested and obtained permission to address a few words to the assembled multitude. He cautioned them to take example by his unhappy fate. Adding that he trusted his peace was made with God, he concluded by bidding them all an eternal farewell.'

He had also asked Reverend Henry Dowling, Tasmania's first Baptist Minister, who attended him while he awaited execution, to amplify his message in a lecture in his chapel. This he did to a full house, mostly ticket-of-leave men and assigned servants, who listened with 'the most breathless attention', many 'evidently affected by the discourse'.

On the scaffold, Conway did not speak, 'but appeared to have suffered dreadfully both from remorse and terror', and had lost his former hard demeanour. Just before the drop fell he joined hands with Jeffs.

So it was that, as the newspapers reported, 'at the usual hour this morning' another two men underwent 'the extreme penalty of their offences'. Blay had shaken hands, as was now his custom before a hanging, with two 'inhuman miscreants' who went to their death holding hands.

Hanging by hanging, Blay was seeing the different behaviours and responses of the condemned, and some gallows scenes were touching. But it was best not to indulge in either empathy or enthusiasm, but rather to maintain a detached countenance.

Such detachment hadn't always been evidenced at the colony's gallows. A *Sydney Evening News* report of the 'good old hanging days', when it was the fashion to 'turn off a dozen before breakfast' in Hobart Town, recalled a fat and fussy governor asking the hangman what was delaying the execution. The hangman said, 'If you please sir, the drop won't work.' To which the governor replied, 'Never mind,' clapped his hands and demanded, 'jump off my lads, jump off.'

No, Blay was grimly determined that the best way for him to keep walking his chosen path was to execute but not engage, doing his best to avoid the undue wrath of anyone, be they sheriffs, colonial administrators, convicts or citizens, and to keep his approach as silent and simple as best he could manage.

He was merely a servant of the law, a small cog in a big empire's wheel, doing what eminent judges and governors ordered, just doing the job, no more and no less.

11

THE BELL TOLLS

Rarely a month passed when Solomon Blay was not required to be the law's final servant. But there was no consistent pattern. While the days of hanging as many as 12 at a time had passed, multiple hangings of two, three, four and five continued. There were numerous individual hangings, sometimes on consecutive days. He could be called to Hobart Town, Oatlands or Launceston, and he had to be ready to join the condemned for their final walk on almost any day of the year, even over the Christmas and Easter periods.

Some hangings attracted crowds of 1000 and more. People attended for many reasons: curiosity, entertainment, vengeance or sympathy. Some were keen to see whether clergy had managed to persuade the condemned to use their final breaths to confess. Some were disappointed when the condemned did not 'dance' and provide some macabre merriment. Some took their children along to demonstrate the consequences of bad behaviour.

Some crimes were so routine and common they excited little interest, or were adjudged so horrid that authorities and newspapers imposed their own censorship and reported little, save perhaps a fleeting reference to an 'unnatural act' or a 'horrific offence'.

The only real consistency for Blay was the bells tolling the hanging hour of 8am. And when a crime, trial and fate of the condemned was of unusual or enormous interest, the bells seemed to toll even louder.

Such was the case in the first week of April 1844, when the hangman had to order 'rope and soap for five'. The *Colonial Times* reported simply: 'Execution — The following individuals suffered the last penalty of the law this morning: George Churchward, George Bristol, John Walker, William Thomas and John Woolley. They appeared sensible of their melancholy position, but no one spoke excepting Churchward, who expressed himself to the effect that he trusted the present awful scene would operate as a warning to all.'

This matter-of-fact brevity underscored the parallels of life in the colony. While the crimes and trial received attention in the *Colonial Times*, the hanging of five men was recorded in a column of brief items headed by consternation about the fees to be imposed at St David's Cathedral for baptisms, weddings and burials, and was followed by details of a match race scheduled the following Monday, 'on the New Town race course, once round, between Mr Kearney's Gimcrack and Mr John Stevenson's Chorister, for 100 pounds aside, the owners to ride their respective horses'.

The men were in a group that escaped Port Arthur in a crude boat made of wicker. Churchward told the court he had been sent to Port Arthur from Sydney, with no hope of indulgence, and had absconded for his liberty. Others said they had suffered for up to

20 years, been tyrannised by severe overseers, given 100 lashes, and chained for up to nine months.

After eight or nine days on the run without food Churchward and his companions, armed with a tomahawk and stones, went to a hut on Betsey Island. But the occupants there pleaded poverty, so they went to other properties.

The men said they wanted to escape unbearable punishment, and only stole enough food as was necessary to survive. One said he had enticed his young 'brother' to join them in absconding and implored the court to extend its mercy: 'He is but a boy ... and I beg of you to give him another chance for his life!'

The court was not persuaded by anything that was said and resolved to hang all five. In contrast to the *Colonial Times*, the rival *Courier*'s report of how 'five unhappy men have this morning closed ignominiously a life of sin and sorrow' was a more fulsome description of a typical hanging.

> The scaffold was erected, as usual, in front of the gaol, within the outer wall; five ropes, ready noosed, were suspended; a military guard stood with their backs to the gaol, and facing them, in the middle of the street, a body of constables.
>
> A crowd of many hundreds filled up the rear-ground, and the windows of the public offices exhibited eager spectators. The crowd consisted, besides men, of scores of women and many children.
>
> Moving into the crowd a female might be seen with two infant children, which she was labouring to elevate at arm's length to enable them to catch a glimpse — of what? — of the ropes by which so many lives were to be taken!
>
> A spectator, whose gruff address indicated a sense of inconvenience from his view being obscured ... commented aloud on the woman's bringing infants to witness such a spectacle, to which she replied coolly 'nothing like example' and turning to the children in her arms she said 'look there my dears ... they'll soon be here and you'll see the ropes put around their necks'.
>
> A buzz in the crowd intimated the presence on the scaffold of the first who ascended, and on turning in that direction, a lad, apparently,

was to be seen bowing to the spectators. His youthful and comely appearance excited expressions of grief and compassion from many present, and the words 'so young' were simultaneously uttered.

His fated comrades now followed successively, accompanied by the Very Reverend the Vicar-General, who appeared to the last to be earnestly applying the preparations and consolations of religion to the condemned.

The ropes were now put round the necks of the victims, and the caps drawn over their eyes.

Just as this operation was about to be performed on one of the number, he stepped back and kissed a companion in fate, and it was an eye whose fountains must have been frozen or dried up that could refuse a tear of sympathy at this last expression of an affection which was more powerful than all other emotions in such a season.

The exterior of man's wretched justice now being arranged, the decent formalities which precede the slaughter gone through, many of the spectators began to move away, satisfied with what they had seen when a sudden noise attracting attention to the scaffold, all was found to be over.

The stretched ropes (which in all the coolness of one familiar to his duties, the executioner was to be observed correcting some disarrangement in) indicated that all had been done which man in hate, or revenge, or fear or aught of dislove, can do to his fellow-worn man, and that five human beings had exchanged the vigour of life and early manhood for that sleep in which the wicked cease from troubling and the weary are at rest.

Blay was quietly pleased. There was no suggestion he hadn't met the challenge of hanging five men simultaneously without mishap, and his determination to evidence a detached professionalism was recognised in the reference to a 'coolness of one familiar to his duties'. Perhaps he had somewhat come to terms with his fate, more able to feel detached. Just as many a convict's sensibilities and spirit was lost after years of punishment and debasement, so more frequent hangings reduced his sense of foreboding and feeling. The condemned's 'indifference' and the executioner's 'coolness' were two ends of the same rope.

Englishman Joseph Syme, who witnessed many of Blay's executions, said the 'apparent apathy with which the unhappy men met their fate was always to us the most humiliating part of the spectacle'.

While their lips would follow the clergyman's prompts, 'they were empty sounds, the soul in a certain sense was already gone', so much so that for the executioner the main part of his duty was already done as 'the kernel was already consumed, the outer shell only remained'.

> They sung psalms, they ate a most abundant meal, they heard the summons of the Sheriff, their arms were pinioned, the halter out about their necks, they heard the solemn and affecting words of the funeral service as the pastor walked before them to the scaffold, the cap was brought over their eyes and they dropped into eternity with more indifference than the ox goes to the slaughter.

While nine out of every 10 condemned to death were 'resigned to their fate', Blay was resigned to his fate but still alive.

Later in the same month, Blay's next 'job', as he called them, was in Oatlands for another double hanging: Alexander Reid had escaped from Port Arthur, and had shot and wounded a pursuing constable; Thomas Marshall had robbed and murdered an old man, and concealed the body in a waterhole at the New Town Brickfields.

Reid was a re-offender sent to Port Arthur, which was only accessible by sea or through a narrow stretch of land called Eaglehawk Neck. Across the isthmus the military established a 'dog line' of ferocious chained dogs, intended to bark and alert guards if a convict managed to get close, or maul them if they got closer. Some dogs were even placed on landing stages in the water in a bid to stop convicts trying to wade past.

The 'dog line' was devised by Ensign John Peyton Jones of the 63rd Regiment:

> It occurred to me that the only way to prevent the escape of prisoners from Port Arthur in consequence of the noise occasioned by the

continual roar of the sea breaking on the beach and the peculiar formation of the land which rendered sentries comparatively useless, was to establish a line of lamps and dogs.

> I ... covered a way with cockle shells as to show a brilliant light on the ground at night and proposed that a certain number of lamps be supplied and rations for a certain number of dogs [initially nine, then increased to 18] to be so placed that they could not fight but eat out of the same trough and render it impossible for anyone to pass through.

Journalist and publisher Henry Melville, who had bought the *Colonial Times* and would produce the first novel published in Australia, Henry Savery's *Quintus Servinton*, described the dogs:

> Those out of the way pretenders to dogship were actually rationed and borne on the government's books, and rejoiced in such soubriquets as Caesar, Pompey, Ajax, Achilles, Ugly Mug, Jowler, Tear'em and Muzzle'em. There were the black, the white, the brindle, the grey and the grisly, the rough and the smooth, the crop-eared and the lop-eared, the gaunt and the grim. Every four-footed, black-fanged individual among them would have taken first prize in his own class for ugliness and ferocity at any show.

The presence of armed guards and ferocious dogs, and talk of sharks in the sea, did not stop desperate men from attempting escape by foot or makeshift rafts and canoes. One convict even disguised himself as a kangaroo and endeavoured to hop his way across the neck, but his plan failed when a soldier decided to shoot 'the large roo'.

Some were more successful, including bushranger Martin Cash, who with Lawrence Kavanagh and George Jones escaped in 1842 by tying their clothes in a bundle over their heads and wading through the water.

Blay would catch up with Cash and Jones in the next month, but now he was dealing with Reid and Marshall.

About 60 people waited at a new scaffold erected in front of the great gates of Oatlands Gaol, the largest regional gaol in Van

Diemen's Land, built by convicts to hold up to 280 prisoners. The massive gates were inside a stone arch, part of an enclosed wall 10 feet (3 metres) high and 3 feet (1 metre) thick.

Fifteen minutes before the hanging hour, the gaol bell began tolling and 'the utmost quiet and decorum prevailed throughout the painful scene', the *Colonial Times* correspondent wrote.

Reverend Henry Gaud had been 'the most earnest and assiduous in affording them spiritual advice and consolation in the gaol' for several days and Reid now exhibited 'the strongest manifestations of piety and contrition'.

Reid told Reverend Gaud he couldn't have imagined that on the eve of his hanging he could attain such a state of mental composure. The only thing that appeared to disturb Reid's mindset, the *Times* correspondent said, was his disinclination to suffer on the same scaffold with the murderous Marshall, whose hardened demeanour and protestations 'became so blasphemous a character as to disincline anyone from holding converse with him'.

Blay escorted the two men on their final steps up to the platform. Reid, 'a man of fine countenance and figure' took his final steps firmly, and briefly addressed the crowd, 'expressive of his resigned frame of mind and anxiety for the welfare of all concerned'. In contrast, Marshall didn't look at the crowd, 'apprehensive perhaps of exciting some expression of the popular feeling', and was 'almost ferocious'.

Blay soon had a noose around each man's neck, and while the reverend was saying prayers for their mercy at the Throne of Grace, 'the dread signal' was given and the platform fell.

The crowd saw what it considered was justice: 'Reid appeared to die instantaneously, but Marshall, who was a man of light weight, struggled for many moments.'

While Reid's body was taken for burial in the town, Marshall suffered the additional penalty of dissection. The bodies were despatched to Hobart colonial hospital for surgeons to further their knowledge of human anatomy and to assist in teaching.

Blay was entitled to know the medical assessment after a hanging, the formal pronouncement of death and whether it came quickly by a displacement of the vertebrae, or whether the bloated or purplish colouring of the face and protruding or bloodshot eyes indicated death had been more of a slow strangulation.

Blay was entitled, but not that interested. His duty was to hang them by the neck until they were dead. He had, and they were.

A week after the Oatlands double hanging, Blay travelled from Richmond Gaol to Hobart Town for the despatching of George Jones, who had escaped from Port Arthur with Martin Cash and Laurence Kavanagh.

In January 1843, posters began advertising 'Reward! Fifty sovereigns and a conditional pardon' for their apprehension, and in May the *Colonial Times* reported that these 'maurauders' had paid a 'domiciliary visit' to the stock station of Mr John Espie in the highlands west of Oatlands.

> ... well aware that this is the season when the winter supplies are laid in at the out stations. They pressed a couple of horses into their service, and carried away a quantity of flour, a bag of sugar, 20lbs. of tea, and a variety of other desirable etceteras. One or two other visits with similar success will keep them comfortable during the winter, and the money and plate they have robbed will be sufficient to pay for information ... Had a more liberal reward been offered for the apprehension of Cash and his companions, they had long ere now been taken and the enormous expense they have occasioned been saved. As however they have as yet taken no life, nor used any violence to females, they could not do a better thing than start for the other side, and apprehend the cowardly murderers of Ward; and we are certain everybody would be glad that by so doing they would thereby save their own lives, obtain a new pardon and a passage to England.

Cash and Kavanagh had been captured and sentenced to death but given a last minute reprieve, much to Blay's annoyance, and were to be sent to Norfolk Island. He was now only required to do business with Jones, who had stayed on the run, not persuaded to give himself up despite Cash and Kavanagh's reprieves. His fate was sealed when he teamed up with James Platt and Frederick Moore in a series of armed robberies, arousing public anger when they reportedly tied an old woman to a bench and applied a hot spade to her legs to force her to reveal where she hid her money, before making off with just £1.

After a massive search, armed constables surrounded the three hiding in a hut near Richmond. The bushrangers opened fire, wounding at least one constable. The police responded by setting fire to the hut. Platt surrendered, but Moore was fatally wounded trying to crawl out, and Jones received a charge of buckshot in the face.

At their trial, in what the *Courier* said was a 'clear and not unmusical voice', Jones said it was true he was an outlaw, but he was 'not the inhuman brute that some of the witnesses introduced against me would lead you to suppose'. He said some of the facts had been exaggerated, the old woman admitted she was only slightly burned, and that firearms usually went off easily during a scuffle.

Jones said:

> You must be aware of also the feelings with which the police regard men who, like me, to gain their freedom, have unfortunately taken to the bush.
>
> I hope your Honour will have some pity for my unfortunate situation; my eyes have been shot away; my condition is deplorable; I know no one about me, nor can I see any man's face; I shall never more see the light of the sun; nor do I know that I am standing in a court of justice, except by hearing what passes around me, and sometimes by what my comrade tells me.
>
> True it is that I am an outlaw; but I have never committed murder; I have never violated the chastity of a woman. Those who know me best, know that I am, and have always been, particular and careful in avoiding shedding blood.
>
> And now, should your Honour be pleased to consider these circumstances, and to recommend my case to the favourable and

merciful consideration of the Executive Council, I will, to the latest hour of my existence, pray for your Honour, I beg.

His Honour begged to differ and passed the sentence of death.

In the gaol hospital, Jones asked a visiting Cash, 'Me lamps is queered. Will they scrag [hang] a blind cove?'

The Executive Council ruled in the affirmative and Blay was given the call to 'scrag' Jones and Platt, the former wearing on his wrist a plaited hair bracelet from a female acquaintance.

It was suggested this was the only occasion of a blind man being hanged in the annals of British crime. Whether Jones was totally blind from the gunshot wounds was not clear; Cash wrote in his memoirs that 'this was not the case as he had previously informed me in confidence that the sight of one of his eyes was partially restored but I was the only person aware of his circumstance'.

Until now Blay had hanged many a man, never a woman. This changed in the spring of 1845.

A wealthy couple staying at the Derwent Hotel in New Norfolk asked their personal maid, Jane Saunders, to go to the larder to obtain an evening meal. But the maid never returned and no trace could be found, until her body was discovered floating in the Derwent with multiple stab wounds.

Three male convicts working at the hotel the night Saunders disappeared were charged with murder, and female convict Eliza Benwell with aiding and abetting them.

Based on the evidence of Keo-Moi Tiki, an indigenous Sandwich Islander, Thomas Gomm, Isaac Lockwood and William Taylor were found guilty of murder, despite their protests of innocence. They were hanged in mid-September 1845, watched by a large crowd — the Cornwall Chronicle said 'the oldest inhabitant does not remember to have seen in Hobart Town, on any similar occasion'.

Lockwood, a former soldier, was described as 'a fine looking young man' who walked 'with a firm military step, with his head erect, and whilst the executioner was adjusting the rope, looked up earnestly towards the beam'. Gomm also walked with a firm tread, but had his head bent as 'one in meditation', and 'raised his hands as far as was possible' before being finally pinioned. Taylor seemed calmer, and 'bowed to the spectators'.

Despite their protests of innocence, the *Colonial Times* was unsympathetic: 'Whether they premeditated the murder or not, the whole treatment of their unhappy victim was so thoroughly brutal that not a single voice was lifted up in deprecation of depriving them of existence in a world their frightful crime had disgraced.' The *Chronicle* said it would have been 'more satisfactory' if the men had confessed to this crime, although they all confessed they deserved death for numerous other offences.

The trial of Eliza Benwell for aiding and abetting took another six days, an unusually lengthy time, with the courtroom packed and a crowd outside. Initially the jury accepted she was innocent, adjudging the murder was unplanned but occurred when the maid resisted the men's advances. But Judge Montagu wasn't happy with the verdict, and told them Benwell was just as guilty for keeping watch during an attempted rape and they should reconsider. An hour later the jury obliged and found Benwell guilty. When the judge sentenced her to death, Benwell exclaimed she was innocent, but prepared to meet her God.

The *Colonial Times* had hoped 'the miserable woman Benwell' would expire with 'a clean breast' by freely confessing. The idea of a woman saying nothing against 'the execrable treatment … by … three destroyers of the poor girl' demonstrated she did not possess 'one single attribute of woman' and proved the adage that an abandoned woman 'is capable of any extent of crime'.

But Benwell continued to protest her innocence, saying that far from 'keeping watch', it was only by accident she had seen Lockwood dragging the maid's body from the building. But it was to no avail, and on 2 October Solomon Blay was required, for the first time, to put his noose around the neck of a woman.

This hanging of four was inevitably going to draw a crowd. Benwell wasn't the first woman to hang, but it had been 15 years since Mary McLachlan had been the first in the colony, and New South Wales and Victoria were yet to hang any women.

McLachlan was a convict-servant who became pregnant, as was common with assigned maids, to 'a person of better education and higher rank in society than herself'. After her baby was born and found dead in the female factory she was found guilty of infanticide, and sentenced to both death and dissection even though women now rarely received that punishment in Britain. McLachlan ascended the scaffold with what the *Colonial Times* described as 'a firmness which is sometimes so much required by men' and her only words were 'oh my God' as she fell.

Now Blay had to ready himself to face only the second woman on the scaffold. A large crowd — variously reported as 2500 and 5000 — gathered as the bells of St David's tolled for Benwell and the three men, and Blay's pulse quickened. The *Launceston Advertiser* reported 'very many females, respectable enough in appearance, as far as that goes, formed a large portion of the multitude'.

Fresh questions frayed his usual detachment. Would women in the crowd try to stop the hanging? Would Benwell collapse on the scaffold? Does a woman die from hanging the same as men? What if he couldn't get them all to die at about the same time? What if her neck wasn't strong enough and her head came off? What would the crowd do if something went wrong? There were many questions but no answers.

Shortly after 8am, he had no choice but to grit his teeth and lead 'the wretched woman' up the steps and place her under 'the fatal beam' alongside the three men. The *Advertiser* said of Benwell: 'The miserable creature appeared nearly insensible, or else so deeply absorbed in thought as to render her almost unconscious of her situation. She uttered not a word.'

Out front, the large crowd watched intently, the grim silence

occasionally interrupted by the noise of 'children, especially boys
... in abundance amusing themselves, so long as they had room
on the pavement to do so, playing leap-frog, marbles and other
juvenile games'.

Blay adjusted the noose around Benwell's neck, put a cap over
her head, and within seconds pulled the trapdoor bolt: 'When the
drop fell, some females near the court-house uttered loud screams,
while several in the crowd were sobbing and weeping.'

Perhaps it was his determination to get it over and done with
as quickly as possible, or perhaps it just reflected the grimness of
hanging a woman, but the *Launceston Examiner* felt the executioner
was a little too business-like.

> The brutal manner in which the man who officiates as hangman
> performed his duty ... was noticed by the police and others, who are
> not insensible to the disgust of such a spectacle.
>
> There was an evident demonstration of indifference, and at the
> same time a sort of professional pride in showing the business-like
> manner in which he could enact his degraded part. Is there not
> something taught even by the reflection that the infliction of capital
> punishment, in the present form, requires an agent whose nature
> must be thoroughly brutalised before he can become qualified for
> the office?

Blay was reminded of the grim affair just two years later, when
another Benwell stood on the scaffold. Charles Benwell, who said
he had been transported after shooting an Irish clergyman and
escaping the noose by pretending insanity, was now facing charges
of cattle stealing and, with a 16-year-old boy, Thomas Wing, of
kidnapping and murdering a timber cutter.

Benwell had forced his victim to carry 100 weight (45 kilograms)
of flour from a timber camp to his hiding cave between Green
Ponds and Jerusalem, then forced him to kneel naked with his
hands tied behind him and to prepare himself 'for the next world'.
After his gun failed to fire several times, and the timber man

fainted twice, Benwell put a fresh cap on his gun and gave it to the teenage boy, telling him to shoot or be shot and burnt himself. The boy reluctantly fired a fatal shot into the victim's back, whereupon Benwell 'sat down and smoked his pipe'.

The *Courier* described the revolting murder as 'scarcely exceeded for cold-blooded atrocity in the annals of crime in any country'. Benwell went on a hunger strike in gaol, adding to public interest. When a large body of constables arrived at about 7.30am to form a line in front of the gaol, some 1000 people, 'including a considerable number of dissolute women and idle boys' had already been gathering for an hour. Then came 'the unhappy culprit, who was assisted up the steps by the executioner, who walked immediately behind, lifting him occasionally under the arm'. On the platform Benwell, haggard and of a 'sickly hue of despair', managed to shuffle along to the drop.

He was not, in fact, the brother of Eliza Benwell, who Blay had executed for the rape and murder of a maid at New Norfolk. According to the *Colonial Times*, he was a man called Power, who had simply co-habited with Eliza Benwell and taken her name. He was tried and condemned as Benwell, however, sharing a name and now a fate with his former paramour, embraced by the same rope.

STAINS AND STIGMAS

As Solomon Blay went about his calling of death, he was conscious the economic and moral sustainability of a colony underwritten and defined by convictism was beginning to be questioned — by officialdom in London and Hobart Town, and among the local settlers, especially in Launceston.

A small illustration emerged in the Eliza Benwell case. While Blay had to remain on sober standby during the week-long trial, Under-Sheriff Crouch, at the direction of the judge, had taken the jury to the Macquarie Hotel each day for refreshment, with the final bill running to £22 17s 6d. But, the *Observer* reported, 'in a sudden fit of economy having seized the authorities, his Excellency offered to bear half the expense only', causing the irate hotel owner to take legal action to receive the whole sum. The paper said it was injustice enough that free settlers were compelled to sit on cases of doubly convicted felons, and that it was a form of 'tax of convictism' that free men on jury duty also had to close their businesses or leave them 'at the mercy of prisoner-servants'.

The 'sudden fit of economy' for Eliza Benwell's jury expenses was a worrying portent for Blay; if there wasn't enough money to support juries in important trials, perhaps the fees for a despised hangman might come under question? And if transportation was deemed so undesirable or unsustainable that it had to end, there would be less call on the scaffold.

Everyone could feel that Van Diemen's Land was in a Depression. The now substantial wool industry was receiving low prices in London after an English recession, and mainland markets for grain and livestock had collapsed. Much of the capital had dried up after investors, graziers and bankers had speculatively supported development of Melbourne after John Batman and John Pascoe Fawkner sailed across from Launceston to found and develop the continent's third major white settlement.

Many colonists were close to insolvency, bankruptcies common, people stopped spending and credit was restricted. Two banks were forced to close, and public revenue sources, especially land sales and taxation, withered.

But still the Colonial Office despatched convicts in record numbers while resisting additional funds. Sir James Stephen, Under-Secretary of State for the Colonies, later admitted it was an 'ill-advised' decision to abandon transportation to New South Wales in 1840 and throw the 'whole current' of 4000 to 5000 convicts a year into Van Diemen's Land.

The 'whole current' included London despatching freedom fighters from the West Indies, Ireland and Canada. They included 58 men from Lower Canada (now Quebec) and 92 from Upper Canada (now Ontario), found guilty of violence against the State and condemned to death. They were instead mostly transported to

Van Diemen's Land, which the governor of Upper Canada, one Sir George Arthur, the despised former head of the colony, said was 'the most humane punishment the wit of man ever devised'.

James Gammell, one of only three Canadian Patriots to escape from Van Diemen's Land to the US with the help of sympathetic American whalers in 1842 — an escape that coincided with Herman Melville's similar 18-month voyage in the South Pacific, inspiring his epic story *Moby Dick* — was welcomed in New York by the editors of the *New York Herald* and *New York Tribune*, and his tales fuelled debate about convictism.

Gammell told them the colony was 'the most remarkable place for drunkenness I ever saw', and 'one of the wickedest, most profane, immoral and degraded places on earth ... Nine tenths of the people are convicts ... some of their crimes are so revolting that I forbear to name them, and as for the London prostitutes they are there in the thousands ... virtue itself would soon be contaminated in such a polluted atmosphere.'

His thoughts, reprinted throughout America, echoed those of Samuel Snow, who wrote a 32-page pamphlet called 'The Exile's Return; or a Narrative of Samuel Snow, who was banished to Van Diemen's Land, for participating in the Patriot War, in Upper Canada, in 1838'.

On his experience with treadmill convicts, Snow wrote: 'The scenes enacted by these wretched men during the hours of darkness were of the most revolting and diabolical character; too dark to be written ... too dreadful to be thought of ... the natural result of herding depraved men together in such a system.'

Queen Victoria eventually pardoned the remaining patriots, including idealistic American lawyer Linus Miller, who wrote in *Notes of an Exile to Van Diemen's Land* of unimaginable scenes, even inside the Penitentiary Chapel.

> On looking about me I could not discover more than twelve, among twelve hundred prisoners, who appeared to be taking any notice of

the service. Some were spinning yarns, some playing at pitch and toss, some gambling with cards; several were crawling about under the benches, selling candy, tobacco etc and one fellow carried a bottle of rum, which he was serving out in small quantities to those who had an English sixpence.

The convict pool of Van Diemen's Land had become international, and the stain of the penal colony was rippling well beyond the local politics and economics of public interest and self-interest. Rising concerns about security cost, sodomy and civility put governors and judges in an impossible position. They faced often conflicting expectations of the Colonial Office and the socio-economic realities in the colony, and unresolved tensions between those demanding strict punishment to maintain public safety and others seeking an end to convictism and more judicial humanity.

The Colonial Office did come to the view that the original assignment system had become too influenced by the attitude of masters rather than fairly reflecting a crime and convict behaviour. Terms of punishment could either be too harsh, little removed from slavery, or, more seriously for London, too lax, with the convicts enjoying better physical conditions than in their homeland, meaning prisoners were not being reformed and potential offenders in England not deterred.

Efforts were made to replace assignments with a probationary system, seeking to maintain original penitentiary principles of punishment and reform through separate confinement and a regime of hard labour, religious instruction and education, but with a more certain reward/punishment ethos at arm's length from the corrupting influence of self-serving masters. Every convict was classified according to the severity of their offences, separated to avoid undue influence from more hardened convicts, and subjected to successive stages of punishment across gaol, labour gangs and more than 80 probation stations hastily established throughout the colony.

But the system was overwhelmed, leading to more misery and restlessness among convicts, idleness, disorder and vice. Settlers were concerned by the increasing law and order risk, rising cost of more police and judicial expenses imposed by London, declining income from cheap assigned labour, and rising 'unnatural crime'.

A report by Franklin's private secretary, Captain Alexander Maconochie, at the request of the English Society for the Improvement of Prison Discipline, received widespread coverage in England. He described assignment as a cruel, ineffectual punishment lottery, and argued that convictism was encouraging immorality, restricting the development of Van Diemen's Land, and staining Britain's reputation.

Maconochie had some strange views — on his voyage out he expounded to passengers his theory that Europeans were once black but had turned white as their brains developed — but on 'penal science' he was more progressive. He believed cruelty debased both victim and the society inflicting it, and that punishment for crime should not be vindictive but strengthen a prisoner's desire and capacity.

His memorandum received support from influential humanitarians, such as Quaker missionaries James Backhouse and George Washington Walker, and members of a British Parliamentary committee convened to report on transportation and its future. The committee, already well disposed to the idea of abolition, embraced Maconochie's evidence about the lawlessness and lottery of life in the colony. It recommended transportation should cease as soon as practicable, gaols built far away from free settlers, more orderly release of convicts, and encouragement for released convicts to return home.

Maconochie's report strengthened the court of public opinion in England against transportation, which is what many settlers wanted. However, they resented his portrayal of a morally degenerate society driven by slave-owning despots.

Governor Franklin also felt compromised by his own Secretary lambasting a system he still had to run, one still dominated by an 'independent party of great wealth and influence', those Arthurite allies and beneficiaries such as the Colonial Secretary and chief police magistrate.

The Arthurites were those mostly involved in Blay's life, and he could see that colonists who had celebrated Arthur's recall and Franklin's arrival as a 'win' were disappointed the Arthurite regime had not been eradicated. Regarding the explorer-governor as a soft-minded liberal, the Arthurites worked zealously to protect their own wellbeing. Franklin was hoist on his own petard of trying to please everyone in a colony where settlers resented English officials ruling over them, officials resented criticism and change, the military resented civil control, convicts resented authority, and everyone feared crime.

Franklin's difficult position was acknowledged by Maconochie, who said 'selfish feelings everywhere predominate ... everyone, from highest to lowest, appeals directly to the governor ... the turmoil in which he lives is incessant' while Lady Franklin said her husband lacked the 'heart of stone and frame of steel' needed in the colony.

Blay, who understood the value of a heart of stone, was not surprised when Franklin was forced to dismiss Maconochie, who became superintendent at Norfolk Island. Here he actively worked with convicts like John Porter, the pirate on Blay's voyage, as he pursued his penal science theories, many of which were embraced in the *Declaration of Principles* at Cincinnati in 1870, a declaration embodying the fundamentals of modern Western penology.

But tensions reigned and the Colonial Secretary, John Montagu, openly questioned the governor's state of mind. Franklin suspended Montagu, but he appealed successfully to the Colonial Office, which in turn censured and recalled Franklin.

Having recalled two governors, and with increasing sentiments of social and economic 'injustice' in the air, the Colonial Office sent Lieutenant Governor John Eardley-Wilmot to the colony in 1843 to revamp the experimental probation system, whose shortcomings in planning, administration and funding had been aggravated by the rising convict numbers and declining economy. Lord Edward Stanley, then Secretary of State for War and the Colonies, regarded Eardley-Wilmot as 'a muddle-brained blockhead', but appointed him because of his interest in criminal law and juvenile delinquency.

When he arrived in August 1843, the self-described 'independent country Gentleman' found a deficit of funds and a surplus of unemployed convicts and unhappy settlers. Like Franklin, he found the Arthurite rump of opposition 'an insurmountable obstacle', but his major insurmountable was the moral stain of the colony.

Tales of cannibalism, homosexuality, sodomy and bestiality disturbed the sensibilities of Londoners. Lady Jane Franklin was among those to tell how eight convicts had escaped Macquarie Harbour, and 'banqueted on human flesh' until only one, Alexander Pearce, remained, captured with human flesh in his pockets — 'it tastes better than fish or pork' — before he was hanged.

One British newspaper, reporting the arrival in the colony of an Anglican Bishop, hoped earnestly that 'the next accounts may not bring word that he has been eaten up'. Governor Arthur Phillip said the sodomites ought to be given to the cannibals to eat, magistrates reported convicts of both sexes living 'as man and wife', and Catholic Vicar-General William Ullathorne wrote that 'scum upon scum, dregs upon dregs' had been poured into a cesspool of degradation which, if not arrested, would be a curse and a plague on everyone.

Barely 10 weeks after his arrival, Eardley-Wilmot sent Lord Stanley a 'private and confidential' despatch, feeling unable to send information publicly 'without outraging decency and creating disgust almost beyond endurance'. Eardley-Wilmot told Stanley of 'horrors' of 'unnatural crime' that generally 'defied description' and were best kept 'as private as possible'. But if the Secretary wanted more details there was 'the most incontrovertible proof' from magistrates and medical men who saw the 'great prevalence of opthalmia', an eye disorder resulting from gonorrhoea, indicating 'the men had diseased one another'. His private and confidential despatch was never made public or printed, and other despatch references to 'unnatural crime' were replaced in House of Commons publications with '****'.

Prison inspectors and magistrates more openly deplored 'filthy and sordid practices' of male convicts in their dormitories, and reported seeing men 'scrambling into their own beds from others, in a hurried manner, concealment being evidently their object'. But the governor's view was that in all 'large assemblies of the male sex, whether in the Army, Navy or among prisoners ... unnatural crime does more or less prevail' and while its occurrence could be reduced it was 'impossible to wholly prevent it'.

Perhaps, Eardley-Wilmot wrote, some 'exaggerated accounts of the existence of the evil' had been sent to England to increase opposition to the probation system. But he assured Lord Stanley and his successor William Gladstone that he would not be found wanting. He was taking every possible precaution and prevention, detailing efforts to increase separate accommodation units, 'lights ... kept burning all night' and 'frequent and unexpected visits ... at all hours'.

Eardley-Wilmot made some ground on the convict economy, securing increased funding for police and judicial costs, more settlers to boost investment, more freedom for conditionally pardoned convicts to move to the mainland and small land grants to ex-convicts. But he lost ground on the moral economy, accused of too many 'amorous affairs' himself, and being 'soft' on 'unnatural crime'.

The *London Naval and Military Gazette* published a scandalous report from its Melbourne correspondent, stating: 'Van Diemen's Land is in a bad state. The men in the bush are almost their own masters, and crimes the most horrible are of daily occurrence. All the females have left the bush, and have taken refuge in the towns, and even there are subject to every kind of insult. Sir Eardley sets a bad example himself. No people of any standing will now enter Government House, except on business. No lady can.'

The governor scornfully dismissed suggestions of 'scarcely concealed concubinage with some of the females received as guests at Government House', but it was harder to avoid the charge that the stain of sodomy was deepening. Judge Algernon Montagu, 'the mad judge', complained 'unnatural crime' had 'exceedingly increased' at least partially due to the decline in imposing the death penalty. He was particularly angered when the governor reprieved bushranger Laurence Kavanagh just 10 minutes before Blay was due to perform his duty. Such intervention, the volatile judge declared, could only be justified by the virtual abolition of capital punishment, and if a jury sentenced a man to hang and the Executive Council issued a reprieve then 'the sooner the Supreme Court is shut the better'.

Six months later Eardley-Wilmot received his own secret despatch from London, advising he was being recalled for failing a significant part of his duty, 'namely the active care of the moral interests involved in the system of convict discipline'. Eardley-Wilmot declared himself 'The Victim of the most extraordinary conspiracy that ever succeeded in defaming the character of a Public Servant'. The *Colonial Times* agreed, saying the governor had been 'murdered'.

Judge Montagu was also removed from the Bench, but not before telling a jury: 'We are surrounded with thieves, burglars and other offenders of the deepest criminality. A worse community, with especial reference to the very large proportion of the convict population, never existed on the face of the globe than in this island'.

Blay only had to scan the newspapers to understand powerful players were wrestling with weighty matters of politics, economics and justice, but while their battles went on, so did life, and death.

Amid the high-level discomfort and discourse about the stain of vice, Blay had to continue dealing with it at a more personal level.

The *Colonial Times* reported that on 12 December 1845, Job Harris and William Collier, two convicts at the coal mines, were charged with an 'unmentionable offence', the rape of a youth while he was held down by six other men. The details, said the *Colonial Times*, were 'unfit for publication', the *Launceston Examiner* as 'too horrible for description', the *Observer* as 'atrocious and unfit for publication'.

Blay hadn't forgotten his fear of sodomy during his chain gang days and could only imagine what the youth must have endured, so this was one job where he didn't have to work as hard to keep any anxiety in check.

Thirteen convicts gave evidence in support of Harris and Collier, but both were convicted and sentenced to be hanged. On New Year's Eve, Blay despatched the two men, along with another man convicted of murderously assaulting his overseer.

The following year another four were hanged for 'unnatural crime', including 19-year-old Michael Lyons, who had been in the colony only 18 months before he was found guilty of misplaced affections with a goat.

Settlers wanting a new identity beyond the imagery of a debauched and blood-stained Hades at the end of the world highlighted the moral stain as a direct consequence of banishing convicts to harsh punishment in close confinement, without religious and rehabilitation support. An anti-transportation push, the country's first potent political movement and genesis of Australia's federation and constitution half a century later, was promoted by a Launceston Congregationalist pastor, Reverend John West, who established the *Launceston Examiner* in 1842.

West was of the view that for the colonies, and Australia, to prosper there was no place for convictism, which he equated to slavery or serfdom, and all its degradations and vices. He wrote essays to argue for a 'federal union of the colonies', and for Australia to join India, Russia and the United States to end slavery and serfdom, and eradicate corruption, brutality and evil. Especially those vile crimes that Christians and governors could not speak of and British Parliament referred to with asterisks.

West was probably the author of a poem published in his own newspaper in 1846:

> Shall fathers weep and mourn, to see a lovely son, debased, demoralised, deformed by Britain's filth and scum?
>
> Shall mothers heave the sigh, to see a daughter fair, debauched and sunk in infamy, by those imported here?
>
> Shall Tasman's Isle, so famed, so lovely and so fair, from other nations be estranged, the name of Sodom bear?

After England sent its last convict ship to Sydney Town in 1840, the island was now taking the lion's share of the Empire's transported felons, as well as re-offenders from Sydney. The colony had become 'the Botany Bay of Botany Bay', West said.

In 1842, a year after Blay's first hanging, the island colony received 5329 convicts, the highest arriving in a single year. Ship arrivals averaged one every two weeks, sometimes two a day.

The surge took the population to 57,471, roughly split between convicts and settlers. But the identity and reputation of the colony was convict and vice driven, despite the earlier view of Governor Franklin that 'the whole state and appearance of society and of the country shew that we do not deserve the bad character which has so unjustly been given us ... and I can most positively state that the originally free portion of the community can bear a very advantageous comparison with that of any other country of intelligence, industry and moral conduct'.

But even British regiments in the colony to help maintain 'civil law and order' were problematic. By the autumn of 1845, nearly 700 members of the 96th Manchester regiment were on duty in 14 locations around the colony, guarding convicts, providing protection against Aboriginal and bushranger attacks, and undertaking various duties not usually associated with normal soldiering.

While some welcomed the red-coated presence as an important and reassuring part of the colony's heritage and wellbeing, others felt the soldiers still evidenced the Duke of Wellington's view that the British Army largely comprised 'the scum of the earth' who enlisted 'for drink'.

Numerous tavern and street brawls with locals who saw them as symbols of continued oppression came to a head when about 50 soldiers took control of Launceston for about 1 1/2 hours. They left their barracks in the early evening armed with 'heavy bludgeons, palings and other weapons', according to the Launceston *Advertiser*, rushed into the Black Swan Inn and began 'attacking every person within reach with the most brutal ferocity', both men and women alike.

Rumours of a riot quickly spread, and locals shut their shops and moved to arm themselves to defend their properties as the soldiers continued their mayhem, smashing windows and heads, before fleeing back to their barracks when other soldiers with bayonets arrived.

The *Examiner* said military insubordination was a serious issue anytime, but more so in a penal colony where convict numbers were rising but soldier numbers were not. A few of the rioters were court-martialled and imprisoned, but no serious inquiry was held. Three British soldiers later changed allegiances to take up bushranging, and were convicted of shooting with intent to kill a constable. They laughed and endeavoured to escape the court when the judge passed the death sentence, but their final salute was in Oatlands to Solomon Blay.

It was all very unsettling for settlers. They were living in a gaol without walls, with uncertainties about assigned convicts, bushrangers, and even 'protective' soldiers. Even 'tench men', those prisoners held in the penitentiary, were allowed to walk freely around the town on Saturday afternoons, which the *Courier* said 'amounts to a serious evil ... the annoyance ... so acutely felt by females that we understand it has become a rule in most families that no female member shall quit home on the Saturday afternoon'.

A hardline approach was pressed by some who saw absolute punishment, and the noose, as necessary to maintain security and law and order, whole others felt the noose symbolised a harsh and failed approach that had passed its use-by date.

Questions of justice were vexing vice-regal appointees, colonial officials and judges, but Blay knew that in the line of Her Majesty's law and order, he was the only one who delivered the ultimate justice and the only one who would personally suffer economically if transportation and the noose was abandoned. His views would never be sought, not that he thought the number of 'jobs' coming his way was likely to decline any time soon. Even in this year of high-level politicking, he despatched 14 men and women, underlining the unchanged reality of the colony's raison d'etre and modus operandi. But more people were looking harder at the hangman's proficiency.

In May he hanged Richard Jackson in front of Oatlands Gaol for rape, an offence the condemned may well have committed, but his recollection had left him due to what the *Courier* called the 'maddening influence of drink'. In front of about 30 spectators, Jackson 'owing to his light weight his struggles were prolonged beyond the usual period of suffering'.

In November, the colony's finisher was again under scrutiny when, in front of about 800 people in Launceston, he hanged Thomas Gillan. Gillan was only about 23, just a few years younger than Blay, originally transported from Ireland. He had repeatedly escaped and been captured, and was now on the scaffold after a robbery and firing at a constable.

A woman shrieked to the hangman to not pull the rope so tight around Gillan's neck, and the *Cornwall Chronicle* also said, 'We think it would be more decorous for the hangman, when he has executed his sad office, to retire to the rear, and not to face the crowd in front of the platform, as he did on this occasion with rather an irreverent air, as if he wished to elicit applause for his (not very honourable) deed.'

Blay was probably not seeking applause, but he was coming to realise his performances on the scaffold stage were no longer devoid of scrutiny, and it was hard to draw a favourable review.

On New Year's Eve he had a triple date with men from Port Arthur: Job Harris and William Collier, for sodomy, and Michael Keegan, an ex-British soldier, for attacking his overseer Joseph Ellis with a spade immediately after he completed 14 days hard labour in chains. The *Courier* said the case was 'mere repetition of many former ones', but beyond that Blay might have thought the name Ellis was familiar, as just the previous month he had hanged Francis Maxfield for stabbing Ellis.

The *Courier* described Ellis as 'a well-behaved man, generally kind to the men under his supervision'. Blay might have supposed the supervisor couldn't be that kind if he had two men try to kill him in consecutive months, but as he had been the source of two hanging fees he wasn't complaining.

The last day of the year was the last day for Keegan, Harris and Collier. The *Colonial Times* reported: 'They were executed on Wednesday morning, at the usual time and place. They died as they lived, apparently callous to the ordinary feeling of humanity. The concourse of spectators was not large.'

The year closed with some of the colony's political and economic strands becoming frayed, but Blay's rope remained tight, ready as ever 'at the usual time and place'.

13

TYING THE KNOT OF MARY

B lay's address moved in 1846 from Richmond Gaol to Oatlands Gaol. It wasn't his first time in Oatlands. Two years before, he had inaugurated a scaffold built in front of the great gates of the town's new gaol, despatching bushranger Alexander Reid and murderer Thomas Marshall, and more recently Richard Jackson for rape.

Blay knew his hanging of Jackson and Marshall, both lightly built, had raised questions about his ability to quickly execute men of any size. But he wasn't one for looking back, and was pleased to be in a new environment after a year at Richmond.

Just before he was moved to Oatlands, he had been called on to despatch an old man, John Phillips, for setting fire to some haystacks. Blay might have been curious that a man who had acquired two horses and savings of £200 felt moved to set fire to a farmer's hay.

What Blay was soon to find out was that arson and Oatlands would provide a connection that would change his life.

Blay had observed the Oatlands development on his frequent stopovers as a passenger on the coaches racing day and night between Hobart Town and Launceston. The duration and hardship of the trip had considerably diminished since Lieutenant Thomas Laycock, the first man to traverse the island, took eight days in 1807 to carry despatches on horseback. People scoffed at a coachman's promise in the 1830s to deliver the basket of mail in less than three days, rather than the usual alternate Sundays, but improved coaches and larger teams of horses working in relay soon cut this time to 15 hours. One major coach operator, Samuel Page, utilised a team of 300 horses with three main fodder depots along the way, including Oatlands.

Roughly halfway between the two main townships, Oatlands had grown from a small military detachment to a major stopover for the competing coachmen and their guards in scarlet coats and white beaver hats. Governor Lachlan Macquarie, who originally explored the area in 1821 and declared it 'a very eligible station for a town', called it Oatlands as it reminded him of a farming area of the same name in his native Scotland, and gave a nod to the Duke of York's Oatlands Palace in Surrey.

The township was the base for Governor Arthur's 1830 drive against the original inhabitants, when 5000 soldiers, settlers and assigned and ticket-of-leave convicts set out with 1000 muskets, 30,000 rounds of cartridges and 300 sets of handcuffs, to herd Indigenous people southward to the Tasman Peninsula.

The plan was singularly unsuccessful, but it didn't get in the way of ambitions to make Oatlands a capital of the interior. Some 80 kilometres of streets were marked out in an 1832 survey, and with the efforts of convict labour the township soon had a flour mill, numerous inns and taverns, and two competitive churches. The Anglicans called on John Lee Archer, the colony's chief engineer and architect, who designed most of the prominent buildings, including Parliament House, ordnance stores at Salamanca Place, the gaols at Richmond and Hobart, and one of the nation's oldest stone bridges at Ross. The Catholics called on Augustus Pugin, the English father of Gothic Revival architecture, who designed Westminster Palace.

But Oatlands was predominantly a military bastion. By 1842, when the whole colony's population was still only 44,000, it had a gaol, the biggest building in the town with its metre-thick stone walls, soldiers' barracks and Supreme Court.

The military focus meant it was somewhat easier for a hangman to avoid trouble and harassment, and Blay could get some peace and quiet walking the banks of Lake Dulverton, which was more a shallow lagoon than a lake. But sometimes, the story was told, he had to walk much further when a coach driver, acquiescing to passengers unhappy to sit beside a hangman, refused him a ride. Tavern talk was that Blay had even been forced to walk the whole 80 kilometres to Hobart Town for a hanging.

Blay's residence in the gaol, part of his sentence, provided free board and lodgings, but he paid the price of sitting among the condemned, embodying the hangman in convict verse: 'The hangman sat as mute as a stone, there he sat in the murky light, he and his shadow alone … when I first took to the hangman's trade, I'd many qualms at the gallows tree, yet I said 'tis law, and those who made the law must answer for such as me … the makers of law have honour and wealth, but I, who finish what they begin, can only creep among men by stealth.'

Blay was allowed out of the stone tomb of the condemned during the day, and as a renewed constable sometimes permitted by the sheriff to reside in the homes of anyone in court facing charges, much to their disgust. He now had income as a hangman and constable, along with the continued opportunity to make a few more shillings selling the clothes and shoes of the condemned.

Beyond the modest financial improvement, Oatlands also

brought Blay into an Irish diaspora including some famous freedom fighters and a young woman who had a burning desire to be transported.

Just as Blay had been forced into crime around Oxford, across the Irish Sea thousands of families also turned to crime to survive the Irish Famine, a period of disease and starvation, despite the country still exporting food to England. In a place no bigger than Van Diemen's Land, the famine left more than 800,000 people dead.

Many turned to petty crime to secure food and clothing, but some had a more desperate desire to escape by being prosecuted and transported. Women in rural Ireland were increasingly committing crimes punishable by transportation.

Mary Murphy was one of them. One of four children, the teenager had stolen money and clothes, but was discharged. She also set fire to a house but was again discharged. Undaunted, in 1848 she and three other young women, including two sisters, set fire to another house with the express purpose 'of being transported'.

Hers was one of about 200 cases of arson reported between 1846 and 1849, part of an explosion which would see Irish women comprise more than 40 percent of the 7000 female convicts transported between 1843 and 1853, and a big percentage of the 12,500 women convicts transported to Van Diemen's Land.

The arsonists were known as 'house and rick burners', the latter a reference to threshing machines taking the place of human labour. Five women who appeared before the Assizes in 1849 were described as 'of profligate character, and without a settled place of abode'. One said she 'set two houses on fire the same night and that she would continue to do so in order that she might be transported'.

A week later, Mary Murphy and three other women were on trial in Cork for setting fire to a woman's house. The court told the women that, strictly speaking, it would be obliged to sentence them to be hanged, but they would be transported 'to deter others from the commission of [this] offence, which was greatly on the increase in this country, where it was heretofore unknown'.

Another convict, Mary O'Brien, made a statement in 1852 indicating many of the arson women knew, or knew of, each other. She said 'four women, Ellen Garrin, Mary Murphy, Judy Macarthy and Mary Macarthy came out in the *Maria*, the ship before us, for burning in the west of Cork, at a place called Ballincorrick ... these girls were tried at the same sessions as myself in Cork ... three of them got 7 years and Mary Macarthy got life because it was she who brought out the fire.'

Mary Murphy's burning wish was granted, the court sentencing her to seven years transportation to Van Diemen's Land. First she spent three months in Cork Gaol, then another three months in a female penitentiary at Grangegorman in Dublin. A surgeon declared many of the women at Grangegorman unfit to sail due to measles and scalp diseases. But Mary received the medical all-clear and, after the sacrament of communion in the prison chapel, boarded *Maria* with another 165 female convicts and their 35 children.

The women were given two sets of clothing for what would be a 109-day journey, one for cold weather, one for heat: two brown serge dresses, a flannel petticoat, two aprons, two cotton jackets, two cotton nightcaps, two neckerchiefs, two pairs of shoes, two pairs of worsted hose and three cotton shifts. The seasick women often froze while they endeavoured to wash their clothing, which was of poor quality for the rough conditions aboard the ship, and it wasn't unusual for some women convicts on arrival to be declared unfit to be assigned to a household.

They were roused each morning at 6.30am to stow their bedding and wash for breakfast, followed by a vigorous cleaning of decks and water closets with lime chloride. Mornings and afternoons were spent learning to read and write or knit, interspersed with lunch, usually with a glass of lime and sometimes wine, then supper and prayer reading. By sundown, all women and children were sent below and the doors locked.

Unlike Blay's *Sarah* voyage, *Maria* did suffer the equator doldrums, becalmed for two weeks. It was becalmed again in the final three weeks of the voyage until, flying the red and white flag signalling the arrival of a ship of female convicts, *Maria* docked in Hobart Town on 23 July 1849. Mary was 19, listed as a 'housemaid', of fair complexion, 5 feet 1 inch tall (1.5 metres), with dark brown hair, long nose and hazel eyes 'with a noticeable squint'.

Mary spent an initial six months on the hulk ship *Anson*, a former warship moored in Prince of Wales Bay to relieve female factory overcrowding and allow women to be trained in domestic skills.

Sometimes housing up to 400 women across its three decks, life on the *Anson* was similar to what Blay had experienced on the *Leviathan* hulk in England. Sitting on the Derwent near Risdon, the women were supervised by Mrs Phillipa Bowden, a former asylum matron of Hanwell Asylum (St Bernard's Hospital) in Middlesex. In between ringing the bells for mustering, meals and prayers, she worked hard to give women like Mary Murphy skills to facilitate 'a means of getting an honest living when thrown at some future time upon their own resources', largely as domestic servants. So they learned to turn raw wool into female clothing and men's shirts, make straw hats and shoes, and become familiar with a laundry and kitchen. A chaplain and schoolmistress provided 'education and instruction as a means of moral influence and training', utilising various trade manuals, books about the birds and insects of Europe, Robinson Crusoe, and self-help books such as *Pursuit of Knowledge Under Difficulties*. Mrs Bowden proudly proclaimed, 'nor is it the least interesting sight in this ship when from 100 to 200 women in uniform parade the deck with utmost decorum, unrestrained, save by the presence of the female officer of their ward' for hygienic exercise.

Female servants were in 'great demand', the *Colonial Times* reported, and said in March 1847 that it was authorised to state that

on Friday the 5th instant at noon, upwards of one hundred women who have finished their period of probation on board the *Anson* will be eligible for private service, and that previous to that hour no one will be at liberty to engage them as servants, or to communicate with them. This precautionary measure has been adopted [so] that the public generally may be placed on the same footing as to obtaining female servants from the *Anson*.

Settlers responded to an advertisement such as: 'Mrs Rex respectfully announces to her friends there will be an assignment from HM *Ship Anson* in the early part of the month, at which time there will be some very good servants (English women). Mrs Rex requests the favour of your orders as early as convenient.'

As an assigned convict, Mary Murphy received a bed, food and clothing. The annual clothing entitlement was one cotton gown, three shifts, three pairs of shoes, three calico caps, two neckerchiefs, one bonnet, two bed-gowns, four petticoats, three pairs of stockings and three aprons. Mary was warned that if she failed to perform satisfactorily, or was blamed for any theft, she could be ordered to the Cascades Female Factory for punishment, which mostly involved washing large quantities of dirty laundry, known as being 'sentenced to the wash tub'.

It was a promising start to be assigned as a housemaid to the town's main surgeon and apothecary, Dr William Stokell, caring for three young children in his substantial 'Harrington House'.

But after only six months the unhappy surgeon took her to court when he found her drunk on the premises. She was sentenced the next day to a month's imprisonment with hard labour in the female factory. Here she was given a black cap, black jacket and black skirt, and her brown hair cut short for hygiene reasons. It was a practice that James Montagu Smith, an English sailor who spent time in the colony, described in his memoirs as a 'punishment feared next to death by the young ones, but they get used to it after a little colonial experience'.

The female factory was established on the site of a failed rum distillery at Cascades, nestled under Mount Wellington. It housed women convicts who re-offended, were pregnant or had children. Expanded several times, it comprised cells, some solitary and with no light, a nursery and hospital facilities, kitchen and laundry. Following major riots in 1839, 1842 and 1843, a government inquiry cited overcrowding, ill-discipline, understaffing, corruption, poor food and inadequate ventilation and sanitation. Another issue was a high infant mortality rate in the nursery, and the influence of the Flash Mob, a dominant group of women preferring to live on the inside rather than be assigned, bullying other women, trafficking goods and lesbian relationships.

After her release from the female factory, Mary was re-assigned to a government official to look after his three-year-old boy, but within a few months she was charged with theft of clothing, valued at about £4, 'not accounting satisfactorily for the means with which she purchased them'.

This time the court imposed nine months of hard labour at the factory wash tub, and ruled she could no longer be assigned to any work in Hobart Town. After nine months of hard washing, including a week in solitary for 'insolence', Mary was released to the Midlands, spending time at the Ross Female Factory before being assigned to a public house near Campbell Town, one frequented by one of her exiled heroes, Thomas Meagher, the freedom fighter said to have created the Irish tricolour flag.

She then moved to Oatlands. Perhaps it was an omen that a small island in the town's Lake Dulverton was called Mary's Island, but the prospects for women convicts were few. In a harsh and predominantly male society, male convicts heavily outnumbered women, sometimes as much as seven to one. They were desired for their cheap labour and sexual services, often falsely accused of theft or insolence when a master wanted the relationship to end, and even dismissed by government committees as 'with scarcely an exception, drunken and abandoned prostitutes'. Some women convicts, like their male peers, were drunks and some had plied a sexual trade, but many more were branded 'prostitutes' merely for living in de facto relationships, and were transported for relatively minor offences, such as theft of money, clothing, food, bedding and drapery.

The reputation of being 'wretched' or 'a whore' was easily attained and hard to lose. Having 'lost' their virtue by having sex outside of marriage, Reverend Henry Fry observed, 'a felon may grow honest [but] lost female virtue is irretrievable'.

Mary wasn't alone in realising that her best prospects might come with marriage. The economy was in difficulty, jobs scarce, income fragile, police numbers dropping rapidly. Many men were also off to join the gold rush in Victoria, so being banished from Hobart Town, and with her 'noticeable squint', Mary was not in a position to be fussy.

Unlike most, she didn't turn her eye away from Solomon Blay. He was one male who wasn't likely to be the source of competition for his company. But he was a strongly built man, by 1849 he had completed his four-year gaol term, received his conditional pardon in 1850, and had a regular job with some government security.

Mary obviously was not deterred by his calling, although was possibly relieved to see that Blay wasn't an extroverted hangman in the manner of Irish hangman Tom Galvin. She'd heard stories back home of him frightening people he'd just met by sneaking up from behind to put a rope around their necks, and of callously calling out to the condemned to 'come out, don't keep the people in suspense, they are mighty uneasy under the swing-swong'.

But a hangman was a hangman, and Blay had seen off more than 100 men and women by this time. The people of Oatlands readily recognised the man no one wanted to meet, as he had seen off a baker's dozen of Oatlanders and been a central player in some of the town's biggest events.

One memorable day came in May 1848, when the *Colonial*

Times reported 'the township this morning presented an unusual scene' due to Blay being called to send four men swinging in unison. Former British soldiers Patrick Shea and James McGough, with James Sullivan, had become bushrangers and shot at pursuing constables. After being given their death sentence, the men used a broken courtroom chair to attack the javelin men and attempt an escape. A fourth man, John Sheil, who had also bolted and was convicted of wounding with intent, joined them on the scaffold where all but one 'wept bitterly' while Blay adjusted the rope.

Three months later he had to draw the fatal bolt on another two bolters, Jeremiah Maher and Thomas Smith, who had stabbed a constable at Jericho. Maher had previously managed to escape from the colony and reach the Mother Country, only to be re-captured and sent back to Van Diemen's Land, where he again absconded, spending time on the run disguised as a Roman Catholic priest with Smith as his assistant. He also attempted to break out of Oatlands Gaol a few nights before his execution.

Mary knew if she committed to Blay she would be taking him 'for better or worse'. She would have been in no doubt his odious reputation could wash over her; she might be heckled and ostracised, she would be alone whenever he set out for 'jobs' in Hobart Town and Launceston. And even if she wasn't denied a ride by a coachman, the atmosphere on board might be uncomfortable, as Blay experienced many times. One winter's morning in 1849, a coach racing from Hobart Town to Launceston had on board a young boy, Thomas McCormack, who later recounted that the passengers 'conversed among themselves, ignoring a well-dressed, staid-looking man of middle-age and thoroughly respectable demeanour' sitting beside him, a man who quietly but engagingly described to the boy anything interesting on the way, 'but not once did he address the guard or passengers nor they him'.

At Perth, the scene of a famous hanging some years before on what became known as Gibbet Hill, the coach stopped for passengers to have dinner. But the 'respectable' man did not go inside to eat beside an open fire, staying out in the cold on the coach roof to eat his meal. Inside, the boy heard the hotelier say, 'I see you've got Solomon with you on this trip,' to which the coachman replied, 'Yes, that cove in Launceston is to be turned off tomorrow, he's a-goin' to scrag him.' The journey resumed, but not the conversation. The wide-eyed boy just stared.

The hangman was used to people avoiding his company, sometimes silently, other times with vitriol and disgust. He would do his best to ignore them, but sometimes he would eventually respond by promising his 'tender solicitude' if they ever came his way. Some people nervously asked questions, but he wasn't inclined to answer. While he was the public hangman, his life, and thoughts, were private.

One man due his 'tender solicitude' was John Stevens, who had murdered Margaret Buttery at Norfolk Plains near Longford. A ticket-of-leave holder, Stevens, who had previously threatened to 'finish her', confronted the woman as she was returning home on Easter Saturday in horse and cart. He got into the cart and shook hands with the woman, before attacking her with a tomahawk, severing the nose from her face. He dragged her from the cart and continued his 'inhuman and murderous attack, and then ran off', according to the *Cornwall Chronicle*. The woman was taken to her master's house where she 'lingered in the most excruciating agony until 12 o'clock, when she expired'.

Stevens was apprehended near the Cressy Hotel. When an approaching constable said, 'I want you,' Stevens replied, 'I thought so.'

Friends said the woman had been his accomplice in thievery in England, but 'he was so mortified that she should forsake him in this colony and get married to another man that he was determined to seek a bloody revenge', the *Examiner* reported.

The *Cornwall Chronicle* thought him an 'unfortunate wretch', callous and indifferent, while Reverend Thomas Butler maintained he was 'deeply sensible of the enormity of his crime, and gave satisfactory proofs of sincere penitence'. Whatever the truth, it made no difference to Blay, who administered the last sentence of the law in front of about 500 spectators. A considerable number of them were children, possibly including young Thomas McCormack to witness the work of his fellow coach traveller.

Blay's working life remained unchanged, but a new personal chapter was emerging. Unlike Stevens, Blay had no deep experience with affairs of the heart. His mother couldn't afford him much love, his own affections had given him syphilis in Oxford, hangovers and solitary confinement in Van Diemen's Land, and the only other woman he had been up close and personal with was Eliza Benwell, who he had hanged.

That had been seven years ago, but now he was enjoying the company of Mary Murphy, someone who provided conversation, company and comfort. One of their conversations would have been his call to hang another Mary, also young and Irish. Mary Sullivan was born in Cork in 1835, another victim of the Irish Famine. As a young girl she had twice been imprisoned for six months for stealing clothes and a church collection box. Her third crime was for stealing quilts, for which she was sentenced, aged 17, to seven years transport.

Arriving in Hobart Town in May 1852, she gave her trade as 'nurse girl', and with a *John William Dare* voyage report describing her as being one of the best behaved, she was assigned to help care for a boy, four years old, and a girl, two years old, while their mother was in hospital and father chasing gold in Victoria.

Less than two weeks in to the role the little girl, Adeline Frazer, known as Addy, was missing, along with some clothes, tea and sugar. The girl was found dead in a water tank, around her neck a narrow piece of calico allegedly torn from Mary Sullivan's petticoat.

Sullivan was apprehended the next day, convicted and

condemned to hang. In the familiar routine, the sheriff signed the authority for his deputy, Thomas Crouch, 'to execute on the 5th day of August the sentence of the law passed on the prisoner, Mary Sullivan', and Crouch in turn called on his operator Blay to execute the sentence.

The *Courier* said the circumstances were extraordinary, given the motive was 'incomprehensible', the girl's indifference when taken into custody and her stoicism during the trial and on sentencing. 'All these circumstances which appeared inconsistent with sanity had led to the belief that upon enquiry her insanity would be proved and her life spared', it said.

When some petitioners sought such a declaration of insanity, and fellow convicts said she was 'out of her mind' and had once been in a 'madhouse' in Ireland, Blay wondered if the insanity argument would rob him of his hanging fee, while Mary wondered if a fellow Irish woman would escape her husband's noose. But a Medical Board decided the teenager exhibited no vacancy or want of perception, merely 'utter callousness'.

The *Colonial Times* painted an unflattering picture of the girl's 'forbidding appearance and sullen disposition', but newspapers also painted Blay as cold and heartless.

But, Solomon and Mary might have discussed, no one really knew what anyone thought or felt, did they? And how could anyone know what was running through this girl's young mind? Who wouldn't look sullen if they were about to be hanged? And was a hangman expected to smile or shed a tear?

Hundreds gathered for the girl's execution on 3 August, only to be told to come back in two days' time due to a newspaper printing error. On the true day of reckoning a vast crowd amassed, watched by a strong body of police and a detachment of military with fixed bayonets.

The teenage girl was tiny even by the average of the day, just 4 feet 7 3/4 inches (1.4 metres) tall, but she walked toward the scaffold 'with a firm and resolute step, and her face and general demeanour indicated a total absence of all fear.' The *Colonial Times* was struck that Sullivan seemed 'unmoved, gazing steadily towards the crowd', and when Blay moved her around to pinion her hands she turned her head back once to continue to look at the crowd.

When he positioned her under the fatal beam and adjusted the rope around her neck the girl betrayed 'no symptom of fear or trepidation'. When he tugged the rope at the back of her pale neck to make sure it was in place, some in the crowd booed.

Towering over the diminutive girl, Blay bent down to put a cap over her head, doing his best to avoid eye contact. He moved away. The girl remained standing 'longer than appeared necessary', the newspaper reported, before the fatal bolt was pulled. The unfortunate girl 'fell through, amidst the silent horror of the crowd'.

The *Courier* wasn't taken by Blay or the girl. He 'appeared to execute his office in a way which had nearly drawn forth loud execrations [curses] from the crowd', particularly when on his re-appearance he 'chucked the rope which was round the prisoner's neck', while she was of 'sullen, morose disposition' and 'her head and features indicated a ferocious and passionate disposition, with strong determination marked in the lower part of the jaw'.

Mary Sullivan had been in Van Diemen's Land just 10 weeks, transported by Irish authorities perhaps believing they had to be cruel to be kind. Now she was dead, driven to her crime by thoughts no one knew. Perhaps in 10 weeks she had already seen enough to feel her life was one without hope, another convict desperate enough to kill and face the hangman rather than endure a living hell.

Mary Sullivan's was the most short-lived and tragic case in Blay's books, but another Irish Mary was firmly in his life.

Blay and Mary Murphy applied for permission to marry, as was required of all convicts. Their Banns, a Church proclamation of an impending marriage to allow anyone to raise any church or civil impediment and thus avoid invalid marriages, were duly announced three times in St Peter's Anglican Church. Perhaps Mary's Catholic faith could not bring itself to bless or marry a hangman.

In mid-January 1853, the lieutenant governor was 'pleased to approve of the solemnization of matrimony between Solomon Blay, ticket-of-leave, and Mary Murphy, ticket-of-leave, both residing at Oatlands'. They married on St Valentine's Day, 14 February 1853. The records showed Soloman [sic] Blay, 'executioner', 33 [sic], bachelor, marrying Mary Murphy, 24, housemaid, spinster.

Blay was in fact 37. It wasn't unusual for a groom to be older than his bride, but it was unusual that this groom's pre-nuptial days were spent in Hobart Town executing two men. On Friday 11 February, he hanged one for shooting a woman after accusing her of stealing £20, and another for 'cutting with intent to kill'.

He returned to Oatlands over the weekend just in time for his Monday wedding, which the *Courier* reported:

> twas the morn of Valentine, when the birds began to prate, that the usually quite township of Oatlands was roused from its lassitude by the gladsome announcement that a marriage in high life, which had previously been more than hinted at in the amatory columns of the *Government Gazette*, was about to take place.
>
> The affair created a little interest in the township, from the position of the favoured bridegroom (Solomon Blay) who holds the distinguished appointment of 'the finisher of the law' for the territory of Van Diemen's Land. They were attended to Church at 8 o'clock (the hour when the bridegroom usually 'ties knots' of a different description) by a highly respectable (?) couple of the township.
>
> We believe that after a short trip to the metropolis the honeymoon will be spent at the gaol, where the bride, Miss Mary Murphy, resides.

Others joked that Blay 'might have been a Ketch, but to Mary he was a useful catch'.

Finally, it seemed, Blay's battle to survive, avoid Norfolk Island imprisonment and 'rise' to a better life was beginning to reap some reward. He was now married, secure in his public service employment, and able to save a few pounds.

After completing his gaol sentences, Blay had moved to a former stable outside Oatlands Gaol. Over the next few years the couple rented whatever they could afford, often from former convicts, even if it was merely a 'skilling', or lean-to, or a small stable converted into a stone cottage.

Mary did her best to squeeze the most out of their income sources: Solomon's base wage and £5 fee per hanging, selling clothing of the condemned and other second-hand material, doing odd jobs at the town bakery, and growing and selling vegetables to the coach trade.

While Blay settled the law's accounts, Mary managed to make regular deposits in the Hobart Town Savings Bank, started by Quaker entrepreneur George Washington Walker in his drapery store for 'the encouragement of frugality, prudence and industry in the community', particularly the 'working classes'. As Mary was unable to read or write, a bank clerk had to match her appearance with her convict record whenever she went in to make a deposit.

The Blays had more of a vested interest in income and capital punishment than any interest and consideration of whether a man, or woman, was fairly or unfairly condemned, or whether hanging served a societal purpose.

After hanging one man for murder, another man later confessed and Blay 'rejoiced when the second man came forward to be hanged, as it meant he would receive another five pounds and the condemned man's clothes', according to a man recalling his childhood in Oatlands in the *Mercury*.

> Whenever anyone was condemned to death the children would climb up on the sale yards fence and wait for hours to see the fun.
>
> But the best fun of all was to watch the antics of Solomon Blay during the hearing of a case in the Oatlands Court. If the accused person seemed likely to escape the hanging Blay would walk out of the court very annoyed, for he realised that if the accused was not

convicted he would lose the 'pleasure' of hanging them as well as getting 5 pounds and a suit of clothes.

Blay might have been annoyed, but he mostly held his tongue, unlike Irish hangman Tom Galvin who, Mary told him, would complain loudly and angrily if a condemned man received a reprieve, thus 'taking the bread out of the mouth of a poor old man'.

Despite clemency denying him the odd customer, the currency of death was slowly improving Blay's finances — a fellow Oatlands resident recalled he 'boasted that he always had plenty of money', and the Savings Bank clerk in Hobart Town must have been quietly impressed with the regularity of Mary's deposits — but there was always more to life than money.

14

REVOLUTION IN THE AIR

B y the time Solomon Blay tied the knot with Mary in 1853, Van Diemen's Land was strangled by a debt of £2 million, paining Vandemonians as much as its continued exclusivity as a destination for the British Empire's 'debris of convictism'.

The dominant convict ethos and economic challenges notwithstanding, the colony had made great strides in the 50 years since the first 'debris' set foot in the colony. Individuals striving for an identity beyond a penal Hades had created a series of Australian firsts: scientific journal, Jewish synagogue, photographic studio, art exhibition, successful circus, public library, ether as an anaesthetic, and exports of apples and wool. Singers and artists were beginning to grace the world stage, the first Royal Society branch outside England was in Hobart Town, and it was the base for important Antarctic explorations and biological and astrological discoveries.

As much as these steps were celebrated, the abolition of convictism had long seemed a step too far. But that all changed on 27 April 1853, when the steamer *Yarra Yarra* arrived in Launceston. Decorated with flags, the boat had barely tied up before the bellman jubilantly announced Van Diemen's Land was now 'a free colony!' On board, after being delivered from London to Melbourne on the *Harbinger*, was the assent of Queen Victoria to a proclamation that 'no more convicts would be sent out'.

This was the culmination of years of fierce argument and lobbying to end transportation, a push which not only set the penal colony on its path to freedom, but was the genesis of political movement, democratic protest and nationalistic endeavours culminating in a new nation of Australia.

Reverend John West, a Congregational minister, author and editor of the *Launceston Examiner* (and later the *Sydney Morning Herald*, whose owner John Fairfax was a friend), was convinced transportation was socially and morally wrong and used every opportunity, from pulpit to press, to drive public support. He realised if all the colonies adopted the same thinking of an anti-transportation league formed in Launceston, and harnessed the mood of Sydneysiders where 8000 protested the attempted arrival of a convict ship in Circular Quay in 1849, the case to London would be irresistible.

In February 1851, John West attended a conference in Melbourne to form the Australia League, with an initial £20,000 fighting fund, the motto 'The *Australias* are one', and a flag comprising a blue ensign with a Union Jack in one corner and five white stars of the Southern Cross representing the five colonies (Queensland was not yet separate from New South Wales).

The nationalist representations gained momentum. Large public meetings were held, and petitions sent to Queen Victoria as emerging leaders like Henry Parkes joined the anti-transportation movement. In 1851, a petition supporting the Van Diemen push for abolition was signed by 16,000 people.

Finally, Queen Victoria and the Colonial Office agreed to end half a century of banishing the Empire's unwanted to the other side of the world. The news carried from Queen Victoria on the *Harbinger* and *Yarra Yarra* was the cause of much celebration, and 'a great demonstration' was designated for every township and village on Wednesday 10 August.

But before Demonstration Day, Mary Blay and the other Irish convicts in the colony had their own celebration, with news that one of their own had escaped. To them it was bad enough that so many Irish men and women had been exiled to Van Diemen's Land after being forced into crime in order to survive or escape. But the British had also exiled many for standing up for Irish interests, convicting them of 'ribbonism', the membership of loosely aligned organisations using quasi-Masonic secret signs and symbols to identify themselves.

Some, like Michael Rogers, a shoemaker of Meath, were transported but escaped and became bushrangers. Rogers was hunted for 'a barbarous murder and diverse other felonies', and within five years of ribbonism his days ended in the loop of a rope.

But convicts like Mary were more drawn to seven better educated and more principled Young Ireland leaders, who had been tried and sentenced for high treason and rebellion in County Tipperary. The men received the sentence 'to be ... hanged until he be dead, his head then to be cut off and his body to be cut into four quarters then disposed of as Her Majesty shall think fit'.

Terrence McManus said from the dock that if he was called to the scaffold he wanted it known that he did not have enmity towards individual Englishmen: 'whatever I may have felt of the injustice of English rule in this island ... not because I loved England less, but because I loved Ireland more'.

Worldwide condemnation saw the seven avoid execution. Instead McManus, John Mitchell, Kevin O'Doherty, Patrick O'Donohoe, William Smith O'Brien, Thomas Meagher and John Martin were sent to the oblivion of Van Diemen's Land as political prisoners by the Colonial Secretary, Earl Grey, the son of the Prime Minister and whose family name was associated with Earl Grey tea. When they arrived in Hobart Town, Mitchell wrote, they found well-built buildings, cabs, stage coaches and guards dressed in red giving 'an old English look to the place, with the names of public houses and homes, reflected the homesickness and identification with her Majesty's Mother Country, eg Rose Cottage, Elm House.'

But Mitchell also saw people who were 'besotted, depraved and loathsome'. A shocked O'Donohoe wrote that nowhere else could 'produce so vicious a population as inhabits this town, where they think nothing of hanging five or six people every morning, some of them old offenders on very trifling charges'.

The Irishmen were offered tickets-of-leave and assignment to different districts with orders not to associate. In return, Governor William Dennison asked that the Irishmen give their word not to escape, something all but one committed to as a serious matter of honour.

Nevertheless, Mitchell noted in his journal that 'the game is not over yet', and the Young Irelanders played a clever game. They continued to meet, sometimes in a remote hut near Lake Sorell and sometimes, the story was told, over a meal on the bridge at Tunbridge, each with a chair within the boundary of their own district.

The authorities periodically revoked their tickets-of-leave, angering Mitchell that such educated and normally well-dressed men, who had been used to overseers respectfully 'touching their hats' when they passed, were now 'clothed in the vile yellow dress of the chain gangs, compelled to work in company with the vilest ruffians that were ever bred upon the earth, and to every indignity which such an abominable friendship could afflict they were forced patiently and silently to submit'.

In his memoirs he wrote of riding around Oatlands to meet his fellow Irishmen, sometimes enjoying 'the spring day [which] has been most lovely ... loading the warm air with a rich fragrance which a European joyfully recognises at once as a well-remembered perfume'. He loved the charm of the central lakes district, which was 'high above all the odious stations, and townships, and the whole world of convictism and scoundreldom', being nearer to the stars than 'the mob of gaolers that welter and wither below' with purer air 'untainted by the lung of lags'.

But the sight of constables and chain gangs, and the presence of a hangman, was one that quickly 'makes us feel once more that the whole wide and glorious forest is after all but an umbrageous and highly perfumed dungeon'.

The Irishmen continued to talk about escaping the perfumed dungeon without dishonouring their ticket-of-leave pledge to the governor.

Now, hot on the news of the end of transportation and 'freedom' in the colony, Blay drew his wife's attention to a report in the *Hobart Courier*: 'Information has reached town of the escape of Mr John Mitchell, the Irish State Prisoner, who was residing upon ticket-of-leave parole at Bothwell ...'

As a failed counterfeiter, Blay could only quietly admire the chicanery. Mitchell 'resigned' his parole to the assistant police magistrate at Bothwell and offered to place himself in his custody. But while the astonished magistrate was still perusing the letter, Mitchell and another man jumped on two horses and sped off, and had not been heard of since. The *Courier* said Mitchell was the 'fourth of the Irish State prisoners who have escaped from the island'.

Meagher, credited with giving the Young Irelanders their orange, white and green tricolour after a visit to Paris, also handed in his ticket-of-leave cancellation to give himself the freedom to escape without loss of honour. He went on to become governor of Montana.

McManus took a ticket-of-leave cancellation as his passport to escape to California. After his death he finally returned to Ireland, after what the Irish press proudly proclaimed 'the longest funeral procession in history, easily outdistancing the return of Napoleon's bones from St Helena'.

Patrick O'Donohe also escaped to the US, and O'Brien, Martin and O'Doherty were eventually pardoned. The men were feted with dinners and gold cup presentations in Melbourne, San Francisco and New York, and Meagher and O'Brien had statues erected in their honour.

But it was O'Doherty's story that Blay warmed to. There were times when Blay needed something 'to steel me nerves', to 'buck me up' and 'help me sleep'. While gaol officials allowed him a quietening rum the night before an execution, it was not always enough, and he would ask an empathetic doctor to find him something in their medicine chest. 'St Kevin' O'Doherty was a doctor in Oatlands.

O'Doherty then went from Oatlands to St Mary's Hospital in Hobart Town, a hospital for the 'labouring classes', where in 1853 he excitedly told Mitchell that activist Patrick Smyth had arrived from New York.

'Transported?' Mitchell asked, as recounted in his journal.

'No my boy, commissioned by the Irish Directory in New York to procure the escape of one or more of us … with abundant means to secure a ship for San Francisco, and to provide for rescuing us if necessary out of the hands of the police magistrate after withdrawing the parole in due form.'

Patrick Smyth had escaped prosecution after Ballingarry by moving to the US to write for the *New York Tribune*, but his passion was for the liberation of his colleagues from Van Diemen's Land. He helped Mitchell spend £80 to buy the fastest horse in the district, Fleur-de-Lis, from the local magistrate, while he bought another speedster, the grey Donald.

The initial plan was to head in separate directions after handing in Mitchell's 'resignation' at Bothwell and for Mitchell to be picked up by a ship in Bass Strait. But this was aborted when the captain sold the plan to authorities. Undeterred, the Irishmen went ahead with the first phase, cheered by locals and unchallenged by constables, one of whom held their horses for them despite the Bothwell magistrate's pleas to 'stop them! arrest them! help help!' and 'stop them in the Queen's name!'

They raced their horses to Hobart Town and laid low until, under the moonlight of 18 July, a tall good-looking Catholic 'priest' quietly boarded the *Emma*, moored on the Derwent. It was Mitchell, who chatted with passengers but studiously avoided an anxious Mrs Mitchell and her children. When they finally reached American soil 'uncontaminated by the oppression, servitude and worse', he received a 31-gun salute, and was heralded as president of the not-yet-established Republic of Ireland.

Dr 'St Kevin' O'Doherty received his conditional pardon as Mitchell was finalising his escape plans. He left Hobart Town for Paris, before finally resettling in Ireland and becoming a member of the House of Commons.

The Young Irelanders' remarkable tales and commitment to fight for freedom with honour resonated with many in the colony, reinforcing that one man's convict was another man's hero, and that survival and escape, or 'deliverance', was a dream worth fighting for.

Now, just a month after Mitchell's escape, Solomon and Mary Blay, and all the convicts and most of the citizens, were ready to celebrate their 'deliverance' at Demonstration Day. It would be the biggest day in the colony's history, marking the end of convict transportation and the 50th anniversary of white settlement.

The dawn of a new chapter began with a thick shroud of fog over Hobart Town, but the air gradually warmed and gently lifted the fog up the sides of the skirt of Mount Wellington, sunshine breaking out to reveal shops closed, ships and houses festooned with flags, and churches ringing their bells for thanksgiving services.

Numerous groups 'with happy faces' made their way to a large decorated storehouse where a 14-foot (4.2-metre) Demonstration Cake weighing 350 pounds (158 kilograms) was carried in by eight men and 'greeted with three tremendous huzzas', for the Queen, the Cessation of Transport and the Jubilee. Amid music, buns, cakes, tarts, lemonade and ginger beer, thousands of children were given a piece of Demonstration Cake and a ticket entitling them to one of 9000 white metal medals struck by the Royal Mint to mark the cessation and the 50th year of white settlement, while those who helped lead the anti-transportation cause were given one of 100 bronze medals.

Additional cakes were sent to the Orphans School, where the orphaned and destitute children of the banished and imprisoned were housed, often in bleak conditions. Just a few years before, the *Colonial Times* observed that behind the orphanage's impressive facade the inside was 'cold, comfortless ... in one room we saw five little fellows blue and shivering with cold, there was it is true a fireplace in the room, but no fire ... never did we see two hundred human beings that exhibited so squalid an appearance as did the majority of the Queen's Orphans.'

Vessels in the Derwent fired several rounds at noon to mark the occasion. The *Colonial Times* reported that 'convictism was dead, and that the loyal and respectable portion of the colonists were rejoicing that their beloved Queen had spoken the word of liberation which again binds the colony to her throne'.

In all the small settlements locals had their own day of flags, prayers, music, dancing, lectures, numerous toasts and fireworks, and some were entertained by 'the magic lantern', an early image projector.

The *Colonial Times* said the one sole 'mourner' was William Denison, the Queen's man in the colony. Governor Denison had been warned some years before by the *Examiner* to be mindful of the people's views on freedom and punishment: 'A statesman half the world distant may be the voluntary author of wrong, but the agent in contact with the people is a witness of the misery he inflicts, and accepts, in the wages of office, the hire and infamy of the executioner'. But on the colony's day of deliverance Denison ordered all government officers not to be seen outside their offices.

The *Colonial Times* said the governor, 'the misrepresentative of his sovereign's feelings', gave the order because 'he knew that most of these gentlemen deeply sympathise with the people, and that they would have considered it no crime to mingle with their fellow citizens' on this 'day of triumph'. 'Let them be comforted: the reign of the withered convict-governor of Van Diemen's Land is at an end: a flash of lightning from the throne has struck him, and he will be forever removed from their sight'. Perhaps Denison felt the fear of one English newspaper that 'the English felonry aspired to alarming domination and the island would become a republic of thieves'.

Local papers, however, rejoiced in painting the day as one of deliverance. The *Launceston Examiner* recalled it was two centuries and a decade since a frail ship, the *Heemskirk*, and its tender, the *Zeehaan*, first ploughed the colony's seas. Such voyages were manned by noble souls in the honourable pursuit of a great south land, not just Dutchman Abel Tasman, but also Frenchmen and Englishmen with names like Marion, Furneaux, D'Entrecasteaux, Bligh, Cox, Flinders and Bass.

But that all changed, the *Examiner* lamented, when the British Government, unable to keep sending prisoners to America, decided to create 'an ultra penal settlement' for its banished and took possession of the island colony for that purpose. The *Examiner* said it was painful to dwell on

> the fetid relics of corrupt administrations … The ghosts of despotic governors with their attendant slaves, composed of rebel spies rewarded for perfidy, perjured men basking in the smile of vice-regal benignity, detected forgers covered by paternal wings from the

merited punishment which the law awards to slanderers, professional cut-throats and highway robbers applauded and patronised by the executive in their efforts to silence and subdue by force the expression of public opinion ... a pageant of selfish and unprincipled rascality often let loose upon society, but hereafter to be regarded as a vision that has passed away forever.

But this dark history had to be recalled to remind people that what they had gained came against 'fearful' odds and they could not 'prize those too highly whose perseverance, activity, and self sacrifice have contributed so largely to the achievement of freedom'.

The *Examiner* said 'suffering brings gratitude' and the path of the just while 'painful and troubled, is yet a shining path'. Its readers, to the tune of God Save the Queen, sang:

Sing! For the hour is come!
Sing! For our happy home!
Our land is free!
Broken Tasmania's chain;
Wash'd out the hated stain;
Ended the strife and pain!
Blest Jubilee!

The *Examiner* exhorted young people to understand the significance of liberty: 'England has her revolutions, from which she dates her career of freedom: America has her revolution, which serves to mark the era of her grandeur, and Tasmania may now boast of her bloodless revolution, for her jubilee the tenth of August, 1853, not only celebrates a period but canonizes freedom. Many have toiled in darkness, and amid discouragements, for your benefit.'

The colony had come a long way from the first landing of 24 convicts from Sydney Town to a jubilee population of 80,000, and, as newspapers boasted, the 'literary, scientific, benevolent and religious institutions indicate the progress of the colony's virtue and piety', such that 'perhaps socially there is not now an Australian settlement to be preferred to Tasmania'.

The *Colonial Times* recalled that early efforts to avert 'the evil' of transportation to 'a place of exile for the most felonious of felons' had been opposed by an influential few with sordid motives, 'exerting all their power to inflame the worst passions of the ignorant ... But the movement became popular, and its potency increased. It was electrical. It crossed the straits and almost at the same instant all the *Australias* were pledged to each other to resist the common wrong.'

The Australian League was formed, and while its ultimate success could not be doubted, the paper said, the speed could not have been anticipated.

> The Supreme Governor of the Universe had decreed that 'the wickedness of the wicked should come to an end'. His inscrutable and overruling providence asserted His way 'amongst the inhabitants of the earth' and brought us deliverance.
>
> Out of the agitation and overthrow of political parties at home, our freedom was evolved, and when least expected the total abolition of transportation to these shores was proclaimed.
>
> This announcement was hailed by the Australian world with delight, and it was deemed right to set apart a day not merely for festivity, but to return thanks to Almighty God for His special interposition which secured the peaceful triumph of virtue to weapons of truth.

Blay enjoyed the celebratory day, even though some of the notions and consequences of political freedom, be it for America, Canada, Ireland or Van Diemen's Land, went over the hangman's head.

But he understood well enough that Her Majesty's cessation of transportation wasn't going to deliver immediate change in his life. A convict-dominated colony would undoubtedly continue to produce candidates for the gallows. In the first four years of the decade in which Blay became a hangman, 15,000 convicts were transported, and in 1849 alone 19 ships, with nearly 1900 prisoners, arrived in Hobart Town. Some were on ships intended for South Africa, Sydney and Melbourne, but which were turned away.

The last convict ship, *St Vincent*, arrived in May 1853. But Blay knew, like the anti-transportationists, the convict tide had some way to run. As journalist Henry Button said in his memoirs, while the 'polluted stream' had finally been stayed it was a matter of waiting for vestiges to disperse or die out.

Blay knew some of them would 'die out' at his hand, and he maintained his simplistic view: he had a job to do, it was the only one he had known or could do, and he would do it until, or unless, it was taken away from him.

Solomon and Mary toasted the 'deliverance', but silently understood and appreciated that the 'polluted stream' had plenty of run left in it.

15

DICKENS AND THE LAST SPECTACLE

As the colony began its post-transportation life, the severity of punishment was beginning to diminish. But it was a slow diminution.

The 'innovative' punishment of forcing prisoners to pedal a large paddle-steamer type wheel to grind wheat or stone continued until the mid-1850s — soldier and author Colonel Godfrey Mundy lamented its gradual disuse because it might still be advantageously used in 'reducing some of the too solid flesh on the peninsular prisoners' — and wasn't outlawed in England until 1902.

Time in the stocks, and public floggings, also continued. A writer in the *Mercury* recalling life in the 1860s said, 'a friend distinctly remembers the stocks at Brighton being in the street leading down to the watch-house, and seeing a man named Gilbert whipping the cat after a heavy drunk with his feet secured in them'.

Public floggings were on the slow decline — an 1846 report said 'only' 516 convicts had been flogged — but not without some lingering regret from those charged with dispensing justice.

In 1865, the Supreme Court regretted it could not order a whipping or the stocks for a 16-year-old Hobart Town boy convicted of obscene language. As late as 1889, a Supreme Court judge told a 16-year-old Launceston boy that just three years ago he would have received the death sentence for assaulting a woman, but now, in what the judge thought was 'a light sentence', he would be imprisoned for five years and 'whipped with a cain, 15 lashes tomorrow and 15 in six months'. The sentence was widely criticised for its leniency, as the 'whipping' was nothing like the flogging of old days and therefore no compensation for a modest gaol term.

Flogging had been a major feature of convictism from the moment the first ships left their English ports and, along with the noose, a compelling symbol of life in Van Diemen's Land.

Novice floggers were taught using sheets of tree-bark and 'woe to the flagellator whose victim's back did not show the necessary amount of mutilation', bushranger Henry Garrett wrote in his memoirs. Thousands suffered

> because they were not able to perform physical impossibilities, and another 10,000 for having committed no greater offence than having the smallest bit of tobacco in their possession.
>
> No excuse was listened to, and if any defence was attempted an extra number of lashes was the result, and the charge was repeated again and again. To incur the ill-will of any of the prisoner or ticket-of-leave 'traps' by either work or look was a terrible crime, from which there was hardly any escape except by murder or suicide.

The fear of flogging, especially on chain gangs or at Norfolk Island, was what motivated Blay to seek refuge as a hangman. He had experienced a whipping on his voyage out on *Sarah*, but that was nothing compared to the brutality of the lash in the gaols of Richmond, Oatlands, Hobart Town and Launceston.

A former convict who became a police inspector in 1851 wrote 'flogging was of daily occurrence', and that one of his convict constables told him, 'My first introduction to the cat was for not lifting my cap to a magistrate — I got 50 for that, and a rough 50 it was. Since then I've kept reckoning gross receipts 1517 — a pretty stiff total sir. But one of the strokes of the first 50 shows on my back today.'

Another convict, Horatio Barnes, 'was sentenced to two dozen every morning 'till he owned to the stealing of a telescope from the Post Officer's office, although he knew nothing whatever of the larceny. For 20 days he was flogged and then sent to Maria Island for 15 months.' Jonathan Kind was accused of stealing a billiard ball. 'He got two dozen pick-me-ups and told to find the ball; knowing nothing of the theft he got 4 dozen more and 18 months in double irons.'

In Launceston, officials went to ask a man who received 75 lashes on a triangle if he would like some tea, but found he was dead. Another survived 3000 lashes in his lifetime.

Convict masters wanting 'misbehaving' assignees punished simply had to give the offender a note to take to the local magistrate, stating the 'offence' and 'desired punishment' — being sent back to the chain gang or a specific number of lashings — after which the prisoner would have to return 'sometimes a weary cruel march of 20 miles' (32 kilometres) to their master.

One former convict, now free with convicts assigned to him, seemed to have 'a fiendish delight in having his men flogged'. A slight misconduct might have been sufficiently punished with a reduction in rations or withdrawal of the weekly ration of rum. This convict-turned-master, however, sent one man off to a magistrate with the customary note, but this convict couldn't resist reading the recommendation: 50 lashes. A colleague later wrote: 'To his horror [he] found that he was to be spread-eagled. Tearing it in shreds and scattering it to the winds he became a changed man — changed (as he afterwards told me in the condemned cell) into a wild beast, every particle of humanity was destroyed in him.' That night he entered the master's hut, took a 'fowling piece' (light shotgun) off the wall and 'scattered the owner's brains' before absconding into the bush to take the path of a bushranger and, finally, to the gallows.

Public floggings were on the wane, but private floggings continued. Public hangings continued but there were more efforts to seek commutation, and newspapers were increasingly critical of hangings being on public display, especially when women and children turned up to watch. But a multiple hanging could still draw a crowd, as Blay expected in the winter of 1855, when he had four men on the scaffold in front of the Hobart Gaol.

The *Colonial Times* said it 'was quite shocking to observe the eager haste of the multitude to be present at the scene of death, and to see hundreds rushing to the spot towards the hour of eight', including many women, some with children at their breasts, and many boys as young as seven.

Unknown to Blay and the crowd, this winter's day would see the last public hanging in the colony.

On the scaffold were John Whelan, Peter Connolly, Edward Heylin and John Knights for bushranging and burglary with violence. The buzz of the crowd, speculating the prospects of a last-minute reprieve or a confession, was stilled when the clock struck eight, and there was 'an awful stillness'. Two minutes passed, then three, then five, and still no one was seen on the fatal boards.

'The suspense was harrowing, the majority not being aware that in this dread interval the priests were performing their sacred avocations, and endeavouring to prepare for eternity those whose souls were being summoned there.'

Finally, after seven minutes, the hanging party arrived. 'Poor Ned, that's him,' and 'Yes, there's Ned,' was heard by men seeing their friend Edward Heylin and 'what we never witnessed on a previous occasion, they burst into tears, some of them weeping like women.'

Peter Connolly jumped the final step to the scaffold, calling out, 'Aarh, and it's the heart and soul of an Irishman they're after taking; if I had to live again I'd shoot them right and left, like ducks [or rats, as another newspaper reported], so I would.'

He had to be restrained so Blay could put the cap over his head, and John Whelan told his fellow bushranger to be quiet.

'The effect of this scene on the spectators was anything but salutary. Murmurs were heard in several directions, and a few referred to the late case of pardon, as compared with this proceeding which they characterised as murder ... The hangman was a long while adjusting the sad preliminaries, when, at length, the bolt was drawn and the four men were launched into eternity.'

Despite the long preliminaries, Whelan didn't go easily. According to the later recollections of a former convict-turned-police inspector, 'Blay made it pretty hot for him on the gallows, as the constable whom Whelan had murdered was a relative [sic] of the executioner. Whelan was 21 minutes choking before he gave up the ghost.'

Whelan had become a poster boy for the community's outrage following the decision to close Norfolk Island in 1853 and ship its 400 inmates back to the colony. At a meeting in Richmond 'to adopt Measures for the Protection of Life and Property', the community resolved that so long as these associates 'and fellow criminals of the convict Whelan continue in this colony, your petitioners cannot but feel that the boasted birthright of all who live under British dominion, security of life and property, and safety of the domestic hearth, are denied to the people of Van Diemen's Land by the inhuman policy of the Imperial Government.'

The *Courier* said convicts were being 'draughted from Norfolk Island and silently distributed through the community', putting it at risk from men like Whelan and Francis McManus. The latter had 'murderously assaulted' a constable in 1847, was transported to Norfolk Island where he stabbed a gaoler to death and was sentenced to solitary for life, but was then released to become a 'savage overseer' of other prisoners before now 'silently' being brought back to the colony.

The *Courier* declared it 'undeniably true' that on being transferred out of Norfolk Island, McManus 'broke away from his keepers, and winding his arms around the gallows, embraced it fervently, swearing that his father, his mother and his sister had been hung, and expressing a desire to share their awful fate'.

So its readers would be 'horror struck' that McManus was allowed to enter private service in the colony, and within 10 days, armed with a carving knife, had repeatedly raped a married woman. It was 'of the highest degree reprehensible' that the authorities should let such desperate characters into the community.

On the scaffold in 1853, McManus decried that he was to be 'butchered and murdered for what I am not guilty of', claiming he had never raped a woman and was 'sorry to see so many women here, come to see their superior, a man, die!'

McManus did not evince scaffold sympathy, nor did the man standing beside him, Levi Allister, who evidenced the other colonial stains of alcohol and sexual crime. A mother had sent her girl of about six to fetch three pints (1.7 litres) of beer from the Red House Inn at Bridgewater, where a drunken Ann Whitbread took the youngster to her own house, gave her several glasses of beer, then laid down beside the girl in bed where Allister's actions would not, the *Courier* said, 'be particularised' and the *Colonial Times* said were 'too revolting' to print.

Two years later, a reward for Whelan's arrest after two instances of 'robbery under arms' was posted amid widespread public alarm. A police inspector described Whelan as 'a fiend in human form', often having his victims strip naked before shooting them.

> At one time while out in the bush [he] stripped a constable stark
> naked, lashing him to two heavy logs and placed the naked shivering

wretch on a bull ant nest, leaving a lump of damper and a pannikin of water at arm's length of the poor victim, but not within his reach, leaving him there. Three days elapsed when Rockey visited the poor constable — he was then just alive — the ants had had a glorious feast, both eyes were eaten out ... but I must go no further, suffice to say the bread and water was found untouched. Rockey had revenged himself on this unfortunate constable because he had been flogged by him when at Port Arthur.

In the end, and after a life of constant violence, imprisonment, escape and defiance, the notorious Whelan was apprehended under benign circumstances, arrested while trying on a pair of boots at a store in Elizabeth Street, the heart of Hobart Town. In his possession was a loaded double-barrelled pistol, a gold watch, £168 and certificate of freedom.

The *Colonial Times* reported the police station was quickly crowded with people excited to get a sighting of 'so notorious a personage', and to see his clothing 'exchanged for a new party-coloured suit from the Penitentiary stores'.

After he was found guilty and sentenced to hang, some still felt Whelan deserved a reprieve, but this was denied by the Executive Council. Whelan admitted that as 'dead men tell no tales' his safest plan was to murder everyone he robbed. On the night before his execution he made a confession:

Hobart Town Gaol, 25th June, 1855.

I John Whelan, alias Rocky Whelan, condemned to suffer tomorrow for robberies on William Kearney and Richard Carpenter, which I acknowledge to have committed with deep sorrow, and in order to make what reparation I can do solemnly declare that I did and being then alone, commit the following murders:

1. An elderly man, between Brown's River and North West Bay, about two months ago; I shot him in the head and robbed him.
2. A young man, (I learned afterwards his name was Dunn), in the Huon Track, about six or seven weeks after Carpenter's robbery; I shot him in the head, and struck him on the head with the butt of the pistol, then robbed him.

3. An elderly man at Bagdad, six or seven weeks ago; I shot him in the head, and then robbed him.

4. A young man on the Westbury Road, about a week after the last murder; I shot him in the head and took away a few shillings.

5. A hawker, near Cleveland, about three days before I was taken; I shot him in the head, and took away several things, most of which are now at the police office.

The full particulars of these murders I have given to The Very Rev. W. Hall, Vicar-general, and the Rev. W. P. Bond, hoping that the bodies yet undiscovered may be found.

I most humbly and sincerely beg forgiveness of the friends of these victims of my cruelty, and hope that the Almighty will have mercy on my poor soul.

John X Whelan. His mark.

The grim 'hot time' hangings of Rocky Whelan and friends brought to a head a simmering debate about the symbolism and effectiveness of public hangings. Some thought the public noose a disgusting, ineffective deterrence, a relic of the past standing in the way of a new order. Others remained fervently of the view the laws of God and man demanded that those who shed blood had to suffer the consequences, and that public hangings instilled faith in the system of law and order.

Prominent settlers like Thomas Gregson, who as a politician would first adopt the term 'Premier', suggested that no convict was considered safely out of society 'until he is hanged', and Irish political exile John Mitchell wrote in his *Jail Journal*: 'Why hang them! Hang them! You have no right to make the honest people support rogues.'

Newspaper editors, politicians, clergy, lawyers, mechanics institutes, temperance groups, settlers and former convicts all had a view, invoking and interpreting various Christian, legal and behavioural doctrines.

Alfred Taylor, a convict descendant and Hobart Librarian who was confined to a wheelchair after a childhood accident, used extensive research to voice concerns about the inadequacies of executions as a deterrent, and the risk that innocents might suffer, a view supported by Bishop Robert Willson and Father John Therry.

Blay's boss, Under-Sheriff Crouch, who had witnessed more executions than anyone else, wanted an end to the 'rum and rope' nexus, or at least the former. He formed the Tasmanian Temperance Alliance to support the lieutenant governor, judges, magistrates and clergy on the influence of alcohol on crime and immorality. A public meeting in 1853 was told 'the average number of executions in this colony for the last 3 years was 12, or one criminal executed each month for crimes induced by intemperance'. Reverend William Bedford, not unfamiliar with alcohol himself, suggested that 19 of every 20 hangings could be traced to drink.

And drink was easily traced. Hobart Town still had 180 public houses — one for every 100 people — and beyond the local colonial beer, porter and ale, more than 180,000 gallons (820 litres) of spirit and 160,000 gallons (730 litres) of wine was imported. The influence of alcohol was to be later acknowledged on the large iron and brass doorknocker on the doors of the new Campbell Street Gaol: a cast face of Bacchus, the Roman god of wine.

The Temperance Alliance said the colony felt anxiety, regret and shame at the 'great and increasing amount of immorality, crime and domestic wretchedness induced by habits of intemperance', and called for prohibition.

The debate over crime and ultimate punishment was largely carried out in the local papers, but was one over which Charles Dickens had strong influence. The *Colonial Times* editorialised after Blay's hanging of Whelan that while the reportage would be 'perused with feelings of intense disgust ... shock our better nature and are revolting to even an ordinary sense of delicacy', it was the role of journalists 'as the historians of our time' to indicate the character of events, and deliver remedies or rebukes as required.

The paper said it wasn't focusing on whether capital punishment was consistent with feelings of humanity, or the dictates of expediency, but death sentences were opposed 'upon every occasion' by philanthropists, Christian philanthropists in particular. Studies had shown the frequent spectacle of public executions had a demoralising impact on the popular mind in Paris, Lyon and Nantes.

> Dickens and others have shown that precisely the same effect is operated upon the popular mind of England ... and the scenes of yesterday prove but too conclusively that here as elsewhere, the same events follow on the same events.
>
> It is idle in the highest degree to speak of such executions occasioning in the minds of the class most sought to be impressed a salutary sense of justice and a dread of the punishment that follows the crime. It is but too evident that no such effects whatever are produced.
>
> It is but too evident that the effect of executions, as at present carried out, is to brutalise, to demoralise, yet more extensively, to render more corrupt and more obdurate, the hearts of the men we seek to terrify and deter.

The Dickens view first emerged when the popular author wrote to *The Times* in November 1849 after joining a crowd of 30,000 for what was billed 'the hanging of the century', the first husband and wife execution in England in 150 years. Frederick and Marie Manning had murdered Marie's wealthy lover for his money and buried him under the kitchen floor, and were to pay the ultimate price at the hands of William Calcraft.

Dickens' letter, written from an apartment he had rented for the hanging, was reprinted in the colony and seen as an independent and respected voice, drawn from his many years as a court reporter and exposure to the world of criminals and punishment.

The description of Maria Manning's scaffold attire of black satin gown and veil had such an impact that black satin remained unpopular for the next 30 years, but it was Dickens' other observations that had more of a lasting impact. In his letter, Dickens said the 'horrors of the gibbet and of the crime which brought the wretched murderers to it faded in my mind before the atrocious bearing, looks, and language of the assembled spectator', and the 'wickedness and levity' of the crowd of adults and children 'made my blood run cold'.

When the day dawned, thieves, low prostitutes, ruffians, and vagabonds of every kind, flocked on to the ground, with every variety of offensive and foul behaviour. Fightings, faintings, whistlings, imitations of Punch, brutal jokes, tumultuous demonstrations of indecent delight when swooning women were dragged out of the crowd by the police, with their dresses disordered, gave a new zest to the general entertainment.

When the sun rose brightly — as it did — it gilded thousands upon thousands of upturned faces, so inexpressibly odious in their brutal mirth or callousness, that a man had cause to feel ashamed of the shape he wore, and to shrink from himself, as fashioned in the image of the Devil. When the two miserable creatures who attracted all this ghastly sight about them were turned quivering into the air, there was no more emotion, no more pity, no more thought that two immortal souls had gone to judgement, no more restraint in any of the previous obscenities, than if the name of Christ had never been heard in this world, and there were no belief among men but that they perished like the beasts.

I have seen, habitually, some of the worst sources of general contamination and corruption in this country, and I think there are not many phases in London life that could surprise me. I am solemnly convinced that nothing that ingenuity could devise to be done in this city, in the same compass of time, could work such ruin as one public execution, and I stand astounded and appalled by the wickedness it exhibits.

I do not believe that any community can prosper where such a scene of horror and demoralization as was enacted this morning outside Horsemonger Lane Gaol, is presented at the very doors of good citizens, and is passed by, unknown or forgotten. And when, in our prayers and thanksgivings for the season, we are humbly expressing before God our desire to remove the moral evils of the land, I would ask your readers to consider whether it is not a time to think of this one, and to root it out.

I am, Sir, your faithful servant, Charles Dickens. Devonshire Terrace, Tuesday, Nov. 13.

Dickens' letter stirred others to urge the Home Secretary, Sir George Grey, to resist the push for executions away from the public eye.

Sir Francis Bond Head, a respected soldier, colonial administrator and author, said in a letter to *The Times* that 'the merciful object of every punishment which the law inflicts is not so much to revenge past crime, as to prevent its recurrence'. Sir Francis said Mrs Manning's last moments 'rather indisputably prove the benefit which society practically derives from a public execution'.

While she had the courage and hardness of heart to murder her best friend, bury him in a grave she dug in her own kitchen and 'with her hands stained with blood' say to her husband 'I think no more of what I have done than if I had shot the cat that is upon the wall!' the woman did not dare to face the terror of a public execution.

Sir Francis said she did not fear death in private — 'she almost succeeded in gradually, and with her own hands, strangling herself' — but about to face the London crowd 'her obdurate heart quailed … and accordingly as her last act she drew from her pocket a black silk handkerchief; requested that she might be blindfolded with it; and having a black silk veil fastened over her head, so as to completely conceal her features from public gaze, she was conducted in slow and solemn procession towards the drop'.

The covered eyes muted 'the terror which the wicked very naturally have of being publicly hanged before the scum and refuse of society!' It was essential, he argued, that criminals be executed in public:

So long as it shall be deemed advisable by us, by laws Divine as well as human, to deprive the murderer of his life, the whole process of his trial, ending in an act of such awful responsibility, ought to be performed in open day, in order that the community may at all events clearly see what it is they are doing — what it is they have done …

If people like Dickens felt the punishment exceeded the offence they could press the country to consider it, and expose an unnecessary harshness or cruelty, but on no account should anyone lose the inalienable right which every member of our Christian community ought to maintain, of witnessing, whenever his conscience prompts him to do so, the legalised execution of his fellow-creatures.

The letters of Dickens — immensely popular in the colony since Henry Dowling, a Launceston printer and entrepreneur, produced the first pirated editions of *The Pickwick Papers*, Dickens' first novel — and Head were reprinted and much read in the colony, not least by Blay, the one resident with the greatest familiarity with public hangings.

The *Cornwall Chronicle*, under its motto of American founding father Thomas Jefferson, 'liberty with danger is to be preferred to slavery with security', said Dickens' 'truths' had been enunciated many times by many people but the 'brutalizing' practice continued.

'We expect some result, however, from Mr. Dickens' letter. He is no speculative writer on penal law, suspected of the bias which is apt to guide the pen of a theorist; but he is a popular author of the age, expressing and speaking to its current feelings and tendencies, and giving these bodily shape and practical effect.'

The *Chronicle* said while public executions in Van Diemen's Land had never had the same degree of 'revolting' features as England, when it came to preventive influence it was persuaded that the publicity of executions 'is anywhere totally inoperative'. Many culprits had been launched into eternity 'amid the half-uttered shriek and sigh of here and there a spectator'. But afterward there was no deeper dread of the punishment of death, most victims 'were, to all appearance ... resigned to their fate', and most people said to themselves 'they don't seem to mind it; it can't be so painful, or so terrible, as we had imagined.'

The *Colonial Times* said whatever opinions were held about the necessity of capital punishment, 'all are united on ... public executions are most objectionable'.

It had been hoped the spectacle of a fellow creature, for the most part in full health, advancing from prison to expiate his crimes against society by public death would have a salutary effect on those of a like mind. But experience had shown this was not the case.

'It is found that so far from originating a horror of his crime, a public execution of the criminal but too often evokes a sympathy with the sufferer. And this we deem to be a fearful and fateful error. Nothing can be more opposed to the philosophy of punitive discipline, or so injurious, in the main to the interests of society.'

If executions had to continue, the *Colonial Times* said, 'they ought to be conducted as to work as little ill as possible', with the simple remedy being to emulate New South Wales' 1852 decision and make executions 'so far as the masses of the public are concerned, absolutely secret'.

> As it is, Justice is blind indeed. She smites, and smites severely, in her righteous hatred of all antagonism to her law, but smiting inconsiderately, perpetuates the necessity for blows which Mercy deprecates, but has no power to stay.
>
> No one can say that the influence of the public execution under such circumstances is likely to be beneficial ... the policy of carrying out the sentence is a matter of opinion, but the impropriety of public executions was never more decisively evinced, and it is to be hoped that the practice pursued in the adjacent colonies of executions within the walls of the gaol will be speedily introduced here.

Blay's despatching of Whelan — whose head was removed post the execution and donated to an English museum — and his associates, drew the attention of the *Sydney Morning Herald*, whose correspondent reported 'a strong feeling has been produced against public executions in the public mind by the last bad scene; they have an evident tendency to de-moralise and harden the spectators, and it is to be hoped that a measure may speedily be introduced to alter the present mode of proceedings'.

A week later, the *Launceston Examiner* said public executions were brutalising, and argued for life imprisonment as the only alternative. Prisoners should be regarded as 'civilly dead to the world', denied all access from everyone, including friends and family, with the exception of the turnkey, chaplain and gaol governor, and only released if their innocence was unambiguously established.

'The being who embrues [*sic*] his hand in blood should not again be turned loose, or allowed the opportunity to repeat the foul crime,' the *Examiner* said.

Time would allow prisoners to repent, or for the innocent an error to be restored, given 'our criminal annals contain cases in which it has been ascertained that capital punishment fell on the guiltless ... nor is the known number small ... unjustly hurried out of time into eternity'.

The colony was suffering too much from 'convictism', the *Examiner* said, with desperate characters too often committing 'the foulest deeds of violence'.

'If it were possible to make a bridge of gold — to give those anxious to leave the means of departure — it would be the cheapest and safest method, but that being impracticable, no maudlin sympathy, no mock mercy, should come between the execution of a just sentence and the sanguinary transgressor of the law'.

If any mercy was to be extended, 'we confess our sympathies are not with the unhanged Whelans, but with the possible victims', the paper said, citing an English poet who said 'he that's merciful unto the bad is cruel to the just'.

The debate had shifted from the merits of capital punishment to whether it should be in public or private. And if hangings were no longer public how to maintain public confidence the death sentence had actually been carried out, and whether anyone should be compelled to attend. The *Examiner* said if hangings were not public, doubt would arise as to whether or not the sentence had been inflicted because it was human nature that 'when excitement prevails, no story is too absurd to obtain credence in a greater or less degree from large circles'. The *Colonial Times* felt there would be sufficient public confidence if attending witnesses signed a declaration attesting the execution had been carried out, together with a certificate by the prison medical officer, with details recorded by the Supreme Court register and published in the *Government Gazette.*

As to whether anyone should be compelled to attend as witnesses, William Champ, a former convict muster master and commandant of Port Arthur (and who would go on to become first Premier in 1856 and later primarily responsible for building Pentridge Gaol), said he knew plenty of men of physical and moral courage who would refuse to attend a hanging.

Blay likely followed the debate in the newspapers with more interest than most, but it wouldn't have escaped him that even those who opposed capital punishment, or criticised his technique, sometimes thirsted for quick retribution when a particular crime offended them.

The newspapers, clergy, community leaders, Charles Dickens and Francis Head all had their say. In the end the government affirmed it was of no mind to stop hangings, but the days of public spectacles were over.

Public hangings officially ceased in 1856 following their abandonment in New South Wales (1853) and Victoria (1854). The new Act to Regulate the Execution of Criminals said it was 'expedient that the practice of executing Criminals publicly should be discontinued ... and henceforth should be carried into effect privately within the walls of the Prison'. Hangings would now be held behind gaol walls, in the presence of the sheriff, under-sheriff, the gaoler and gaol officials, any constables and military deemed necessary to be in attendance, and any adults who the sheriff saw fit to accept, such as the press, and any magistrate who desired to attend. They were required to sign a declaration that the condemned were 'hanged by the neck until his body was dead', with a penalty of up to 10 years gaol for any false declarations.

This meant Rocky Whelan and friends in 1855 were Blay's last public hangings in Hobart Town. His last in Launceston was the previous year when some spectators cried out 'murder!' when he first appeared on the scaffold to hang Thomas Kenny for setting fire to a stable and a valuable mare, and George Willey for robbing and assaulting a 'notoriously bad character'.

Inside the gaol yards, convicts re-erected scaffolds within the walls, and dug holes of about two metres under the scaffold trap to spare prisoners a dreaded walk up a ladder and ensure the hanging was not visible from outside the gaol walls. It didn't stop people gathering to peer through the gaol gates as a horse-drawn hearse arrived, to try to see dead men hanging from the beam, but there would be no more public viewings.

Blay could have no regrets about the end of public hangings. It was hard enough to put a noose around someone's neck and hang them until they were dead without doing it in full view of people who might be crying, booing, calling him a murderer, protesting a victim's innocence or contemplating revenge against the man with his hand on the rope.

His work would now be done behind gaol walls, but the hanging days were not over.

A silhouette of Solomon Blay, one of a series of sculptures beside the Midlands Highway, near Oatlands. Locals told the story that at times he had to walk to Hobart for a hanging because coachmen, or other passengers, refused to have him on board. Sculpture designed by Kooper Tasmania (formerly Rural Design), Folko Kooper and Maureen Craig, 2004. Image courtesy of Southern Midlands Council.

The signature of Solomon Blay on a letter written to Her Majesty's Governor Charles Du Cane, seeking his co-operation to overcome an unsuccessful attempt to escape a life of hanging and financial difficulties. Reprinted from The Penitentiary Chapel Historic Site, p. 41, G. Brown, D. Burton, E. Mercer, P. Mercer, B. Rieusset, 2007, Tasmania: National Trust of Australia and 40 Degrees South.

Convicts like Solomon Blay were rowed to prison hulks. Here they lived in
wretched conditions and undertook hard labour on the banks of the Thames before
being loaded onto transportation ships. *Prison-ship in Portsmouth Harbour, convicts
going aboard*, hand-coloured etching, Edward William Cooke, 1828. Image courtesy
National Library of Australia, AN905845.

Hobart Town in 1833, much as Blay would have seen it on arrival. This view of the
town was sketched and painted by watercolourist and draughtsman Louis Auguste
de Sainson during a French expedition. The scene was taken from the Domain. *Vue
de la rade de Hobart-Town, Ile Van-Diemen*, hand-coloured lithograph on Indian
paper, Louis Auguste de Sainson, 1833, Allport Library and Museum of Fine Arts.
Image courtesy Tasmanian Archive and Heritage Office, AUTAS001131821043.

Manacled and whipped along by soldiers, convicts ploughed fields, pulled wagonloads of stone, and powered wagons on the country's first railway. *A convict ploughing team breaking up new ground at the farm – Port Arthur*, printed postcard, A. C. Dreier postcard collection, 1926. Image courtesy State Library of Victoria, H22182.

The original gaol at Murray Street was created to house re-offending convicts and convicted settlers. Although built of inferior bricks, it remained the town gaol and scene of Blay's hangings for more than 30 years. *His Majesty's Jail, Hobart Town*, lithograph, Henry Melville, 1834, W. L. Crowther Library. Image courtesy Tasmanian Archive and Heritage Office, AUTAS001126077080.

GOVERNOR DAVEY'S
PROCLAMATION
TO THE ABORIGINES
1816.

"Why Massa Gubernor" said Black Jack. "You Proclamation all gammon"
"How blackfellow read him-eh? He no learn him read book"
"Read that then" said the Governor, pointing to a picture.

This proclamation was released by the Colonial British Government in Tasmania, with the intention of graphically showing the supposed equality in the treatment of white settlers and Indigenous people. *Governor Davey's Proclamation to the Aborigines 1816*, etching and watercolour on buff paper. Image courtesy State Library of Victoria, H14164.

On the wooden scaffolds at Hobart, Launceston and Oatlands, the execution party comprised the under-sheriff, hangman, gaol superintendent, guards or javelin men, and clergy to minister words of comfort to the condemned. © Illustration by Simon Barnard. Published by The Text Publishing Company. Reproduced with permission from *A-Z of Convicts in Van Diemen's Land*.

Paul Samuel (left) was one of few native born prisoners to be sentenced to death. He was condemned for rape in 1869, but reprieved. *Paul Samuel*, photograph, 1874.

William Campbell (middle), also known as Job Smith, was the last man hanged for rape. *William Campbell*, photograph, 1874.

James Sutherland (right) set fire to a house and fatally shot the owner in 1883. After his hanging a plaster cast of his head was made. *James Sutherland*, photograph, 1883.

Variously attributed to A. H. Boyd and Thomas Nevin. Image courtesy National Library of Australia.

As photography came to the fore in the late 19th century, inmates of Campbell Street Gaol were not excluded. The faces of inmates, men and women, old and young, were closely scrutinised by some for 'evidence' of intelligence, criminality and brutality. Reprinted from *The Penitentiary Chapel Historic Site*, p. 20–1, G. Brown, D. Burton, E. Mercer, P. Mercer, B. Rieusset, 2007, Tasmania: National Trust of Australia and 40 Degrees South.

Blay positioned the condemned to stand on a wooden trapdoor before putting a noose around their neck. By the 1900s the scaffold was housed inside a small shed-like room at Campbell Street Gaol, until 1946. *Campbell Street Gaol, Hobart – Trapdoor in the Execution room*, photograph, Wilf Elvey, 1955. Image courtesy Tasmanian Archive and Heritage Office, NS2340/1/23.

EVOLUTION AND EXECUTION

As Charles Dickens' influence came to bear on public executions, the evolution of the colony caught Charles Darwin's eye. He retained fond memories of his visit to Hobart Town on the *Beagle* in 1836 — the evenings of fine dinners and Italian music after spending the day collecting the plants and insects that bolstered his developing theories.

One of his close friends was Joseph Hooker, a botanist-explorer and friend of Sir Joseph Banks. He visited the island with the *Erebus/Terror* Antarctic expedition and befriended William Archer, a prominent colonial landowner and naturalist, and Ronald Gunn, a botanist and former convict superintendent. They regularly sent plants to Kew Gardens, run by Joseph's father William Hooker.

In 1854 officials in Van Diemen's Land, which was beginning

to become better known as Tasmania, made an unsolicited grant towards the cost of publishing Joseph Hooker's *Flora of Tasmaniae*, which he dedicated to Archer and Gunn. In the foreword he supported the theory of evolution as brought about by variation and natural selection, the first published statement in support of Darwin's radical thinking.

Darwin was delighted that the colony supported the book. 'What capital news from Tasmania,' he told Hooker. 'It really is a very remarkable and creditable fact to the colony. I am always building veritable castles in the air about emigrating, and Tasmania has been my headquarters of late. It really is a very singular and delightful fact, contrasted with the slight appreciation of science in the Old Country.'

Four years later Hooker helped present the historic paper of Darwin and Alfred Wallace, challenging the assumption that plants and animals were unchanging, to the Linnean Society of London, followed in November 1859 with the publication of Darwin's *Origin of Species by Means of Natural Selection*.

Various aspects of the colony's evolution pleased Darwin and friends. Further evolution came in 1856, when Queen Victoria formally authorised Van Diemen's Land becoming Tasmania, honouring Dutch seafarer Abel Tasman for his 1642 voyage. Blay might have smiled if he'd been aware that the man being honoured had died in drunken disgrace, apparently in a ditch, after he tried to hang, without trial, two impudent sailors.

That same year the colony also gained self-government, but matters of heads of state mattered less to Blay than heads to be noosed in his first non-public execution under the New Criminals Execution Act. The gallows were now placed in a secluded section inside the prison yard of the Hobart Town Gaol in Murray Street, enclosed within a wooden fence and covering 'to render the sad ceremony as private as possible', the *Colonial Times* reported.

Blay noted that there was more than the usual fussing by officials keen to ensure things went smoothly and there be no public doubt that a hanging sentence was fully delivered. Outside, a military guard was alert to any trouble from those still gathered in the hope of witnessing a 'private' execution.

After leaving two condemned men hanging for an hour, the sheriff, under-sheriff, gaol keeper, two javelin men, two constables and two magistrates all signed a certificate stating: 'We the undersigned do hereby declare and testify that we have this day been present when the extreme penalty of the law was executed on the body of Thomas Rushton/John Mellor, lately convicted at the Supreme Court held at Hobart Town, and sentenced to death, and that the said Thomas Rushton/John Mellor was in pursuance of the said sentence "hanged by the neck until his body was dead."'

Then some personal news: Blay finally received his pardon. In the *Government Gazette* in February 1857, last in the list of those gaining their free pardon was 'Solomon Bleay [sic], *Sarah*'. It was 20 years after his arrival, six years longer than his original sentence.

In the winter the *Government Gazette* revealed the crumbling old Murray Street gaol was closing and Blay would soon be plying his trade in a new Campbell Street facility, expanding the existing Prisoners' Barracks Penitentiary into the larger Gaol and House of Correction. A new execution yard was placed on the side of an existing penitentiary chapel designed by John Archer, the colonial engineer and architect, who dusted off a cruciform shape he had proposed for an aborted new gaol in 1829. He put the chapel atop a new cellblock of 36 solitary cells, known as the 'dust hole' because they were only 27 inches (70 centimetres) high, with little ventilation and no light. The cells and chapel, which housed 1000 convicts and up to 500 members of the public wanting to reserve their own pew for £1, all housed within high stone walls crowned with broken glass.

Newspapers speculated that with telegraph posts being built for the Electric Telegraph, the old Murray Street site could be its terminus. The *Cornwall Chronicle* was especially taken by the possibility of the symbol of the past, the 'Bastille of Tasmania' evolving into 'the new state of things'. A place of crime and woe which evidenced the fine line between the paths of vice and virtue might now be central to the connection of men hundreds of miles apart: 'How many scores, or may we not say hundreds, have passed from its unhappy precincts into eternity, expiating lives of crime and blood by the ignominy of a public execution!'

The paper hoped that

> rather than any permanent record of its existence we shall learn that this memorial of a by-gone state of things is itself to pass away … not one stone of it is to be left upon another and that its site no longer a Golgotha [but] may become connected rather with that new order of things which we may congratulate ourselves has begun.
>
> What a leap from the age of gaols and stripes, and chains and public executions on crowded scaffolds, to that age which has begun in Tasmania, of Electric Telegraph!

But despite the end of transportation, a new name for the colony and excitement about new technology, the state-sanctioned terminus of life remained, along with the old technology of rope. And although Blay was now free, he was a long way from being free of hangings.

Notwithstanding their questioning of capital punishment, newspapers were quick to amplify public thirst for punishment the next year when the murder of a 14-year-old boy walking to school along Kingston Road, Hobart Town, caused an uproar. The boy had been dragged off the road and after suffering 'an unmentionable crime' had his throat cut.

His father, Captain C. S. Chamberlain, bitterly castigated a system that sent people like the convicted man, George Nixon, to a colony of free settlers, especially when the *Mercury* revealed Nixon had been transported from Britain for murder. The grieving father said: 'Such infamous characters were not known to the community, although the government were well aware of them and who, like lions and tigers, preyed upon the public, and destroyed their children. We are told, he said, to look after our daughters, but now, Oh! Dreadful! We must look after our sons!'

The *Courier* said, 'The blood of young Chamberlain cries for vengeance and retribution cannot too quickly follow the crime.'

The public were now not permitted to witness the law's ultimate vengeance, but nearly 2000 people still turned up on the day of sentencing to try to catch a glimpse of Nixon. Convicted largely on circumstantial evidence, he declared, 'I do not say so out of hardness or braveness but I have nothing to say except that I'm innocent.'

The first executions at the new Campbell Street Gaol would be no different to those Blay had experienced at Murray Street; he would be using the same scaffold beams and trapdoor.

The new gaol's inaugural victim was Alexander Cullen, who late on a winter's night drunkenly attacked his female companion with a tomahawk, gave his naked child to a neighbour and said that 'you'll never see me more'. He was later pulled from the Derwent, ranting and raving that 'Betsy, Betsy, I've done this for you'.

On a February morning in 1859, Blay read of the death of Thomas Lascelles, the officer in charge of guarding the very first convicts to arrive direct from England on the appropriately named *Indefatigable* in 1812. But there was nothing to read of another death at the same time: Solomon Blay Sr had died, aged 82. Father and son hadn't seen each other since 1835, when they were scrapping about in Oxford before being separately transported. Blay Sr died in Liverpool asylum in New South Wales, where hangman Alexander Green was also assigned for 25 years after the gallows became too much for him.

Later that same day Blay readied five ropes: three for bushrangers Daniel 'Wingy' Stewart, William 'Flowers' Ferns, Peter 'Black Peter' Haley, convicted of shooting at a chief district constable; and two for John King and William Davis, for murders on Christmas Day.

Up to 100 bushrangers ranged the colony at any given time.

They often robbed without more than the threat of violence, raiding cottages in pursuit of food and clothing, and were often given shelter by sympathetic former convicts.

Their activities were so common that in May 1858 the *Courier* simply headlined one report 'The Bushrangers', and gave a matter-of-fact account simply using the nicknames of those involved:

> On Saturday about seven o'clock 'Wingy' and his companions paid a visit to Mr Brown, at Cluny, and remained there nearly three hours. They tied Mr Brown's hands behind him, they served the man servant in like manner, and ransacked the house, taking with them when they departed a revolver by Dean and Adams, with a gold watch and chain belonging to Mr Brown. They enjoyed themselves upon bottled ale and wine, and took some with a gallon of rum away, after they had compelled the servant to get tea for them in the kitchen, which they partook of one at a time. They returned a gold chain which they took from Miss Ibbot, as they were told it was a keepsake, and also a silk dress belonging to Mrs Brown.

But sometimes bushrangers became more violent, or used firearms in a bid to avoid capture.

Five months later, the *Courier* reported police had found the notorious bushranger Daniel Stewart, alias 'Wingy', and his mate William Thornton, alias 'Sydney Jim', in a central highlands hut where they had been harboured for 18 months. In the capture, Stewart was wounded and Thornton killed. Stewart told the inquest into Thornton's death that the constables opened fire without a word: 'We were both shot before a word was spoken to us by the constables; we could have been taken as easily as children, and that without ill-usage; but we were shot like dogs, and beat about with the butt end of their guns after we were helpless.'

The jury found Thornton was killed by gunshot and bayonet wounds, but they did not attach any blame to the constables for not taking him alive. When it came to fatally shooting bushrangers, 'justifiable homicide' was a predictable finding. Thornton's life was over, a life that had seen him transported for seven years for stealing chickens, and in the next 20 years enjoy only four years of freedom while persistently trying to escape the iron fist of penal settlements in Sydney, Norfolk Island and Van Diemen's Land.

Thornton's surviving colleagues went before the Supreme Court on 26 January 1859, facing charges of shooting 'with intent to kill and murder'. In the crowded courtroom they pleaded not guilty, before Stewart, his wounded arm in a sling, rose in his chair and pointed to a woman in the court and said, 'I wonder you have got the cheek to come here, you harlot.'

The chief justice, Sir Valentine Fleming, exclaimed, 'What is all this?'

Stewart replied, 'I can prove, your Honour, that that woman was my harlot for more than two years, and then she betrayed me!'

The chief justice said, 'I know nothing of that, but I cannot allow this interruption.'

Stewart then said, 'I'll not be quiet whilst she is in Court. She was my harlot for two years, during that time she harboured me, and then she took Government money and betrayed me. Go out you false, cruel harlot! You false, cruel, perfidious wretch, get out!'

The woman withdrew and the case continued, with the men's defence unsuccessfully arguing doubts about identity, whether their guns were loaded and whether the shots were actually aimed at a man, not known to them as a district constable, or merely to stop his horse-drawn carriage.

Five days later a crowd gathered early for their sentencing, and when the doors were opened 'the rush which took place was tremendous, and in a very few minutes every available space was occupied'.

Chief Justice Valentine Fleming first quickly dispensed sentences on a man for stealing barley (two years hard labour) and another for uttering a forged money order (four years). Then he dealt with two Christmas Day killers: William Davis, convicted of murdering a French Canadian, Andre 'Frenchie' Cassavaut, near New Norfolk with an axe after an all-day drinking binge, and John King who shot his drunken de facto in the Bull's Head Inn, saying, 'There shall be no more rows here, for I'll blow her brains out, and then I'll be hung like a man.'

Blay heard that King had asked upon his arrest, 'Do you think I shall see Solomon Blay?' Now King had the answer. The judge put on his black cap and pronounced the death sentences on both.

Then he turned to the three bushrangers as court officials closed the doors of the court to stop more people trying to squeeze in.

Asked if he had anything to say, Ferns explained he had absconded because he had been sentenced to four years for a crime of which he was innocent, and maintained the shot had been fired at a horse to stop him in his tracks, not at the driver:

> Since I've been in the country I have never been three months in trouble, never had a sentence except the four years I spoke about, and I think it is very hard now that my life should be forfeited for what I never done. We had plenty of opportunities of hurting people, and never done anyone any harm and I hope that you will take that into consideration. That's all I've got to say.

Stewart's lawyer argued there was no evidence directly connecting him to the shooting at a man, and that apart from some minor offences all three men had, up to the time of the alleged offence, 'borne excellent characters'.

But the chief justice had a different character assessment, saying the three men and the deceased Thornton had 'banded together to pursue a lawless career of violence and plunder'. He characterised Stewart's record since he had been transported in 1842 for horse-stealing as one of 'rebellion and resistance to lawful authority'. Just when he had become free of servitude and had an opportunity of honest work he took to sheep-stealing and was sentenced to transport for life at Norfolk Island, where he was clearly engaged in 'continuous rebellion'. And even when he returned to Hobart Town and became a ticket-of-leave holder in 1855, eligible to serve a master and with a degree of liberty, he had chosen another path.

Ferns had 18 prior convictions before being transported in 1850 for seven years for stealing lead, and had been within a year of being 'as free as the air to have earned an honest livelihood but instead of that you took to the bush'.

Similarly, 'Black Peter' Haley, a South African transported for horse-stealing, was convicted with a similar offence within a year of his arrival, and sentenced to transportation for life at Norfolk Island. On his return he also had the chance to make amends for the past, but had absconded to the bush.

Chief Justice Fleming told the three men: 'You must have been well aware, that if the band of justice overtook you, your lives would be forfeited. It is not to be endured in this colony that men, like yourselves, should go about marauding, and through their violent and lawless acts, keep whole districts in feverish alarm.'

Reflecting the community anger about the return of convicts from Norfolk Island, the judge said the safety of settlers and their property 'in their isolated loneliness' had to be protected, and he was confident the Executive Council would not issue a reprieve because it shared his duty of affording protection to society.

Blay was used to the tension of occasional delays due to petitions for clemency and possible reprieves, but this time he had to wait, five ropes at the ready, for what became known as 'the hanging sessions' before he could do his job.

In October 1858, Parliament passed a new 'Offences Against the Person Act' but the drafting was flawed because it didn't perpetuate the same sentences for crimes under the old Act. This presented a problem, as it meant three bushrangers sentenced to death were now truly in limbo, condemned not to stay on earth but barred from going to the next life.

Parliament, which had been adjourned, was brought back to close the loophole, whereupon some politicians argued the bushrangers were suffering an injustice, and there was an undue and unseemly haste in trying to pass retrospective legislation. MP John Gregson asked, 'What have these convicts done? There are greater robbers in the country than these men', citing government officials who had 'stolen' their salaries by being of no benefit to the people.

A petition for reprieve secured 160 signatures, including members of the jury, and the constable allegedly shot at. Blay wondered if he would be denied his fees, but his concerns were eased by the *Courier*:

> It is painful to have to vindicate the supremacy of the law, which is the only bond that holds society together, when it can only be vindicated and society can only be protected by the sacrifice of life.
>
> The question which arises in this case is clearly whether the lives to be sacrificed are to be those of innocent people, or the lives of reckless, vicious and incorrigible men?

The paper said England always had some distant colony to which an incorrigible offender could be transported for life. But with the worst criminals foisted on Tasmania, and Norfolk Island closed, the colony now had no place to further transport men securely away from 'further outrage on mankind'. A life sentence only turned the criminal loose again within a few years, so there needed to be a resolution when criminals' liberty was 'incompatible with the peaceful existence of industrious and moral people'.

If Rocky Whelan had been previously executed for killing a woman at a farmhouse in New South Wales, the paper said, it might have spared four honest people he later murdered.

The *Courier* said there was no reason to depart from the deliberate, regular and firm administration of the law. Until the colony could provide for permanent incarceration of the miscreants which England and other colonies inundated it with, then it would be 'better and cheaper for Tasmania, instead of having to sacrifice human life, to pay large rewards and incur perpetual expenses for the apprehension and punishment of apparently incorrigible offenders, to return them in every case, after serving their sentence, to the custody of police in England'.

A few days later, Blay was informed the Executive Council had rejected the reprieve bid, and the *Courier* showed its weariness with those seeking to forgive bushrangers just because they hadn't killed anyone:

> Times have been when bushrangers traversed this country in dangerous parties, and acted as champions of the oppressed prisoner class. They professed, like Robin Hood, to take from the rich and give to the poor. They shot arbitrary magistrates, cut off the ears of cruel overseers, or tied them to a tree and administered to them a taste of the flogging which they sometimes procured undeservedly for the prisoners under their rule. Much romantic incident surrounds those doings of a dark age, and probably at some future time they may be moulded by literary genius into instructive lessons for human guidance, drawn from a phase of social life which, it is hoped, can never recur.
>
> There is nothing of romance about the career of the bushranger now, who becomes nothing more than a petty thief, prowling about the country as a terror and a scourge, and taking by force of arms the means of existence from those who have hardly earned them.

According to the *Courier*, the colony had evolved to the point where even the humblest labourer could now rely on the law for protection, rather than take his chances with the corrupt and tyrannical magistrates of the past: 'The result of the case of Wingy and his accomplices will prove to many other desperate men ... that we have arrived at a stage of civilisation at which the law of the land is too strong ... to permit it of being outraged with impunity, even in the wildest fastnesses of our island. Sooner or later justice will assuredly overtake the evil-doer.'

Receiving the news that justice had overtaken them, and that there would be no reprieve, Ferns was said to have 'trembled', Haley 'struck with paralysis', Stewart 'unmoved'.

The night before the execution Blay was, as usual, inside the gaol steeling himself for the next day's full hand. He didn't need the

Courier to tell him this was 'the most exciting event of the week in Hobart Town'.

Nearby, Under-Sheriff Thomas Crouch talked to all five condemned men. The two Christmas Day killers, John King and William Davis, said they wanted it known that 'it is drink had brought us to this'. Ferns told him, 'It was my misfortune when very young to lose both my parents and I was left to the care of an old grandmother, who foolishly let me have my own way in everything. Naturally self-willed, I could not bear to be crossed, and so I grew up determined to have my own way. And I did have it, for I went heading into sin, and here I am at last.'

On their last morning, the condemned men shook hands with the clergy, under-sheriff and gaoler, but Stewart refused. 'I don't want to shake hands with anyone. This is worse than a savage government, to hang ---- men for doing nothing at all.'

On the scaffold, Blay bound the legs of the five together with leather 'to prevent mishap', and put nooses around their necks and caps over their heads.

Stewart demonstrated 'a reckless demeanour' but Ferns said 'good bye' to everyone and, standing next to Haley, who 'appeared more dead than alive, his countenance … ghastly' said, 'Give us your hand Peter.'

His voice choking with emotion, Reverend Arthur Davenport read the first Psalm as the men held hands: 'Have mercy upon me, O God, according to thy loving kindness, according to the multitude of thy tender mercies blot out my transgressions.'

Blay waited for the signal to draw the fatal bolt. It was, the *Courier* said, 'an awful moment, a fearful thing, to gaze upon five human beings, then in full health and instinct with life, and to know that in an instant they would all be in the agonies of death'.

The drop fell, its 'heavy thud being the only sound that announced the suspension of the criminals'.

Reverend Davenport sank to his knees for a final prayer that

God would be with the men in their last moments, and 'then all was still: the law had been vindicated, and outraged society appeased'. While there was some muted discussion that Blay hadn't adequately taken into account the different body weights and rope drop lengths to effect five quick and simultaneous deaths, the law and a lust for vengeance was satisfied.

King had openly asked the question on the minds of all captured criminals: 'Do you think I shall see Solomon Blay?' Much had changed in the colony, but some things did not change. The answer for many condemned remained in the affirmative.

17

LONG AND SHORT

In 1860, a team of 11 cricketers representing Launceston in a match against Hobart Town were 'rather disgusted at having as a fellow passenger the public executioner, Solomon Blay', the *Cornwall Chronicle* reported.

When they made their disgust clear, Blay might have been tempted, as he occasionally did to a taunter, to suggest he would afford them 'tender solicitude' if they should meet on the scaffold, or emulate a New South Wales peer who told an unhappy co-passenger, 'Don't you get excited Mister ... one of these days I'll have you standin' before me, and then you'd be glad of any company you can get.'

The cricketers would have been more disgusted the following day if they witnessed their fellow passenger's hanging of Henry

Baker, as 'the struggles of the wretched being for nearly 10 minutes afterwards showed that life was not so easily extinguished'.

Baker, convicted of murdering a woman, was allowed out of his cell early to wash, in full view of the gallows, but he seemed unconcerned and took 'a hearty breakfast of bread, coffee etc'. He wasn't to know his death would take almost as long as his last meal.

Whenever asked, Blay maintained he performed his 'jobs' in a professional manner.

'When I have to deal with a friend I finish him off in a decent manner', he said towards the end of his career, maintaining he made due calculations for a victim's height and weight, and the necessary drop length, to ensure a quick breaking of the neck rather than longer suffocation.

But there were plenty of indications that his self-taught training did not mean victims were always finished off in 'a decent manner'.

A year after the 'hideous' hanging of Henry Baker, Blay was back in the northern capital for a triple hanging: John Hailey for multiple murders, John Chapman for assault and attempted murder, and Patrick Moloney for a fatal stabbing.

Hailey, born in Scotland and known as 'four-fingered Scotty' having lost one thumb, had been convicted on his own plea of the 'terrible murder' of a man at Fingal. Chief Justice Sir Valentine Fleming said he had 'outraged all laws, human and divine'. On the day before his execution he also confessed to killing two women, including the vicious rape and axe murder of a woman at Cleveland in front of her two children.

In its Town Talk and Table Chat column, a *Chronicle* correspondent wrote that on arrival at HM Gaol at about 7.45am, he was ushered into a sort of lobby 'with a comfortable fire burning', to meet several others 'awaiting to regale their morbid appetites with the disgusting feast in preparation for them'.

One of them was Mr Solomon Blay, 'dressed in a modest suit of black, having on a broad brimmed hat'. Others included Dr George

Maddox, to pronounce death; Mr Robert Clabburn, a dentist, there to take a cast of Hailey's head; and Dr Ernest Wigan, to collect Maloney's body for scientific experiment.

Conversation, in which Blay took part, flowed with 'ghastly geniality' for almost 10 minutes. They discussed the merits of the different prisoners' cases, their demeanour since conviction, Hailey's confession, the merits of a plan for a monster picnic for the upcoming Queen's Birthday, 'and pleasing reminisces of former executions'.

The conversation ended with the arrival of the sheriff, and the group followed him from the lobby to a yard in the centre of which was a detached building containing the condemned cell. The 'three unhappy men' were brought out and 'the executioner now approached the throng bearing in his hand the significant implements of his office, in the shape of three lengths of stout whipcord, and three white cotton bags or caps', the *Chronicle* correspondent wrote.

On reaching the top of the scaffold to take their place each kissed the rope, and Hailey whispered something to Blay — perhaps the most frequent request of a hangman to 'make it quick' — who 'placed the ropes round their neck, and tied up their heads in the cotton caps he had provided for that purpose'.

> Very few more words or prayers were spoken, when the executioner grasped the handle attached to the fatal bolt, which he strongly pulled, and the drop fell with a loud thud. Maloney and Chapman ceased to exist almost instantly with scarcely a struggle.
>
> But very differently did the wretched Hailey depart his life. For if ever mortal agony was intense, that miserable miscreant suffered it. For a few seconds after he fell he was still; he then commenced several spasmodic struggles, kicking with his feet and striking on with his hands, during which the cord which had bound his arms became loosened.
>
> The executioner lifted him by the rope and let him fall suddenly, swinging him to and fro as he would a cat. He [Hailey] now raised

his hand and grasped the rope by that portion just above his neck. The executioner kicked it away with his foot, until the blood issued from the back of it. This was repeated several times. For as fast as the executioner kicked away the hand, it resumed its grasp of the rope swiftly and tightly, until evidently the mighty strength the arm possessed became weakened by the rapidity with which it moved and was removed.

Then the grim functionary ceased kicking and pushed it away with his hand, swaying the body again and again by the rope. Still the sufferer seemed to retain with desperate tenacity the great principle of life. This lasted many minutes until at last endurance could bear no more, the arms gradually seemed bereft of motion. The body quivered, shook, and gently became still.

Solomon Blay then with his pocket handkerchief coolly wiped his hands, which were covered with blood, and stood over his victim steadying the rope until it ceased to vibrate. It was truly a sickening sight, and cannot be adequately described.

Now the parties assembled were called into the middle of the yard by the sheriff, 'who was greatly affected, and who in a voice almost stifled by emotion' read aloud Hailey's confession to previous crimes:

I, John Hailey, now lying under sentence of death in the Gaol, Launceston, and about to appear before the judgment sent of God, do declare and confess, that I was the unhappy man who caused the death of Mary Stack, near Cleveland, about three years ago. I further declare that the suspicion that fell on a man named Charles Challis, was entirely without foundation, as no one but myself had any act, deed, or knowledge of the death of the said Mary Stack. I also declare, and confess, that I caused the death of Julia Mulholland, and that no one but myself had any act, deed, or knowledge of the death of the said Julia Mulholland. Drink, bad company, and the neglect of my duty to Almighty God, led me to commit the dreadful crimes of which I have been guilty. Oh that others would take warning by my sad fate. Death and eternity are before me. May God, for Jesus' sake, take pity on my poor soul. (Signed) John Hailey, alias, Robert Magattny.

Blay did not want to hang around for the posthumous confession, or for the arrival of three plain coffins under the scaffold and Dr Maddox's formal verification that 'the vital spark had fled'. As steeled as he was to keeping the demons of death at bay, as detached as he had become to hanging fellow human beings, Blay knew this was a botched job. He truly had blood on his hands and a grim memory that could never be washed away.

The hanging was widely condemned in the colony and beyond. One writer said sarcastically that for 'the lovers of torture' Hailey had provided value for their money by struggling to stay alive before his 'legal kicking to death', and said burning of heretics was meagre cruelty by comparison.

Hailey continued to provide 'value' even after his hanging. He was anatomised, and then six years later a phrenology speaker at the Launceston Mechanics Institute produced Hailey's skull, pronouncing it 'the worst possible description of a head ... more of the conformation of a baboon than that of a human being, and the murderous angle from the eye to the centre of the ear was there'.

Blay, as ever, sought to put any hanging horror behind him with the help of a constitutional rum. He wasn't one to look back, and this wasn't the first or the last time his proficiency was questioned.

Over the years, newspapers frequently suggested not every victim had been sent off 'in a decent manner'. Thomas Marshall, 'a man of light weight, struggled for many moments' (1844), Richard Jackson 'owing to his light weight his struggles were prolonged beyond the usual period of suffering' (1845), Eliza Benwell's execution was performed 'in a brutal manner'(1847), Rocky Whelan was given 'a hot time ... 21 minutes choking before he gave up the ghost' (1855), Henry Baker 'struggled for 10 minutes' (1860), John Hailey was bloodily kicked and his body had to be swayed 'again and again by the rope' (1861), Hendrick Witnalder 'for some four or five minutes ... considerable muscular action was apparent in his limbs' (1863), Daniel Connors 'probably on account of its lightness the sufferings of the wretched man seemed to be prolonged' (1868), Patrick Kieley's end was 'suggestive of the intense agony endured' (1869), and John Regan's 'struggles continuing for about a quarter of an hour' (1870).

One British soldier claimed in his memoirs that Blay allowed one victim too much rope 'with the result that the unfortunate man came down on the lid of his coffin which was in accordance with the then practice kept below the drop, and smashed it ... as life was not extinct [the victim] had to be finished off by Solomon Blay clinging to his body and strangling him. It was a most revolting sight'.

In 1884 there was uproar when the doctor, examining the body of Henry Stock, a 5 foot 4 inch (1.6 metre) tall, powerfully built man, said he had not died of a dislocated neck but from suffocation.

The 'considerable astonishment and indignation' was reported interstate and raised in Parliament, where the attorney-general admitted that three years prior the Colonial Office had recommended the colony lengthen the four-foot (1.2-metre) drop.

The attorney-general said that Blay's modus operandi 'corresponded' with English hanging practice, save for the drop, 'which has always been about 4 ft [1.2 metres] only in Tasmania'. This ignored the fact that the drop length was the most crucial factor, and the 'short drop' length had been abandoned 30 years ago in England. The Colonial Office now belatedly recommended the colony follow suit, and London's recommendation was referred to the deputy sheriff to 'consult with the executioner'.

But it was not thought desirable, the attorney-general said, to interfere with the hangman's modus operandi, 'as the present hangman, Solomon Bleay [sic], had executed 196 [sic] persons without mishap'.

The attorney-general maintained the length of the drop for Stock was 'an exception' at nearly 8 feet (2.4 metres). Asked about the finding of suffocation, the medical officer had claimed that on an 'incomplete' examination he could not detect a fracture or dislocation, but expressed no conclusive opinion.

The attorney-general's revelation about the attachment to the short drop demonstrated that Blay's efforts to finish off the condemned 'in a decent manner' was well behind the thinking of England. It evidenced his technique had not changed much based on his own experiences, or he simply didn't care to change even when hangings went awry. His colonial masters were apparently not too interested in the pursuit of more humane hangings, and London paid scant attention to what was happening at the end of the line.

The four-foot short drop was the crude legacy of early hangings, when a short rope and fixed knot noose meant death could take as long as 20 minutes and crowds enjoyed the spectacle of victims 'dancing with a stranger'. It was stopped in England in the 1850s when an Irish doctor, Samuel Haughton, developed equations for a more humane execution in a paper 'On hanging considered from a Mechanical and Physiological point of view'. Using his equations, a new 'standard drop' of 4 to 6 feet (1.2 to 1.8 metres), intended to quickly break the neck, causing immediate paralysis and probable unconsciousness, quickly spread to most English-speaking countries and judicial systems with an English origin. But not to Van Diemen's Land.

While Blay continued with the outdated short drops, a further advance came in 1872, when William Marwood advocated the 'long drop' of up to 10 feet (3 metres) for lightly built men, and an improved 'running knot' on the side of the neck between the ear and occiput, or back of the skull, to better effect breaking the neck. A longer drop was intended to more quickly fracture the spinal column at the neck, helped by the careful placement of the noose to jerk the head back as the noose tightened.

Experienced English hangmen knew that getting the calculations wrong could be disastrous: a head might be decapitated, the victim's feet might simply drop to the ground below, or the neck vertebrae would not break and there would be an agonisingly long strangulation or suffocation.

Marwood's successor, his friend James Berry, a former Bradford policeman and one-time boot salesman, took his calling seriously. He had business cards stating 'James Berry, Executioner', and saw his role as the last link in the 'chain of legal retribution', as honourable a role as that of a policeman chasing a criminal, a prosecutor making the case, and a judge passing sentence.

Berry further developed Marwood's 'long drop' thinking, paying 'the greatest attention' to ensure

> for each person executed … sufficient length to cause instantaneous death by dislocation rather than by strangulation … [but] not so great as to outwardly mutilate the victim.
>
> If all murderers who have to be hanged were of precisely the same weight and build it would be very easy to find the most suitable length of drop, and always to give the same but as a matter of fact they vary enormously.

In fact there were numerous variables, such as height and weight — prisoners sometimes gained or lost considerable weight in their final days — and whether the condemned had a strong or weak neck.

And there had to be sufficient space for the body to drop and hang. There were the odd occasions when a condemned man dropped to solid ground, necessitating readjustment and replay. Blay, however, was not known to have emulated his New South Wales peer Albert Green, who once grabbed a pick axe and shovel and began digging a hole beneath a man's feet to better effect his suspension.

Done 'well', the victim's drop caused the spinal column at the neck to quickly snap, normally between the second and third vertebrae, while the tightened noose allowed no air into the lungs, putting the victim into a coma.

Hanging with little or no drop caused death by strangulation, the body's weight tightening the noose at the trachea, forcing the base of the tongue upwards to prevent breathing and restricting blood flow to the brain by either jugular vein or carotid artery. The condemned died painfully, taking between 10 and 20 minutes. The physical struggling and any uncoordinated limb movement or convulsion gave rise to the depictions of hanged men as 'dancing and jerking like a freshly landed fish', 'dancing on nothing' or 'dancing with a stranger', and that a hangman like Blay was 'a real life empire's marionette on a string, with string in hand'.

The 'dancing' was seen by many for decades as entertainment. A *Sydney Evening News* correspondent recalled how a Hobart Town warder in the 'good old hanging days' was watching two men, one old and one young, in the condemned cell on the night before their execution. A conversation about dancing led the two to competitively demonstrate to each other their 'double beats', 'shuffles' and 'steps'. The next day the old warder watched as the younger man, 'being lusty and heavy, broke his neck in the fall, gave a few convulsive shrugs, and died peacefully. The old man, being emaciated and light, was not so fortunate as to be strangled right off, and in spite of his bonds he kicked convulsively and drew up his knees after the foolish fashion of hanged men generally.' The cynical warder exclaimed: 'Well I'm blest if the old'un isn't the best dancer of the two after all.'

During the dance of death, the victim's face could become engorged and livid as the brain filled with blood, causing blood marks on the face and burst capillaries in the eyes due to excessive blood pressure, and the pressure of the noose could cause the tongue to protrude. Sphincter muscles sometimes relaxed and caused effusions of urine and faeces, and some prisoners had penile erections due to the pooling of blood in the lower body.

Brain death in a well-executed hanging typically occurred in about six minutes, but the heart could take much longer, as an Adelaide doctor proved in 1897 when he monitored the heartbeat and pulse at the hanging of a healthy, medium-sized, well-built man of 40 years and found the heart did not stop entirely until 14 minutes and 45 seconds had passed. Total body death usually occurred within 30 minutes of the brain cells being starved of oxygen, but Blay's victims were usually left hanging for an hour, as was the British custom, to ensure they were truly 'hanged until dead'.

Ultimately, whether the hangman delivered a quick and 'decent' death or a slow and agonising death was only known to the condemned, and they couldn't tell the tale.

Even James Berry's most diligent approach wasn't enough to spare him two decapitations. Aged just 40 he had enough and took early retirement to write and speak about his experiences in a lecture tour billed as *The Late Hangman — The Man Who Will Entertain You With Exciting Episodes*. He became a firm opponent of aspects of capital punishment.

Blay might have wondered why someone who hanged people would now openly say some hangings were a mistake. Hangmen in England might fuss with their ropes and drops, and ask themselves whether victims were truly guilty of murder or truly deserved to be hanged. But in this isolated and distant part of the world he would continue to practise 'hanging by the neck until dead', just as the law demanded, doing it his way, silently, and in his own 'decent manner'.

18

THE LAST WOMAN

The absence of the milkman on his early morning run was the first sign that something was amiss in Hobart Town on Monday 7 January 1862. Residents went to check on John Coghlin at his lodging house, and Blay soon picked up the neighbourhood whisper that the milkman would not be doing his run today; his throat had been cut, his face and head battered.

The 60-year-old milkman lived in a cottage behind the Baptist Chapel with his wife. Born Margaret Galvin, she was one who legitimately could have been described as one of the 'damned whores', the epithet readily slung at almost every female convict, having spent six years in the trade in Ireland. But that was not why she was transported to Van Diemen's Land. After an 1846 trial of two men who shot and killed a cripple, Galvin falsely swore to authorities that another man was in fact the killer, and she was charged with 'wilful and corrupt perjury' and sentenced to seven years transportation. Some speculated the victim had refused to pay for her services as a prostitute, others that she had the intent of being transported.

After arriving in the colony in 1847, the diminutive 5 foot 2 inch (1.57 metre) 29-year-old 'housemaid and plain cook' was assigned to a successful sheep-breeder near Campbell Town. But a more affluent environment didn't keep Margaret from some of her habits, and she was soon given a month's imprisonment with hard labour for being drunk and absent.

But by the time she was in her forties, Margaret was a free woman and married to an older man, milkman John Coghlin. They rented out a room to lodgers, and drank their income.

Neighbours, including Thomas 'Blind Tom' Arnold, were well familiar with the couple's drunken disputes and Margaret's frequent threats to kill her husband, but the Sunday of 6 January was not to end as another familiar day.

It began with the couple having a rum before breakfast, then alternating sessions of beer and rum. When Margaret refused to hand over a shilling to buy another half-pint of rum, her husband took her into the yard to hit her until he secured the shilling and acquired more rum, which they both drank. That night the quarrelling resumed, and Coghlin again hit Margaret with a piece of wood and pushed her out of the house.

'Blind Tom' heard Margaret pleading with her husband not to hit her and a patrolling constable also told the couple to behave themselves, but it wasn't to be. The constable later saw Coghlin, who could barely stand, trying to enter closed public houses for more rum, while his wife tried to bribe 'Blind Tom' to secure more rum for herself.

In the early hours of the morning the constable again saw Margaret outside her home, waiting, she said, for her 'old man' to come home. A little time later a fellow policeman heard Margaret cry out from inside her window, 'Oh Lord! Bless me, he's come home and cut his throat.' Inside, they found the milkman in his bed in a pool of blood, his throat cut with a razor in one hand. But it was a doubtful suicide: he also had nine other serious wounds on his face and head.

After a two-day inquest at the Bull's Head Inn the Coroner found Margaret 'not having the fear of God before her eyes but being moved and seduced by the instigation of the devil' had murdered her husband.

En route to the female factory to await trial she confessed, saying her husband had woken her around 12.15am, pulled her out of bed by her hair, called her a 'bloody whore' and thrown a piece of iron at her. The bar missed, but Margaret said, 'I was the worse for drink … I turned back in passion, and took up the bar, and struck him with it … I destroyed him.'

Because he was dying 'so hard', she 'felt so sorry that I got the razor and cut his throat'.

Her lawyer, a young Englishman on his first case, argued for manslaughter due to intoxication and provocation. He told jury members they had 'a holy privilege of stepping between Mrs Coghlin and the grave', and that 'for my sake, for the sake of justice, for the sake of mercy, I implore you to record a verdict that you will never have the occasion to regret'.

Chief Justice Sir Valentine Fleming said the jury had to consider whether the accused had received justifiable provocation or whether under the influence of ungovernable passion she caused her husband's death. Personally, he thought it 'improbable' Coghlin had thrown an iron bar at his wife, and after just 10 minutes the jury agreed and found Margaret Coghlin guilty.

Dressed for sentencing day in black, a trembling Margaret heard the judge say this 'evil act can only be attributed to that curse of all curses, drink', and that he thought her 'insensible' to the awful position she was in.

'Now it only remains for me to perform the most painful duty which man is compelled to perform,' he said, and reached for his black cap.

Blay read the next day that the condemned woman said she accepted the verdict: 'I deserve this and a thousand deaths if that were possible for the horrible crime I have committed.' But as she was led away she urged 'all women take warning by my awful fate', and to 'remember Blind Tom', suggesting that an all-male judicial system couldn't understand evidence about physical abuse and provocation.

The community was more empathetic than the judge. Most of the colony's newspapers suggested she was more 'deranged' than hardened criminal, and that her case to avoid the noose was at least as strong as that of a man recently reprieved after being sentenced to death for stabbing his mother-in-law, with a strong suggestion of rape.

The all-male Executive Council was not moved, prompting the *Launceston Examiner* to comment sarcastically:

> We presume hanging and reprieving are regulated by no fixed principle, except, perhaps, that the worst and most dangerous criminals are saved to commit more murders, and the least dangerous are sent out of the world.
>
> The wretched penitent provoked woman who snatched up the iron bar hurled at her by her husband, and in a moment of passion killed him is to be executed, but the monster who violated his own mother-in-law and deliberately all but murdered her designing to put her out of existence is to be saved for the benefit of other females who may have to travel lonely roads in company with such a character.
>
> There is a morbid and disgusting sympathy with crime and criminals, which is a very bad symptom of the moral condition of this colony.

Coghlin was attended at the female factory by Catholic Bishop Robert Willson, Father George Hunter and nuns from the Sisters of Charity, then moved to the Campbell Street Gaol to be the first and only woman to hang there.

Walking through two heavily hung gates, past the doorknocker featuring Bacchus, the Roman god of wine, she passed beside the gaol superintendent's two-storey stone cottage, bordered by a low hedge and with passionfruit and climbing roses over the verandah and balcony.

But the further Margaret walked the more the prison's real face became evident: high stone walls, prisoner muster areas and eight convict gangs (including public works, Government House, Royal Society garden, quarry, mechanics). She could hear the sounds of the print shop producing thousands of labels for the Royal Society garden, shoemakers and tailors meeting government orders, blacksmiths producing seats for the cricket association, carpenters making school desks and mattress makers producing hospital bedding.

She would have seen the same 'strange collection' that a *Mercury* correspondent recalled in 1882: 'There they were, young men and old, the foolish only and the felon, thrown together in one motley family ... some were the lowest and most brutalised type, among this class were the murderer, the ruffian assaulter, the notorious thief, the card sharper, the old and practised swindler, the clever forger, the drunkard.'

The correspondent said the black leather caps on their shaved 'criminal visages' helped conceal 'their vicious propensities and villainous characters ... they were in truth a forbidding repulsive lot ... yet very far from unintelligent ... a villainous shrewdness and a perverse cleverness writ in man a cunning, gleamy eye and heavy brow ... and a dogged determination ... the style of the gait were as the translated speech of the artfully calculate daring crime.'

It was regrettable, the correspondent wrote, that younger 'well featured' fellows in gaol for more minor offences and some older men, of whom 'respectability of look still clung' but were guilty of common assault, were forced to be 'in the jug' as equals with 'not only the refuse of modern colonial society but the very dregs of the most abandoned of the convict element'.

Foolish or 'dregs', they sat together in the mess-room. Margaret Coghlin could see rows of close-cropped men saying 'amen' to the grace 'bless o Lord these thy good creatures to our use and by them fit us for thy service through Jesus Christ our Lord', before a lunch of coarse bread, meat and potatoes. Their daily ration was two ounces (56 grams) of flour, one pound (450 grams) of bread, a half pound each (225 grams) of meat and vegetables, and a half ounce each (14 grams) of salt and soap.

Toward the back of the precinct the 'model' prison had tiny underground cells for those given a month in solitary, allowed outside for just an hour a day in a narrow five-yard (4.5-metre) enclosure, and further back again the condemned yard and cells, constructed on what had been the western transept of the penitentiary chapel.

Margaret's condemned cell was one of two, just 13 feet by 9 feet (4 metres by 2 metres), with double doors, the outer of wood cased with sheet iron, the inner of stout open iron railing. Inside was a bed, table and chairs. A small double-barred window had a gas burner fitted outside, burning from dusk to daylight to throw light into the final refuge. On the ledge was a Douay Bible and Testament, and a book of devotions called *The Garden of the Soul*.

Under gaol Rule 66, 'Prisoners Condemned to Death' were to be confined 'to some safe place within the Prison' and provided with prison clothing, allowed any dietary needs as directed by visiting justices or the medical officer, and 'exercise in the open air for a reasonable time every day'. During the day she could walk about the brick-paved condemned yard, covered overhead with wire netting to ensure no files or knives could be thrown in.

Margaret was expected to wash her face and hands daily, and feet 'at least once weekly'. Tobacco, cigars and pipes were only allowed with the sheriff's permission in the exercise yard, and his permission was needed for any visits by relatives, friends and legal advisors.

Inside her cell at night, checked every 15 minutes by a warder, she could see the coda of the condemned on the walls, men who knew they had a date with Solomon Blay. There were rough sketches of men hanging and scaffolds, the words 'hanged like a dog', and drawings of sailing ships. Another had scratched out his last days, 'Tuesday 1, 2, 3, 4, 5, 6, 7'. Another had written that 'underneath this dismal cell lies the body of poor old Bell, old he lived and old he died, and at his finish nobody cried, where he's gone or how he fares, nobody knows and nobody cares'.

At 6am on 18 February, Coghlin took her final meal in the company of another female prisoner, before she prepared to take her last steps across a short narrow bridge-way to the scaffold.

Just before being led to execution, she put her X mark on a statement drafted and later handed out to the Press by the Catholic Bishop:

> I acknowledge fully the justice of my sentence, I deserve this, and a thousand deaths, if that were possible, for the horrible crime I have committed. Drink, the curse that has been on me, strong drink, has caused all my misery — everything has been sacrificed for strong drink. May God in mercy to my poor soul, for Jesus' sake, have pity on me! Oh! May all women in particular, take warning by my awful fate. Oh! Let all fear the hour of death! Oh! Eternity, eternity! Oh! That I had kept my pledge! How fatal was the hour when I broke it! I die in peace with all mankind. May all forgive me whom I have injured, offended, or scandalised, by my evil living. Oh! Jesus, in pity, have mercy and spare my poor soul; for thou alone art my refuge, and my hope! Jesus, Jesus, Jesus!

Blay and his wife Mary might have speculated during the trial if the woman was related to Galvin, the notorious Irish hangman, but as usual the hangman kept contact and conversation with the condemned to a minimum.

The *Mercury* reported that on her final day Coghlin was 'much thinner than at her trial', clad in deep mourning, and 'most humanely, her eyes had been bandaged, before she was led out from her cell, so that she could see nothing that was passing around her. Her face was blanched, and her lips were colourless; she also trembled greatly, so much so that she had to be supported.'

Blay supported the blindfolded and trembling woman to the scaffold, as she endeavoured to repeat the litany of the Bishop and Reverend.

With a noose around her neck, she prayed earnestly and audibly until just as she uttered the words, 'Lord Jesus have mercy on me!' Blay released the drop, which fell with a thud. The female prisoner who had kept her company in her final hours 'shrieked loudly, thus deepening the horror of the scene', according to the *Mercury*, before fainting.

One of the penny pamphlets published later that day said:

> This morning at eight o-clock while many thousands of thoughtless persons were about their daily business, Margaret Coghlin, the unhappy Murderess of her husband, was standing on the brink of Eternity, and within a few minutes of appearing before her Just Judge. She had dipped her hands in the blood of her husband … she had taken that life which no one has a right to take but He who gave it … the unfortunate woman's case ought to be a dreadful warning to us all, no matter in what situation of life we are placed.

The pamphlet said after the drop fell the woman 'struggled for about a minute or two, still striking her breast in prayer, but soon all was over, and her soul in Eternity.'

It had been 33 years since the first woman, Mary McLachlan, had been hanged in the colony for infanticide, a crime no longer punishable by death, 19 years since Blay's first hanging of a woman, Eliza Benwell, and 10 years since the hanging of Mary Sullivan. Now it was all over for Margaret Coghlin, the last woman to hang in the colony. Blay had done his 'job', and he walked from the new gaol seeking an old comfort, something a little stronger than milk.

Berry's Table of Drops (1885)

		8 Stone	9 Stone	10 Stone	11 Stone	12 Stone	13 Stone	14 Stone	15 Stone	16 Stone	17 Stone	18 Stone	19 Stone
		Cw. Qr. lb.	Cw. Qr. lb.	Cw. Qr. lb.	Cw. Qr. lb.	Cw. Qr. lb.	Cw. Qr. lb.	Cw. Qr. lb.	Cw. Qr. lb.	Cw. Qr. lb.	Cw. Qr. lb.	Cw. Qr. lb.	Cw. Qr. lb.
1 Ft.		8 0 0	9 0 0	10 0 0	11 0 0	12 0 0	13 0 0	14 0 0	15 0 0	16 0 0	17 0 0	18 0 0	19 0 0
2 "		11 1 13	12 2 23	14 0 14	15 2 4	16 3 22	18 1 12	19 3 2	21 0 21	22 2 11	24 0 1	25 1 19	26 3 9
3 "		13 3 10	13 2 15	17 1 14	19 0 13	20 3 11	22 2 9	24 1 8	26 0 7	27 3 5	29 2 4	31 1 3	33 0 1
4 "		16 0 0	18 0 0	20 0 0	22 0 0	24 0 0	26 0 0	28 0 0	30 0 0	32 0 0	34 0 0	36 0 0	40 0 0
5 "		17 2 11	19 3 3	22 0 0	24 0 22	26 1 16	28 1 11	30 3 3	33 0 0	35 0 22	37 0 16	39 2 11	41 2 15
6 "		19 2 11	22 0 5	24 2 0	26 3 22	29 1 16	31 3 11	34 1 5	36 3 0	39 0 22	41 2 16	44 0 11	46 2 5
7 "		21 0 22	23 3 11	26 2 0	29 0 16	31 3 5	34 1 22	37 0 11	39 3 0	42 1 16	45 0 5	47 2 22	50 1 11
8 "		22 2 22	25 2 4	28 1 14	31 0 23	34 0 5	36 3 15	39 2 25	42 2 7	45 1 16	48 0 26	51 0 8	53 3 18
9 "		24 0 11	27 0 22	30 0 14	33 0 23	36 0 16	39 0 18	42 0 19	45 0 21	48 0 22	51 0 23	54 0 25	57 0 26
10 "		25 1 5	28 1 23	31 0 14	34 3 4	37 3 22	41 0 18	44 1 4	47 1 21	50 2 11	53 3 1	56 3 19	60 0 9

From this table of the striking force of falling bodies of various weights, falling through different distances, Berry calculated the 'drop' required on the basis that the striking force required was 24cwt.

After he decapitated a condemned man, James Berry revised his calculations for falling bodies at different drop lengths, trying to ensure death by breaking the neck. It still didn't prevent 'bungles' and near-decapitation. Reprinted from *Executioner: Chronicles of James Berry*, p. 335, S. Evans, 2004, UK: Sutton Publishing.

NOTICE
TO TICKET-OF-LEAVE MEN.

Police Department, 21st February, 1842.

NOTICE is hereby given, that I am authorised by the Lieutenant-Governor to offer the Indulgence of a Conditional Pardon to such *well-conducted* Ticket-of-Leave Men as will serve in the POLICE, as hereinafter stated, at the expiration of their respective terms of Service: viz.

TICKET-OF-LEAVE Men, whose term of Transportation is Seven Years—to serve with good conduct for Six Months.

Ditto, ditto Fourteen Years—ditto One Year.
Ditto, ditto Life—ditto Fifteen Months.

It is, however, to be clearly understood, that no Pardon will be issued under these Regulations until such Ticket-of-Leave Men shall have been in the Colony for either Four, Six, or Eight Years respectively, according to their terms of Transportation being either for Seven Years, Fourteen Years, or for Life.

Men wishing to enter under these Regulations are to address their Applications to the CHIEF POLICE MAGISTRATE, and send them through the Police Magistrate of the District in which they may reside.

M. FORSTER,
Chief Police Magistrate.

Convicts could receive a ticket-of-leave, a form of parole, about halfway through their sentence. They received some freedom, but had to remain within a designated area, report to police regularly and behave. They could progress to an eventual full pardon. Ticket-of-leave convicts were recruited to the police force to boost numbers. *Notice to Ticket-of-Leave Men*, photograph, Archives Office of Tasmania, 21 February 1842. Image courtesy Tasmanian Archive and Heritage Office, AB713/1/11680.

19

SEX ON THE SCAFFOLD

Solomon Blay was now well known as the final hand of justice for those convicted of high-profile murders, bushranging, robbery under arms and shooting with intent to kill.

But there were also crimes that received less publicity, crimes of homosexuality, sodomy and bestiality kept quiet by judges and editors uncomfortable with some of the consequences of a society isolated from 'normality': men and women hardened to self-interest and survival, deprivation of sexual and other freedoms, disproportionate male-to-female ratio, restrictions on marriage, rampant alcoholism, long periods of confinement in solitary or close confinement with others of the same sex, and few curbs on power-based homosexual behaviour.

Many of the convicted were quietly sentenced to isolated cells at Port Arthur or Norfolk Island, with prosecutors, defenders and judges conspiring to keep the cases short and out of the public eye.

The newspapers obliged, self-censoring details that were seen as 'unfit to disclose', 'not fit to meet the public eye', or 'of the most revolting character, and are wholly unfit for publication'.

The papers referred to such 'evil' crimes obliquely, governors spoke of them in private despatches without any detail, and clergy would not discuss what was 'unspeakable'. Anti-transportationists and reformers saw 'unnatural' evil as symbolic of a convictism that induced immorality, restricted development and stained the reputation of Britain and the colony.

The Crown solicitor, Alban Stoner, told a House of Lords committee in 1847 that while there were nine convictions for 'unnatural' crime between 1841 and 1845, this 'gave no idea of [its] prevalence' because the attorney-general ignored 'a great number of depositions' to avoid bad publicity.

So while capital punishment was designed to be a public deterrent it was often in comparative silence that men were hanged for an 'unnatural offence', or a 'nameless offence', ranging from sex offences involving young boys and girls, including family, and with oxen, mares, pigs, goats and calves.

Unfit for the public eye, perhaps, but not unfit for Blay. From the very start, in 1842, he had to hang teenage boys and older men for committing 'an unnatural offence' upon girls as young as three, five, six and 10.

In one typical case in 1860, Martin Lydon, transported for striking a superior officer in the British Army, was charged with 'an unnatural offence upon a child of tender years', the sexual assault of a nine-year-old girl who was looking after her younger sister. Lydon left behind a hand-written statement that the little girl was not abused in the manner stated at his trial, but he deserved to die for the drunken attempt.

In a second statement addressed to 'all men at Port Arthur' he said,

> I write this with my own hand. I am about to die. Tomorrow at this time I shall be in my grave. Mine has been a life of degradation and sorrow. Ten years old I began to disobey my parents. At 16 I became a soldier. In a moment of anger, I struck an officer of my company for which I was flogged; this ruined me. I hated the army after that, and took to drinking. Then more violence, for which I was transported. The vileness of Norfolk Island turned me into an animal. I often said a long time ago, and only three weeks since … that I did not care about being hanged. This was my wicked flashness. God knows I now see the difference. The devil put these fool's words in my mouth. Every man about to die must fear the judgment of God. May God have mercy on my poor soul. I die in peace with all people. May all forgive me what I have done wrong to them. May the drunkenness that brought on this misery be a warning to all of you. Martin Lydon.

Charles Flanders had also been drinking in a public house in Bagdad before the 10-year-old daughter of his drinking companion was found strangled in a fern gully. In a final statement, Flanders, 39, denied some of the self-incriminating statements that officials alleged he made, but having taken up the Catholic faith he would now 'freely forgive from the bottom of my heart any who may have meant by unfair means to convict me', and begged 'forgiveness of all of whom I have injured in all my life in this world.'

Newspapers reported Flanders had changed considerably since his trial: his frame had become attenuated, he was 'deadly pale' and 'bore traces of much mental suffering'. Flanders kept his eyes closed from the time of his leaving the cell until Blay put the cap over his head, all the time calling earnestly upon the Almighty to have mercy on him.

A female acquaintance revealed that Flanders had a uniquely personal connection with his fate: he had made both the grate in the condemned cell and the ironwork which was part of the scaffold.

While he did not know it, Blay was the last executioner in the colony for crimes of carnal knowledge (1859), buggery and sodomy (1863), and rape (1875).

England's 'Acte for the punysshement of the vice of buggerie', piloted through Parliament in 1533 by Thomas Cromwell, defined buggery as an unnatural act against the will of God and man. The Act also allowed King Henry VIII to use the law, and his spies, to convict and execute any monks and nuns, and seize their monastery lands.

In the 19th century the British Navy was said to be built on 'rum, sodomy and the lash' and held together by 'the golden rivet', notwithstanding an edict since 1627 that 'If any Person in the Fleet shall commit the unnatural and detestable Sin of Buggery or Sodomy with Man or Beast, he shall be punished with Death by the sentence of a Court-martial'. Sailors received as many as 1000 lashes for consensual sex, while captains and lieutenants were executed. Around the time Van Diemen's Land was first colonised, there were more hangings in England for sodomy than murder.

British officials knew that in its penal colony the absence of women risked all sorts of undesirable behaviours, the predominance of males making it 'impossible to prevent the settlement from gross irregularities and disorders'. They still, however, embarked on half a century of male-dominated transportation.

Some sought more women as an antidote to sodomy and to discourage the rape of 'respectable' women, but officials often had little respect for any women under their charge. Early governors described female convicts as 'a disgrace to their sex', 'utterly irreclaimable', the 'refuse of London'. Others dismissed all convict women as little more than 'damned whores', and a government report in 1837 dismissed them as 'excessively ferocious' and 'all of them, with scarcely an exception, drunken and abandoned prostitutes'.

While this was an exaggeration, some women who chose prostitution to overcome poverty in Ireland and England had been transported, and some male convicts had also been transported for sexual offences. Convict ship captains often tolerated sexual freedom on the long voyages as 'politic', and for some there was an opportunity to engage in 'abnormal' sexual behaviour well away from family.

The penal environment was conducive to power-based homosexuality. One convict recalled a convict flagellator using his position to gain sexual favours from other inmates, and male and female prisoners in gaols and chain gangs employed coercive influences.

Reverend John West described some of the sexual behaviour as being like a scene from 'Pandemonium', the capital in John Milton's epic poem *Hell in Paradise Lost*. Vandemonian settlers feared such pandemonium. Reverend Robert Crooke, a convict department chaplain, said that 'the blood runs cold at the thought of a sodomite being the servant of a respectable household'.

But amidst brutal sodomy born of isolation, desperation and power, there was genuine love, evidenced since the island was first mapped.

Explorer Matthew Flinders, who first circumnavigated the island from 1798 to 1799, wrote of his co-explorer George Bass that 'there was a time when I was so completely wrapped up in you, that no conversation but yours could give me pleasure; your footsteps upon the quarterdeck over my head took me from my book and brought me upon the deck to walk with you'.

In 1846 a convict sentenced to hang for mutiny, often a naval euphemism for sodomy, wrote Australia's first same-sex love letter:

> Dear Jack, I hope you won't forget me when I am far away and all my bones is mouldered away. I have not closed an eye since I lost sight of you. Your precious sight was always a welcome and loving charming spectacle ... the only thing that grieves me love is when I think of the pleasant nights we have had together. I hope you won't fall in love with no other man when I am dead and I remain your true and loving affectionate lover.

Same-sex behaviour in gaols and female factories was often consensual.

At Maria Island, superintendent James Boyd wrote: 'One night I found that eight men had removed the separation boards and were sleeping together under most suspicious circumstances ... two of the eight had the bold and disgusting effrontery to tell the visiting magistrate that they had never heard sleeping together prohibited at other stations where they had been.'

Boyd said the lack of surveillance meant 'immorality and crime must reign triumphant', and described the use of night-tubs as an indecent practice 'ruinous to morality'.

At Norfolk Island, visiting magistrate Robert Stewart wrote: 'On the doors being opened, men were scrambling into their own beds from others, in a hurried manner,' and at Ross House of Correction, he described the indecent assault of one female on another as typical of the 'filthy sensuality so prevalent among female convicts'.

At the female factory in Hobart Town, the lieutenant governor said women inmates had 'their fancy women, or lovers, to who they are attached with as much ardour as they would to the opposite sex, and practice onanism to the greatest extent'. A group of same-sex couples, called the Flash Mob for the 'flash' language of thieves, gained and dispensed favours inside and outside the factory and, according to the Colonial Times, ensured factory discipline was 'bad and rotten at the very core, tending only to vice, immorality and the most disgusting licentiousness'.

Dr William Irvine, a superintendent and medical officer, described one prisoner as 'one of the pseudo male individuals' whose presence was sought out by 'those addicted to these most depraved and abominable habits'. He believed some women had a 'preternatural development of an organ peculiar to the female, the "clitoris", which enabled them to assume partially the function of a male', while others used 'artificial substances, mechanically secured to the person from the substitute for the male organ', a practice he considered worse even than masturbation as it caused 'palpitation and functional, if not structural, diseases of the heart'.

Homosexual behaviour was exaggerated by some to evidence all that was wrong with convictism and transportation, encapsulated in a poem by Reverend West in the *Examiner*: 'Shall Tasman's Isle, so famed, so lovely and so fair, from other nations be estranged, the name of Sodom bear?'

Colonial Secretary William Gladstone, who would go on to become British PM four times, asked Charles Joseph La Trobe, former superintendent of Port Phillip District, to investigate every penal institution in the colony. He concluded the probation system was 'a fatal experiment' because 'vice of every description is to be met on every hand, not as isolated spots but as a pervading stain'. Numerous probation stations were closed, sleeping arrangements re-designed to allow more separation and scrutiny, battens fixed between beds to 'prevent the continuance of such abominable vices', night lamps installed so patrolling officers could see every bed, and warders given slippers lest their footsteps provide a warning.

In 1846, the *Examiner* extolled the virtues of 'a new invention' in London, by which convicts could be housed at night in a 'panopticon', the name referencing Panoptes, a Greek mythological giant with a hundred eyes. The concept was to allow a watchman to observe (*-opticon*) all (*pan-*) inmates from a central position without them being able to tell whether they are being watched or not, with the inmates sleeping separately such that 'not a breath can be uttered that must not be heard by the overseer', and the men put on a sleeping roster so they never spent successive nights together.

While officials tested 'theories' of custodial design and sleeping management, others argued repression had its own risks. Alexander Maconochie, Governor Franklin's Secretary and later commandant of Norfolk Island, felt 'unnatural acts' were caused by inappropriate management of prisoners. His view was that 'if we actively employ our prisoners, and by suitable means cultivate in them the daily practice of manly and social value, they will protect themselves from degrading vices better than we can protect them by walls and bolts'.

England had its last hanging for sodomy in 1835. James Pratt and John Smith were visited by Charles Dickens in their final days, and the magistrate who committed them to trial later wrote to the Home Secretary arguing sodomy was a crime with no injury done to any consenting individual. And, he said, it wasn't fair that wealthy men could engage in homosexual behaviour because they could afford private space with little chance of discovery, while men like Pratt and Smith were condemned only because they were forced to use a room in a lodging house and were easily spied upon.

But the two men were hanged at Newgate Prison, and the lodging room owner transported to Van Diemen's Land.

That was the end of hangings for sodomy in England, but on the other side of the Empire nothing changed. Partly on the back of concern about the extent of unnatural crime being a stain on the colony and the Mother Country, transportation ended in 1853, but it wasn't until 1863 that Blay performed the last hangings of men convicted of 'buggery' and 'sodomy'.

Hendrick Witnalder, described as a Kaffir native from South Africa, and a 14-year-old boy were charged with an 'unnatural offence'. The boy was found not guilty but Witnalder, who was not defended, was sentenced to hang.

He had served in the Cape Rifles but was involved in a 'mutiny' in 1838, court-martialled and transported to New South Wales, where he was treated for venereal disease, dismissed as a 'worthless little Hottentot', then convicted of raping his master's wife in 1846 after a wage dispute, and transported to Hobart Town for life. Witnalder was conspicuous because of his small stature, colour, dress and drunkenness. One newspaper said he was 'long so familiarly known to the inhabitants of Hobart Town', another that 'the diminutive Caffre goes about arranged in military clothes'.

After spending Christmas awaiting his fate, at 3.30am on the day of his appointment with Blay he asked to be joined by a Reverend and they spent several hours in prayer. Witnalder told the clergyman he was too weak to make any statement on the scaffold, but asked that he tell people he was 'perfectly innocent' of the crime for which he would suffer.

Witnalder bowed and saluted the witnesses in attendance inside the Campbell Street Gaol. He watched Blay attach iron weights at his feet in an attempt, the *Mercury* reported, to prevent or shorten 'the death struggle' given his comparative lightness. The newspaper reported 'he appeared to die easily', although despite the weights for about 'four or five minutes considerable muscular action was apparent in his limbs'.

Six months later Blay was in Launceston for the hanging of Dennis Collins, for another 'unnatural offence'. Collins, a Chelsea carpenter transported for theft, ascended the scaffold and told those present he was innocent but he had no desire to live, was reconciled to death and meeting the Almighty, and would die for those who had given evidence against him.

Witnalder and Collins became the last men to hang for 'unnatural offences' in the Empire.

The first photographs of same-sex couples were taken at the base of Mount Wellington in the 1890s. But the 'stain' attitude didn't dissolve, and for the next 100 years Tasmania would have the world's highest rate of imprisonment for consensual male sex.

Twelve years after the last sodomy hangings, Blay saw off the last Tasmanian man for rape.

Job Smith, 55, was serving an eight-year sentence at Port Arthur for forgery. He was regarded as a good prisoner and appointed a wardsman, allowing him some liberty.

Late in the afternoon of 27 February, when prisoners should have been secured for the night, Margaret Ayres, the housemaid for the prison's Anglican chaplain, went into the bush to look for her master's cow and came across Smith. Asked about the cow, Smith pointed in a direction where the girl headed until becoming aware she was being followed. After she slipped and fell to the ground, she said, Smith used considerable violence and raped her, threatening to kill her if she told anyone.

Smith's defence claimed there was no evidence of him assaulting the housemaid, he was just one of six prisoners free at the time, and the girl had failed to notice Smith had lost the use of one of his arms.

The jury rejected the claims, but others pleaded his case. As Blay began his preparations, a lengthy letter in the *Mercury* on Friday 28 May by 'Clemency' argued that execution for rape would only encourage more rapists to commit murder 'on the principle that the dead do not speak'. He said the girl's life had been spared, there had been no execution for rape for many years, the evidence was quite circumstantial, the girl's character for morality and truthfulness might be questionable, and information had emerged at Port Arthur about the veracity of some of the original statements.

The attorney-general ascertained from the *Mercury* that Clemency was a lawyer, Thomas Sheehy, so he telegraphed Port Arthur's commandant to furnish any additional information by express messenger. The next morning, a Saturday, the Executive Council met at Government House but deferred a final decision as the express messenger had not arrived. The attorney-general telegraphed the commandant to ask what the messenger was bringing, and was told it was 'unimportant'.

The messenger, a senior constable, finally arrived at 10pm on Saturday, 'his horse completely knocked up and himself jaded' after the 95-kilometre ride. The documents discredited or cast doubt on Clemency's arguments. Late as it was, the attorney-general went immediately to see the governor, who agreed to recall the Executive Council the next morning. The council resolved there was no cause to change course, and Smith would be terminated 48 hours later.

For his final meal, Smith asked for some bread, cheese and beer, but according to the *Mercury* when he left the cell for his execution 'the refreshment remained untouched'.

Inside, he had scratched his name alongside others on the stone wall of the cell of the condemned.

20

FLEEING THE NOOSE

By the time Solomon Blay was in his fifties, he and Mary had managed to accumulate a tidy balance of about £250 and began thinking it might be time to finish with being the colony's finisher.

The nerves and demons that had beset him at the start of his hangings had dissipated but not disappeared. He had hardened himself to the task, something he had now done close to 200 times. Two hundred bells tolling for the condemned and for him. Two hundred times he had tightened the noose around someone's neck, enduring his own life sentence. Dispensing death was stressful enough, even after so many, even after a rum or two and even after doctors provided something to 'steady me nerves and let me sleep' and to 'buck me up' — which might have simply been prescriptions for brandy or opium — but now any shortcoming in his work was openly castigated and sometimes booed.

What he thought was being suitably and professionally detached, newspapers described as 'brutal'. What he thought was a respectable role in the chain of justice was described as being the 'degraded' role of a real-life Ketch from Punch and Judy. What he thought were his just rewards of the condemned's clothing was described as being 'the Fagin of the mortuary'.

Blay was the most despised and demonised public servant in the colony. The ultimate in denunciations was to describe someone as less worthy than the 'common hangman' or 'not fit to be a hangman'. Those campaigning for an end to transportation and convictism saw him as the personification of all that they wanted to banish in the land of banishment. Anti-hanging proponents asked why, if life was a gift of God, would man 'take the scaffold for vantage ground, lecturing upon this sacredness of human life [and] hire a man to kill a man?'

Ordinary people aware of his identity might show their disgust at coach stops or in the streets and inns. Even the club of justice, of which he thought he was a member, did him no favours, as in 1860 when he summoned a woman for 'scratching his face and throwing stones at him' only for the case to be dismissed. Again, in 1872, he summoned another woman for using abusive language, but the magistrate dismissed the case as one of a 'trumpery nature' best resolved by a fine of five shillings.

It all went with the territory. Previous hangmen had been similarly ostracised, the *Examiner* reporting that 'a feeling approaching to horror was excited when his calling and character became known'. His mainland peers had not fared well: John Harris simply 'disappeared' from his post in Melbourne, replaced by former Van Diemen's Land convict William Bamford, who lost an eye in a brawl and was frequently in trouble as a drunken vagrant, and in Sydney Alexander Green was scarred after an axe attack and had been committed to a lunatic asylum.

And the scaffold business was beginning to slow. After 18 hangings in each of 1856 and 1857, in 1860 there were only six, and subsequent years saw hangings of three, two, one and then two. Then there were two years when Blay had no call for rope and soap, two of only three years in the colony's history there had not been a hanging.

While Blay was weighing his options, Mary was disappointed her husband would miss St Patrick's Day celebrations in 1868, more so because he was off to Launceston to hang an Irishman, Daniel 'Little Dan' Connors. The barbarous murder of Ellen Moriarty at Longford was a celebrated case because of the crime (the woman's body was found with her intestines ripped out and tossed aside), and the trial (Connors launched a wholesale attack on everyone for prejudice: lawyers for denying him a fair trial and clergy for neglect).

According to the *Mercury*, Connors 'reviewed the evidence with considerable shrewdness, and criticised the characters of some of the witnesses for the prosecution'.

When the judge began exhorting him to prepare for the worst, Connors said:

> I don't want to hear any more --- sermons from you.
>
> His Honour: Don't interrupt me, sir.
>
> Connors: Give me my sentence and have done.
>
> His Honour: I shall say what I desire. Your life is due to society as an expiation of the crime you have perpetrated. I say I hope you will pay the most earnest attention to your spiritual advisers, and obtain that mercy from above which you cannot get here. The sentence of this Court upon you, Daniel Connors, is that you be taken from hence to the place from whence you came, and from thence to a place of execution, and that there you be hanged by the neck until you are dead! And may the Lord have mercy on your soul.
>
> Connors: May you get back to England.

Newspapers said Connors' 'bravado' dissipated after the trial. In the condemned cell, he regretted his courtroom rage and was 'very sensitive to any kindness exhibited towards him'. He spoke at length with others about his life, giving rise to a popular pamphlet, and engaged with clergy until late into the night before his execution.

Blay and some prisoners had finished erecting the scaffold in the inner gaol yard the previous day in his full view 'and it is said to have been inspected by Connors during its erection'.

The Executive Council met at the Club Hotel to review the pending death sentences against Connors and two others, Ephraim Booth, for the rape of an eight-year-old girl, and Patrick Daly, a blind man, for an 'unnatural offence'. The Council commuted the latter two sentences to life imprisonment, but resolved that Connors' 'should take its course'.

At about 5.30am on the morning of his execution, Connors asked to see Blay. '[He] had an interview with him. During the conversation the latter mentioned his regret that Connors should have been so foolish as to place himself in such a position, when he replied that he was an innocent man,' the *Examiner* reported.

Two hours later, Blay was back in the cell for business. He shook hands with Connors, as was his custom, pinioned his arms, and with two javelin men walked him to the scaffold.

Dressed in grey prison clothing, Connors ascended the steps leading to the platform, 'pale and anxious looking'. But 'with a free springing tread' he stepped from the drop to the front rail, and calmly made a statement to gaol and sheriff officers and about 30 people allowed inside to watch:

> To the public I am very grateful to the visiting magistrates, and likewise to Mr Cox (Governor of the Gaol) and all the officers of the gaol for their attention to me. I am going to die now on a charge I say before God and man I never had a hand in, or took any part whatever. I sincerely forgive all my presenters ... and I hope the Lord will have mercy on my soul.

After Connors stepped back to the centre of the platform, Blay put the rope around his neck, the calico cap over his head, and drew the bolt.

Notwithstanding the earlier dawn chat between executioner and condemned, one in which the hangman probably heard, as ever, the plea to 'dinna hurt me' and 'make it quick', death did not come so quick. 'The body swung round, and probably on account of its lightness the sufferings of the wretched man seemed to be prolonged. The legs moved, twitched, and contracted for 10 or 12 minutes after the drop fell', said the *Cornwall Chronicle*.

It was after this St Patrick's Day episode that Blay told Under-Sheriff Crouch he'd had enough. The man who had appointed him 18 years and 200 hangings ago didn't dissuade him. Crouch passed the news to the sheriff, who passed it to the attorney-general, who informed Parliament 'the hangman is worn out in the service'.

Whether he agreed he was 'worn out', Blay's thinking was clear. He could still do the job, but all the cold gaols and travelling had worn him down, and the work was virtually gone. But he couldn't do anything else and a hangman wasn't going to be employed by anyone. Too many people gave him a hard time. He would never get any real peace and would be found out in the other colonies. He should go back to England where no one knew him.

While Blay made his plans, the government resolved that 'should it unfortunately prove necessary to call the services of such a functionary into requisition, other arrangements will be made', such as utilising a hangman from another state. It announced Blay had retired on a pension, prompting some newspaper suggestions that 'the hangman's occupation is gone, for Blay is hale and hearty'. In Parliament, one member quipped he 'must have been starved out', and another 'congratulated' the government for issuing a pension to someone who 'has not had a patient on his hands for the last 3 years'. Both comments were greeted with derisive parliamentary laughter.

Having resolved he had reached the end of his days in Tasmania, in the winter of 1868 Solomon and Mary withdrew their savings. Their money, ironically held in a new Hobart Savings Bank building on the site of the old Murray Street gaol, was first used to book a passage on the *Southern Cross* as 'Mr and Mrs Murphy', Mary's family name. They were anxious to avoid the experience of a former hangman, who had also endeavoured to escape and start a new life in Sydney but, according to the *Examiner*, the passengers 'one and all, protested against his company and he was turned ashore'.

Two days later they quietly boarded the steam ferry, a former blockade runner in the American Civil War, for its regular run to Melbourne. Within a week they were aboard the new *Somersetshire*, bound for England with its cargo of 48,000 ounces (1300 kilograms) of gold, wool, tallow and meat.

The escape trip came just a few months after Queen Victoria's 23-year-old son, his Royal Highness Prince Alfred, the Duke of Edinburgh, visited Tasmania as part of the first Royal tour of Australia. He was greeted in Hobart Town by close to 20,000 people, with 5000 children singing 'Ode of Welcome', a night-time maritime procession of 30 boats with torches, bonfires up and down the Derwent shoreline and Mount Wellington, a ball for 1200, shooting contests, cricket match and a regatta.

The Royal visit also served as a final chapter in the Empire's decimation of an ancient civilisation. At the regatta, the Duke delighted in meeting fellow 'royals': Aboriginal woman 'Queen Truganini', one of the last 'full-blooded' Aboriginal Tasmanians, who presented the prize for a duck hunt, and her consort, William 'King Billy' Lanne. Lanne had been the youngest child in the last Aboriginal family captured in the Black War, and was the last so-called 'full-blooded' Aboriginal Tasmanian man. The *Mercury* later reported he was not particularly proud of his ancestry, and had objected to a photograph taken of him for the 1866 intercolonial exhibition as being 'too black for him'. But, it said, 'he was a pure-bred Tasmanian Aboriginal and as black as a sloe [a dark-coloured berry]'.

Despite the royal patronage, 'King Billy' Lanne died the following year from the effects of alcohol, cholera and dysentery. The misery of his people continued in death: before and after burial, Lanne's body parts, including head, feet and hands, were removed by various scientists, including those from the Royal College of Surgeons of England and the Royal Society of Tasmania, in a dispute over who should possess the skeleton and remains of the 'last Tasmanian man', as newspapers called him.

Blay failed in his attempt to find safe haven in the homeland that had banished him. His true identity became known, and the retirement plan quickly frayed.

The reason he left the colony, Blay later wrote to Governor Charles DuCane, was because after 'upwards of 30 years [as] public Executioner in Tasmania', he had suffered failing health and been put on the pension list. He had been 'advised medically if it was in my power to seek a change of climate'.

'Having stored a little money, I thought perhaps Melbourne would be a benefit to me, but such was not the case and I then proceeded to England', Blay wrote, although not explaining why he only stayed in Melbourne a few days.

In England, the couple bought 'a cottage and piece of ground outside London', the hangman

> believing that I could live unknown and quietly in my retreat, but such was not to be. It soon became whispered about that I was the Executioner from Tasmania and as a matter of course there was no more peace for me in the land of freedom.
>
> At last I was obliged to sell my home at a fearful sacrifice to preserve my life and that of those dearest to me and return to Tasmania where I would not be molested.

Just shy of a year after leaving for England, Solomon and Mary Blay were despondently back on board the *Roxburgh Castle* for more than two months sailing to Melbourne — a longer trip than usual after the ship was becalmed at the equator doldrums for nine days — and then the *Southern Cross* to Hobart Town.

They were back with much of their life savings gone. While presumably cognisant the governor would have wondered why Blay returned to the colony and climate from which he wanted to escape, in March 1870 the executioner nevertheless sought vice-regal sympathy for 'how I have been situated and to what extreme loss I have been subject in my voyage to England and, I may say, my compulsory return'.

His escape effort had 'dried up my purse', so to overcome his financial position Blay felt he had no choice but to again serve as a hangman. He had applied to the attorney-general for reappointment, which was agreed to, but 'to my surprise there was but £28 or thereabouts added to my pension, making my salary but £52 per annum, whereas formerly I received £80 per annum, and did not consider it too much for my office'.

And previously while he had been 'in the habit of dealing in a small way in the country district ... I am unable through poverty to begin again, having no funds but my salary of £1 per week'.

So Her Majesty's 'most humble servant' had an uncommon proposal for His Excellency: to 'offer the Government my pension for any sum they may think equitable, so that I may have a little capital to begin with again. At the same time I will faithfully engage to perform my duty whenever called upon to do so'.

His Excellency might have been taken with the innovative notion of someone 'selling' their pension, and perhaps wondered if Under-Sheriff Thomas Crouch had helped craft the eloquent letter. But six weeks later the Colonial Secretary's Office recorded: 'Solomon Blay is informed in reply to his petition praying that his pension might be commuted for a fixed sum, that the Government regret they are unable to recommend a compliance with his request as the provisions of the Superannuation Act do not admit of retiring allowances being commuted.'

So a disappointed Blay had no choice but to continue as hangman, a role he wanted to end, in a place he had sought to escape, on reduced remuneration, with fewer funds to his name, and fewer hangings on the books. He was at least fortunate the government had not appointed a successor in his absence.

The *Mercury* had been dismayed that 'some malicious slanderers have been circulating reports to the effect that certain respectable tradesmen of the town have applied for the vacancy', statements that could only be made by 'the very lowest of humanity, wretches too unworthy even of the hangman's office', but applications had not been sought.

The government had said it would deal with the need for a hangman if the occasion demanded, but the occasion didn't arise while Blay was absent, and on his return it was easier for the under-sheriff to have his long-standing 'finisher' back on hand for any executions rather than find a newcomer, or rely on the availability of a hangman from Melbourne or Sydney.

The attorney-general explained there had been 'a vacancy in an important office, in the Sheriff's Department, the executioner. Mr Solomon Blay was found to be a pensioner for a small amount and in preference to sending to Victoria, Mr Solomon Blay received the appointment'.

The issue of being on the pension list but also drawing a salary continued to attract attention. In 1873, the *Examiner* noted that the pension list included £21 15s 4d to Mr Solomon Blay, in addition to £28 4s 8d as the salary of the executioner, and a further £10 as expenses for executions.

> As the executioner and Mr Blay are identical, we wonder what this official does for the money? Surely Tasmania is not in such a flourishing state that she can afford the luxury of a State hangman? It is positively disgraceful that we should be called upon to pay this amount when the country cannot afford it. No doubt, if we would pursue our inquiries further it would be found that this gentleman is found comfortable quarters and sumptuary rations at the expense of the public. The marvel is that some of our members did not kick against this reckless expenditure.

But unlike everyone else in the judicial chain, the most comfortable quarters for Blay and his wife was a rental property and small second-hand goods shop in Argyle Street, close to the execution yard at Campbell Street Gaol.

On the ledger of reputation there was also no comfort. In November 1869, the *Cornwall Chronicle* reported that Solomon Blay 'arrived here by the mail coach from Hobart Town yesterday morning' and continued:

Some new arrival may enquire who the ---- is Solomon Blay?

Mr Solomon Blay is an old and efficient public servant whose onerous duties are in a direct line and perfect accord with those of the Judges, Executive Government and Sheriff of the land.

After his last appearance here, on St Patricks Day 1868, when on behalf of the Sheriff he officiated in a solemn ceremony at the gaol, Mr Blay's name having been enrolled on the pension list with those of our retired great public functionaries, side by side with a bishop and a judge, Mr Blay felt disposed for a time to retire from active service, and taking his passage on board the *Southern Cross* proceeded to Melbourne, and from thence per clipper ship *Stirlingshire* [sic] to London to revisit the scenes of his youth.

He may have ascended Mont Blanc or he may have went up the Rhine, he may have made the whole continental tour as laid down in the latest guides, but on the other hand he may not.

The business at the Old Bailey would form an attraction to a legally constructed mind such as Mr Blay's which he would find it difficult to resist.

In whatever way Mr Blay expended his time in the old worn out country we dignify by the term home, it is gratifying to know that none of the fascinations of the day were sufficiently powerful to detain him there.

He found new theories propounded there thoroughly antagonistic to the interests of all artists in his line and profession, and he returned with a longing gaze to that southern clime where the good old British institutions he admired still exists on an apparently firm though less public basis than when he commenced his duties and practice.

Disgusted with the democratic tendencies of the age, on the decline and fall of the Disraeli Ministry and the assumption of power by those levellers Gladstone and Bright, maybe Mr Blay paid his passage, or worked it — can't say which — back to the land which provides pensions, or employment, or both, for such veteran functionaries as himself.

The veteran 'functionary' was in Launceston to hang Patrick Kieley, a ploughman convicted of murdering his wife Bridget. He had deserted her some years prior and moved south, during which time Bridget married another man, Matthew Clarke. A year later Kieley returned to Deloraine, whereupon Clarke turned Bridget out after discovering her and Kiely in his house, followed by Kieley returning to his home another night to find her with Clarke.

After throwing the pair out and unsuccessfully asking police to charge Bridget with bigamy and Clarke with housebreaking, Kieley confronted the woman, demanding to know, 'Are you coming along with me?' When she replied, 'No I am not,' he said, 'If you don't keep out of my sight I'll job this rail through you.'

A week later a neighbour asked Kieley where he was going, and he said, 'Going down to Paddy's Scrub to kill Biddy.' Told he was too drunk to know what he was doing, Kieley asserted he well knew what he was doing. He was later seen in a public house, exhausted, bloodstained and asking for a drink. 'It's all over now and can't be helped,' Kieley had said.

Bridget was found with her throat cut. Kieley was found guilty, but the jury unsuccessfully recommended mercy because he had been motivated by jealousy. Kieley, who admitted drinking seven glasses of rum before he 'could determine to commit the murder', spent many days listening to clergy but not eating, his diet being likened to a strict fast in Lent, to the point where Dr George Turnley 'considered it necessary to support [him] by a little stimulant in the shape of wine', to help the clergy 'succeed in as far as it was possible in bringing the murderer into a fitting frame of mind for the awful change awaiting him'.

The awful change was once more in Blay's hands. He went through the well-worn routine and drew the bolt.

But about two minutes after the drop fell, 'the iron shod heels of the boots could be heard striking tremulously against each other, for half a minute, in a manner suggestive of the intense agony endured by their wearer'.

When the body finally hung still and lifeless, those watching turned away to 'breathe more freely outside the scene of the judicial tragedy, and to gaze on one of the brightest, fairest, and most peaceful scenes imaginable — the view down the silvery Tamar glancing as brilliantly in the morning sun as if neither sin or death had yet entered so beautiful a world'.

21

LITERARY IMPRINTS

Solomon Blay's one attempt to escape his hangman life had failed. Many convicts had also tried to escape and a few succeeded, including Irish and Canadian political exiles. But for most there was no escape, no matter how hard or often they tried, as English author Anthony Trollope found.

Trollope was among those who founded the Arts Club in London in 1863, 'for the purpose of facilitating the social intercourse of those connected with, or interested in Art, Literature or Science'. The literary intercourse of authors and poets was often drawn to the Empire's southern extremity and its rich metaphor for cruelty and isolation.

In the armchairs of the private club in Mayfair, London, Trollope was persuaded by Charles Dickens to visit the colony. Dickens frequently referenced convicts in his own writing, including the famous Fagin, and characters transported to Australia, such as John Edmunds in *Pickwick Club*, Wackford Squeers in *Nicholas Nickelby*, Uriah Heep and Mr Littimer in *David Copperfield*, and Abel Magwitch in *Great Expectations*.

As editor-in-chief of the weekly periodical *Household Words*, Dickens published many articles about the Empire's exiled. He declined a lucrative offer to visit, but his two sons, Alfred and Edward, migrated in 1869.

Trollope visited Hobart Town as part of a 12-month tour of Australia and New Zealand. At Port Arthur, which once housed 3500 men but now held the final 500 paupers, invalids and lunatics, Trollope was drawn to an old man called Dennis Dougherty. He was only 14 when he deserted his regiment in Londonderry and was transported for 14 years, starting a life of resistance that cost him nearly 3000 lashes in Sydney, Norfolk Island and Port Arthur for absconding, disobedience, neglect, insubordination, insolent language and disorderly conduct.

Trollope described him as 'all his life fighting against law, who has always been controlled but never tamed'. But now the old Irishman admitted he was 'broken' at last, and after a life of escape, rebellion and torment 'there he stood, speaking softly, arguing his case well, and pleading while the tears ran down his face for some kindness, for some mercy in his old age'. He told the author, 'for 42 years [I] had never been a free man for an hour … I have tried to escape, always to escape … as a bird does out of a cage. Is that unnatural, is that a great crime?'

Dougherty, who finally ended one of the longest tenures at Port Arthur with a ticket-of-leave in 1876, just a year before the gaol closed, featured in Trollope's articles published in London and reprinted by the *Mercury*.

> How to manage convicts, how to get work out of them without the least possible chance of escape, how to catch them when they

did escape, how to give them liberty when they made no attempt to escape, how to punish them, and how not to punish them, how to make them understand that they were simply beasts of burden reduced to that degree by their own vileness, and how to make them understand at the same time that if under the most difficult circumstances for the exercise of virtue they would cease to be vicious, they might cease also to be beasts of burden — these were the tasks which were imposed, not only upon the governors and their satellites, not only on all officers, military and civil, not only on the army of gaolers, warders and such like, which was necessary, but also on every free settler and on every free man in the island.

Trollope described the hangman as 'a great and well-paid official', one of 'the undignified extremities of a long tail of repressive but dignified officials. For no one who had cast in his lot with Van Diemen's Land could be free from the taint of the establishment.'

The author described convict assignees as 'slaves' in a colony with a name that 'had a sound which had become connected all over the world with rascaldom' and was 'harsh with the crack of the jailer's whip'.

But Trollope acknowledged the universal truth that 'horrors are always so popular that of course such tales are told the loudest', and gave a nod to the successful lives of many former convicts, the good behaviour of many assignees and the fairness of many masters.

'Van Diemen's Land had not a great reputation. It had a name that seemed to carry a taunt in men's ears. But it was prosperous and fat; and unless when bushrangers were in ascendancy, the people were happy,' Trollope wrote. The land and climate profitably produced 'almost every plant and almost every animal that thrives in England', so men were able to become rich, and the colonial settlements of Launceston and Hobart Town were prosperous on the back of cheap labour providing good roads, handsome buildings, public gardens, schools and hospitals.

The colony was becoming better known in kinder terms — Trollope wrote 'everything in Tasmania is more English than

England' and told his hosts that, like Charles Darwin, 'could I choose the colony in which I was to live, I would pitch my staff in Tasmania'. The 'isle of Hades' was now growing a reputation as 'the apple isle', with 120 varieties developed from the country's first seedlings planted in 1788 on Bruny Island, businessmen promoting the 'summer isle of Eden' and the 'sanitorium of the sunny south'. The air, Trollope said, was 'perfect', and Edward Braddon, a settler who went on to become Premier, said it was 'to that of England as cream to skimmed milk'.

The convict stain was also being diluted by fresh thinking, the importing and exporting of ideas about freedom and nationalism.

Around the time of Trollope's visit, local lawyer Andrew Inglis Clark was an active member of literary and debating societies, and a student of the American push for independence. He was especially interested in how the Young Irelanders' push for freedom had been influenced by the Italian Risorgimento (resurgence) of Giuseppe Mazzini, 'the beating heart of Italy'.

Clark had a portrait of Mazzini in every room of his home in Hobart Town. At the 1876 annual dinner of 'young ardent Republicans' at the American Club, he declared 'the principles ... proclaimed by the founders of the Anglo-American Republic ... to be permanently applicable to the politics of the world'. He hosted American author and preacher Moncure Conway when he visited the newly proclaimed city of Hobart in 1883, and in turn Conway introduced Clark to leading American writers and thinkers, including Oliver Wendell Holmes, who fuelled Clark's admiration of the American Constitution and its democratic and republican ideals, and his conviction of their applicability for Australia.

Blay knew Clark as the barrister who had appeared for many clients destined for the gallows. His talk of 'revolution' unsettled some, including the *Mercury*, which attacked his 'ultra republican, if not revolutionary ideas' as being akin to those of Communists.

The ambitions of Clark and others echoed those of John West, who arrived in the colony a year after Blay as a 29-year-old member of the Colonial Missionary Society. His ability to prosecute his anti-transportation and pro-federation views from his congregational pulpit and printing press was a lasting influence on the public conscience of Australia.

After several years of fruitless campaigning, at a large public protest meeting in 1850 he won acceptance of a plan to engage and unite every organisation and influential man opposed to continued transportation. This led to an abolitionist conference in Melbourne in 1851. Then the Australasian League for the Prevention of Transportation was formed, where West stressed that 'Australians are one' and should act together in spite of artificial boundaries.

His two-volume history of the young colony, *The History of Tasmania*, in 1852 was a foundation stone of Australian historical writing, and as editor of the *Sydney Morning Herald* his editorials and articles under the name 'John Adams' were the first substantive treatment of the question of federation.

Just as West was concerned about constitutional unity and national wellbeing after the gold rush, the younger Clark saw federation as a solution to inter-colonial rivalry over tariffs. He drafted a constitution bill, and worked with Samuel Griffith, Edmund Barton and Charles Kingston to develop a constitution that was the basis of Australia's federation in 1901, with Barton as the first Prime Minister.

Blay could sense how much had changed after decades of isolation. People and ideas moved freely to and from Italy, America and France. The island was now linked to the mainland by submarine telegraph cable, electricity allowed telegrams to be sent, and a Launceston schoolteacher, Alfred Biggs, made Australia's first long-distance telephone call a year after Alexander Bell's breakthrough.

It was a different world from Blay's early days, when information was tightly held by colonial rulers, correspondence exchanged by slow ship voyages, and literary connections made through pirated editions of Charles Dickens' *The Posthumus Papers of the Pickwick Club*. Blay was old enough to have come across Isaac 'Ikey' Solomon, a javelin man and flagellator said to be the model for Dickens' character Fagin in *Oliver Twist*.

Isaac Solomon was convicted at the Old Bailey, but managed to escape to Denmark and then America, and finally to Hobart Town, where Governor Arthur had him returned to London. He was re-sentenced and re-transported for 14 years, back to Van Diemen's Land.

He met Blay at Richmond Gaol, and again later when he used his ticket-of-leave to set up a tobacconist shop. He joined the Hobart synagogue, the first in Australia, largely funded by Judah Solomon, transported with his brother for receiving stolen goods, after the government refused support for non-Christian organisations.

It was perhaps the only synagogue in the world to have numbered benches for convicts. And Hobart was perhaps the only place in the world where three unique 'Solomons' — counterfeiter-hangman, thief-merchant and receiver-philanthropist — could cross paths in a unique place.

Dickens never followed 'Ikey' to Van Diemen's Land, but he went close to accepting a £10,000 offer by Englishmen Felix Spiers and Christopher Pond, who ran the Cafe de Paris in Melbourne. They had seen the commercial opportunities after arranging the first English cricket tour of Australia, and wanted Dickens to take an eight-month reading tour, telling him of the advantages of 'the study of life and character in an entirely new field, and the benefit he would confer upon these colonies by making them better known in the Mother Country'.

Dickens declined, but other literary giants did travel. Emulating Anthony Trollope, Samuel Clemens, better known as Mark Twain, visited Hobart Town in 1895 as part of a tour of the British Empire to help extricate himself from a debt of $100,000 after a failed investment in a revolutionary typesetting machine.

In his account *Following the Equator*, Twain said, 'English law was hard hearted in those days. For trifling offences which in our day would be punished by a small fine or a few days confinement men, women and boys were sent to this other end of the earth to serve terms of 7 and 14 years, and for serious crimes they were transported for life. Children were sent to the penal colonies for seven years for stealing a rabbit.'

He had been horrified that some men in England were being sentenced to 25 lashes, but 'no man had been found with grit enough to keep his emotions to himself beyond the ninth blow' and 'humane, modern London couldn't endure it'.

But 25 lashes was nothing compared with what he found in Tasmania: 'They gave a convict 50 for almost any little offence, and sometimes a brutal officer would add 50, and then another 50 and sometimes more. In Tasmania I read in an old manuscript an official record of a case where a convict was given 300 lashes for stealing some silver spoons. And men got more than that sometimes.'

Twain said convict life was so unendurable that once or twice despairing men got together and drew straws to determine which of them should kill another in the group — 'this murder to secure the death to the perpetrator and to the witnesses of it by the hand of the hangman!'

Twain said he quoted such incidents as 'mere hints' of what convict life was like. And while some of the convicts were 'bad' people, most were probably not noticeably worse than those left behind in England.

> We are obliged to believe that a nation could look on, unmoved, and see starving or freezing women hanged for stealing 26c worth of bacon or rags, and boys snatched from their mothers and men from their families, and sent to the other side of the world for long terms for similar trifling offences ... And we must also believe that a nation that knew ... what was happening to those exiles and was still content with it, was not advancing in any showy way toward a higher grade of civilisation.
>
> If we look into the characters and conduct of the officers and

gentlemen who had charge of the convicts and attended to their backs and stomachs, we must grant again that as between the convict and his masters, and between both and the nation at home, there was a quite noticeable monotony of sameness.

Like Trollope, Twain was taken with Hobart Town, declaring it 'the neatest town that the sun shines on' with 'perfect air', and observing that 'in speech and manner your Australians have a sort of frank and friendly way that lacks something of the English reserve ... they develop a certain similarity to the people of the United States'.

The *Mercury's* correspondent was pleased to find the white-haired, pilot-capped Clemens a quiet and polite man, not keen to dazzle with 'pyrotechnic wit' like a 'literary snob'. But while he admired Mark Twain the humourist, it was the 'misfortune' of the cigar-smoking Mr Clemens to be an American and 'thus imbued with American attitudes about patriotism and English values'.

Literary observations by the likes of Dickens, Trollope and Twain gained considerable local and overseas attention, but they weren't the first to be fascinated by Solomon Blay's world.

Convictism was the origin of Australian writing. The country's first book of general literature was Thomas Wells' account of bushranger Michael Howe in 1818, a convicted highwayman who arrived on the first convict ship *Indefatigable*, and called himself 'Lieutenant Governor of the Woods'.

The first staging of an Australian play was David Burns' *The Bushrangers* in Edinburgh in 1829, and Henry Savery wrote *The Hermit in Van Diemen's Land* in the first volume of Australian essays in 1830, and the first novel, *Quintus Servinton*, in 1831.

English author Mary Grimstone settled in Hobart Town to write *Woman's Love* in 1832, and Charles Rowcroft published his first novel *Tales of the Colonies, or The Adventures of an Emigrant, Edited by a late Colonial Magistrate* in 1843, and in 1846 *The Bushranger of Van Diemen's Land*. Escaped convicts penned *The Exile's Return* in 1849 (Canadian Samuel Snow) and *Jail Journal* in 1854 (Young

Irelander John Mitchell). Emily Dickinson invoked Van Diemen's Land in her poetry in 1862, and novelist Caroline Leake started a long line of fiction with *The Broad Arrow* in 1859, which informed Marcus Clarke's *For the Term of his Natural Life* in 1874.

Much of the writing centred on real and metaphorical notions of heaven and hell, paradise and punishment, deliverance and death. Solomon Blay's role was frequently alluded to. He was the one most familiar with the very real world of punishment and death, and now he was about to be drawn to the memoirs of someone he had long prepared to hang.

22

MISSING CASH

Already aggrieved by his failed return to England and the personal and financial cost of his public service, Solomon Blay's sense of injustice was heightened when the Mercury Steam Press produced 2000 copies of *The Adventures of Martin Cash*, a green-covered book of 179 pages.

Blay was spending his twilight hanging years as quietly as he could manage, but he would occasionally be confronted by someone who wouldn't let him forget the past, leading to what one newspaper described as a 'warfare of words' with 'Old Sol'. At Hiddlestone's grocery store and in favourite inns he crossed paths with another white-haired man, the man he long complained had 'escaped him' — bushranger Martin Cash, who he first met 30 years ago on a chain gang at Jerusalem before their lives took different but ever-intersecting paths.

Billy Graham, an office boy at the *Mercury* in the 1870s, later wrote of an unpretentious little pub in Liverpool Street, where his father and others made merry over bread, cheese, rum and foaming Cascade beer drunk out of pewter pots. It was reminiscent of the many old pubs of Hobart Town, with sawdust on the floor and red curtains on their windows, frequented by what Graham said were 'such people as Dickens used to describe'.

'Solomon Blay was a frequent visitor to that pub and I knew him well. He was a tall gaunt fellow, with grizzled hair and beard; a silent morose man, even in liquor. Still he took in good part any reference made to his profession by boon companions.'

Another frequenter was Martin Cash: 'He was then a snowy haired genial old man who lived out Glenorchy way, and brought fowls and eggs to market occasionally.'

The two relics of the convict era were living out their days as free men, but with unique storylines.

Blay the hangman and Cash the bushranger had danced on the same stage of life and death, but while the hangman despatched most members of Cash's gang, he was not to put the noose around their leader's neck. Cash went within minutes of being hanged by Blay for killing a policeman, but survived the sentence to become known as the only Australian bushranger to die of old age, and in his own bed. Blay too would die an old man, but not in his own bed, and without getting his man.

When they first met on the Jerusalem chain gang, Blay was washing laundry, Cash breaking rocks. Both wanted to escape. Chain gangs were a perilous environment, as convicts used every ruse to serve their own interests and overseers used every opportunity to inflict punishment. A bonus 'slant', or feed, was given to the provider of any information, such as a man planning to abscond or having tobacco in his possession. Irrespective of whether it might be true, such information delivered a minor reward to the informant and summary punishment for the victim.

Cash said in his memoirs:

No matter how well a man conducted himself he was not safe, as at
any time he might be denounced by his fellow prisoners, without the
possibility of defending himself.

    For the first week I remained at Jerusalem I had not an opportunity
of making my escape from this abode of wretchedness, where gaunt
starvation, tyranny in all its revolting forms, and treachery existed
to an unlimited degree. It was a perfect reign of terror, but as I was
determined to make tracks as soon as possible, I endeavoured to act
on the square to all parties.

Cash recalled Blay behaving 'in the character of a good man' at
Jerusalem, and 'a few days after my arrival he was summonsed to
Hobart Town in order to get initiated into the mysteries of tying the
noose, and where two unfortunate men awaited his introduction to
another world'.

    Cash escaped the chain gang and went on to gain notoriety as
head of a 'Robin Hood' gang, known as Cash and Company, which
largely concentrated on the well-to-do and left poorer farmers
and settlers in peace. In his memoirs, Launceston journalist and
subsequent mayor Henry Button said the gang behaved 'with
something like chivalry ... women and children were treated with
marked consideration and respect, a peculiarity due to the influence
of the leader who declared that he detested bloodshed and violence'.

    At one point when his 'paramour' had been arrested for receiving
stolen goods, the gang even wrote to the governor:

Messrs Cash & Co beg to notify His Excellency Sir John Franklin
and his satellites that a very respectable person named Mrs Cash is
now falsely imprisoned in Hobart Town and if the said Mrs Cash
is not released forthwith and properly remunerated we will in the
first instance visit Government House and beginning with Sir John
administer a wholesome lesson in the shape of a sound flogging,
after which we will pay the same currency to all his follows.

The note was signed by Cash, Kavanagh and Jones.

Chivalrous intent or not, it seemed inevitable that Cash's bushranging days would eventually end, either from the muskets of pursuing police or the hands of Solomon Blay.

Notwithstanding his declared aversion to bloodshed, and his 'chivalry', Cash was furious when in 1843 he found his 'Mrs Cash', his 'paramour' Bessie Clifford, was living with another man in Hobart Town. Despite being on the run, he set out to confront and kill her. He and fellow gang member Lawrence Kavanagh ventured into town disguised as sailors, but were recognised.

Kavanagh was wounded and captured but Cash escaped, only to be recognised again when he came back for Bessie a second time. He was captured after fleeing into a dead-end street and fatally shooting one of his pursuers, later discovered to be a constable. Under-Sheriff Crouch was one of those who heard the cries of 'Stop thief!' and 'Stop Martin Cash!' and gave chase, and helped ensure Cash was not beaten to death but would survive so as to be hanged by his man Blay.

Cash stood with his arms folded during his trial, wearing a blue jacket and green handkerchief over his head wounds, presumably to emphasise his argument that the arresting police had unnecessarily beaten him. But, unsurprisingly, Cash was convicted of killing the constable, and awaited his reunion with Blay.

'A day or two previous to that appointed for my execution, and when returning from the gaol yard to my cell, on passing the cookhouse I overheard one of the men telling some person to keep out of my sight, but the party spoken to was not so refined or delicate in his feelings and consequently came to the door, disclosing to me the features of my old friend Solomon Blay.'

'Well Martin,' he exclaimed, 'how are you getting on?'

'I'm in the best of health,' Cash replied with a wry smile, 'and passed on to my cell, being perfectly aware that he was called down from Oatlands for my especial benefit.'

In his memoirs, Cash said that while it was his misfortune to be in the condemned cell, Blay was fortunate to still be the hangman.

He recalled the time when Blay, after 'getting into high life and becoming a government officer', took it into his head during the New Town races to 'exercise his old profession' with an accomplice and broke into a cottage and

> having secured what was moveable was in the act of making tracks but on some of the neighbours giving the alarm they were apprehended.
>
> For this Solomon received a sentence of transportation for life. What became of his mate I do not know, being a person of very little importance whose case received no particular attention.
>
> But I do know that while Solomon remained in gaol, the only consideration which appeared to annoy him was the loss of his very high position in society, resolving upon various expedients (in order to establish his claim) to a renewal of office, former services being the ground upon which he mainly depended.
>
> The Government … being anxious to secure the services of the dexterous person, restored him to office under certain restrictions.

Cash mused that while Blay was merely 'a functionary of some notoriety', the hangman saw himself as 'still a man of the world, and thought he had better hold a candle to his sable majesty. He therefore embraced office and any other restrictions, namely that in lieu of four years [*sic*] to Norfolk Island which his sentence involved, he submitted to take it out at four gaols, Launceston, Oatlands, Richmond, and Hobart Town, one year in each respectively'.

Now Blay had journeyed from Oatlands for Cash's 'special benefit', and was within the appointed hour of ending his good health. But the bushranger maintained his optimism.

'I shall ever remember a dream which I had while waiting to hear my doom,' he wrote. 'I imagined that I was attacked by a large black snake which I succeeded in destroying after a most determined struggle. I augured favourably for this dream, and for the first time it occurred to me that my life might be spared.'

Perhaps the black snake was a metaphor for the noose. He and Kavanagh were given an unexpected reprieve when Judge Algernon Montagu visited the gaol and gave the under-sheriff a warrant to postpone the imminent execution for 14 days, countermanding his own co-signature on a Lieutenant-Governor-in-Council warrant issued only 24 hours before. It wasn't clear whether the unpredictable Montagu had been swayed by opponents of capital punishment — including his own father Basil, a British jurist who was a good friend of poets Samuel Coleridge and William Wordsworth — the pleading of womenfolk who had been courteously treated by the bushrangers, or had his own doubts about the validity of the sentence.

Lieutenant Governor Sir John Eardley-Wilmot felt he had no choice but to defer to the Law Lords in Britain for their judgment. But because it was impossible to get despatches to and from England inside many months, he still had to act when Montagu's 14-day adjournment expired. He commuted Kavanagh to life imprisonment at Norfolk Island, and respited Cash 'until Her Majesty's pleasure could be known'.

The gaol-keeper was among those moved to tears by the obvious relief and gratitude of the two men. Cash wrote: 'There is no man who can have any just conception of the feelings of the wretched culprit who knows and can reckon the fleeting hours he has to live but the man placed in similar circumstances. I returned to my dungeon with as light a heart and as much satisfaction as if it had been a palace.'

Blay was probably less satisfied, but at least Cash was in the condemned cell under sentence of death, respited but not reprieved. He might have grimaced as he saw Cash accept the parade of cakes, sweets, fruit, books and other indulgences sent by well-wishers, as was permitted for those in the condemned cell. But Blay had reason to remain confident that he would have the final say.

In the meantime, he had the final word on one of Cash's former accomplices, George Jones. He had taken a charge of blinding buckshot when arrested in a shootout, and doubted anyone would 'scrag a blind cove'. But he was wrong.

Still Cash waited for his fate to be known. And still his luck held.

The first Roman Catholic Bishop, Robert Willson, was looking for opportunities to promote the elimination of the most severe aspects of convictism. After talking with Cash he took up his case with the governor, who already tended to the view that reform was more important than punishment.

Based more on the humanitarian instincts of the two men than a fine point of law — that while the bushranger had killed a policeman, he didn't know he was a policeman — His Excellency signed the commutation papers. Judge Montagu visited the gaol to tell Cash that after more than a year in the condemned cell he had been spared Blay's rope.

Instead, he would be sent to Norfolk Island for life. 'You are lucky to be alive, Cash, but while there is life there is hope,' the judge said.

Life perhaps, but not much hope. Cash well knew brutality, corruption and sexual and physical abuse was endemic, but the island was about to enter a new level of brutality. After a dispute about eating utensils, a despairing, lash-weary William 'Jacky-Jacky' Westwood decided he had nothing to lose because he was no longer 'living', and led a bloody uprising in which four constables were killed by club and axe.

Westwood was transported when only 16 for stealing a coat and cruelly whipped by his first farm master, and now reflected the unchanged outcome of what even Governor Arthur noted 20 years before: 'Some convicts have felt the effect so much of the dreariness and of the hard labour upon them that they have actually committed murder for the purpose of being sent to trial,' and cited a convict killing his friend 'despite there being no quarrel between them: the prisoner could not account for the feeling but that he was weary of life'.

Now Westwood would face John Price, who had just arrived from Hobart Town as Norfolk's first civilian commandant, with a reputation for severity as a convict muster master and then stipendiary magistrate, a pretentious monocle and a family crest featuring a dragon's mouth around a human hand dripping blood.

The manipulative Price, the foundation for Maurice Frere in Marcus Clarke's *For The Term of His Natural Life*, occasionally evidenced sentimentality but, fresh to Norfolk, he needed to demonstrate to 2000 prisoners who was in charge and kill off any lingering thoughts of rebellion. Of the hundreds involved in the uprising, Price picked 26 to pay the retributive price, including Cash's companion Kavanagh.

Blay probably read reports in the *Hobart Town Advertiser* and *Courier* with more than passing interest, unsurprised by the involvement of the 'notoriously bad' Kavanagh, but surprised Cash was said to have 'had nothing to do with the uprising ... he is a very quiet, industrious, well-behaved person who principally amuses himself with making straw hats'.

Cash was well behaved because Price, who had previously told Cash when he appeared before him in court 'you will not best me Martin', now told the bushranger, 'if you'll act on the square I'll lay up to you ... it's a bargain is it?' There was an upside to staying on Price's good side.

Kavanagh, Westwood and others waited as the authorities in Hobart Town despatched a justice team to Norfolk: the attorney-general, a barrister as acting judge, some clergy, and an unidentified convict travelling by the name 'White', who would be the hangman. It wasn't deemed necessary to send any counsel to defend the convicts.

Eleven men were quickly convicted alongside Westwood, the man who had actually committed the murders, and the hanging orders were given.

In a final letter, Westwood put a tragic human face to the brutality of convictism, declaring he did not grieve for the end to his 'earthly career'. Indeed, he said, 'I welcome death as a friend. The world, or what I have seen of it, has no allurements for me.' He said that for stealing a coat as a youngster, before he understood responsibility, he had forfeited his birthright and been torn away from his parents, brother and sisters. Since then he had been treated 'more like a beast than a man, until nature could bear no more', and while he had committed murder it was of those who for years physically and mentally tortured, half-starved and flogged men 'in what I call refined cruelty, carried on by Englishmen under the British Government'.

In his own writing, the former errand boy from Essex concluded his anguished cry from the ugly edge of the British Empire:

> The strong tyes of earth will soon be wrentched, and the burning fever of this life will soon be quentched, and my grave will be a heavens, a resten place for me Wm. Westwood.
>
> Sir out of the bitter cup of misery I have drank from my sixteenth year, ten long years, and the sweetest draught is that which takes away the misery of living death. It is the friend that deceives no man. All then will be quiet. No tyrant will then disturb my repose, I hope. Sir, I know bid the world adieu and all it contains. Wm, Westwood, his wrighting.

Cash visited Kavanagh the day before his execution. The two men embraced and Kavanagh apologised for an earlier putdown that Cash had become a 'government' man, to which Cash replied, 'I never bore ye a grudge Larry. It's a sad man I am to be seeing ye here in this trouble,' and recalled how 'you were a good mate to me in the bush Larry. Some fine times we had together'.

Kavanagh replied, 'We've paid heavy.' He said that while he had gone about his life 'the wrong way', and done 'a power o' things wrong' to the shame of his mother, he wasn't involved in the crime for which he was to be 'scragged for' but 'I've earned it for many another deed, so what's the difference?'

The two sat for some time in silence, their hands clasped together until a priest said it was time for Cash to leave.

'Goodbye then Martin, pray for me.'

'Goodbye then Larry. May God be good to you.'

On 13 October 1846, Kavanagh and Westwood and 10 others were led to a scaffold with 12 greased nooses dangling from a beam, some describing such scenes as akin to seeing tassels on a cord. The unknown hangman pulled the bolt and the floor fell away, leaving 12 men writhing, spinning, convulsing and swinging, until they were all still.

'The melancholy example was made this morning,' Fielding Browne, the Hobart barrister acting as judge wrote in a report to Hobart Town. 'The island since I have been here has been perfectly quiet, and, I should hope, under its present management, will continue so.'

The leader of Cash and Company was now its last surviving member and, after keeping Price onside by alerting him to potential vengeful attacks, was rewarded by becoming one of the first prisoners to be moved back to Hobart Town when the closure of Norfolk Island began in 1847, a closure opposed by settlers. Some 6000 people signed a petition to London, seeking the removal of 'the penal stigma' and relief from the 'quintessence of wickedness' and 'enormities' of sodomy that would surely come from a return of the 'Black Norfolkers'.

Blay would have found it hard to accept that someone like Cash could be sentenced to death for killing a policeman only to be reprieved and sent to the supposed hell of Norfolk Island, where he survived on a relatively 'easy' billet. And now, with the help of Commandant Price, he was coming back to Hobart Town with an appointment as constable, a fresh ticket-of-leave in his pocket and Mary Bennett, a convict servant he had married on the island.

For Blay, battling to survive with his own Mary after a lifetime of public duty and public odium, it must have seemed an injustice.

Cash didn't take up his constable duties, but instead became overseer of gardeners in the pleasant surrounds of Government House Domain. He lived in a small cottage with Mary and a new son, gaining increased respectability and a pardon, and spent some time in New Zealand before returning to 160 acres (64 hectares) of land near Glenorchy. Here he cultivated fruit and vegetables to sell in a market in Hobart Town, and enjoyed a drink with other old lags, former sailors and whalers.

He befriended an Irish immigrant, James Burke, transported in 1848 for striking a sergeant in the British Army. The result was *The Adventures of Martin Cash*, his first-hand life story published in 1870 as a biography in autobiographical style.

The *Cornwall Chronicle* described the book as 'a faithful account of one of the most notorious and daring bushrangers even known in Tasmania'. It was a 'faithful history of a period of trial, now happily past, [and] takes its place among the literature of the colony as an interesting and important record', although more recent arrivals might think the contents 'exaggerated fables' given the 'present happy, secure and unexciting condition of affairs'.

Blay must have winced at the *Chronicle's* portrayal of Cash: 'The hero has long since passed from the ranks of crime to that of reputable citizenship, and no more highly respected farmer, kind friend, or pleasant neighbour lives among the beautiful hills of Glenorchy than Martin Cash.'

The book attracted the attention of English romantic novelist Marcus Clarke, who four years later included some of Cash's stories in *For the Term of his Natural Life*, which Mark Twain said was a 'brilliant and fascinating' tale. But the Cash book wasn't to give its writer or subject a happy ending. Burke died a pauper before the memoir was reprinted with 10,000 copies, and before its acclaim as one of the best biographies in Australian literature and a classic of Tasmanian literature.

And less than a year after his life story was published, Cash lost his only son, also called Martin, to rheumatic fever. The old bushranger lost his enthusiasm for life and became a heavy drinker. In late August 1877, the 'celebrated' bushranger went to the Lord Rodney tavern in Salamanca Place and told the landlord he was ill but had been refused admission to Hobart general hospital. The landlord let him stay and be attended for a few days by a doctor, who said his poor health was 'accelerated by intemperance'. Cash then returned to his Glenorchy home, where he passed away.

Originally transported for house-breaking, the Irish farm boy had, like Blay, been banished across the world as a young man, celebrating his 19th birthday en route to Van Diemen's Land. Cash's official convict record described him as having 'remarkably long feet, a very swift runner', and for 50 years he had indeed been able to stay one step ahead of the noose.

23

ROPE SHADOWS

After a lifetime hanging someone at least every month, sometimes five at a time, there were now long periods when Blay had no need to pack his rope and soap.

The convict 'look' was still readily cited, with visitors like the chaplain accompanying Prince Alfred, Duke of Edinburgh, reporting 'unmistakeable convict faces' and aristocratic Frenchman Marquis Ludovic de Beauvoir their 'dark, fierce faces'. American actor Joseph Jefferson saw in the audience of *The Ticket-of-leave Man* play 'men with low foreheads and small, peering, ferret-looking eyes, some with flat noses and square, cruel jaws, and sinister expressions — leering, low and cunning — all wearing a sullen, dogged look as they would tear the benches from the pit and gut the theatre of its scenery if one of their kind was held up to public scorn'. Author Henry Nesfield wrote of their 'hangdog, cringing look'.

Hangdog look perhaps, but the outlook on hanging had shifted. Some 190 of England's original 200 capital punishment offences had been abolished, and judges were putting on their black caps with much less frequency. Blay hadn't done any business with those convicted of arson and bestiality since 1855, carnal knowledge since 1859, sodomy since 1863 and violent assault since 1864.

But there would always be those whose torment or determination to deliver their own justice would generate a call for rope, and bushrangers had not yet been consigned to history.

Blay had returned to Oatlands in 1860 for one last time, to hang John Vigors, said to have been involved in seven murders. He solemnly declared he was free from the blood of all men, and did sketches in his cell: on paper he drew several guns, pistols and swords, and on the floor a representation of a scaffold.

Other de rigueur despatches in the early 1860s included Robert Brown for raping a three-year-old girl, Martin Lydon for 'an unnatural offence' on a nine-year-old girl, William Mulligan for rape, Hendrick Witnalder for sodomy, a 'deplorably ignorant' Bernard Donahue for attacking his master with a frying pan and spade, John Nash for shooting a man just a few months after being reprieved from another death sentence.

And sometimes men committed crimes that were even harder to comprehend. In 1865, Blay was called to hang William Griffiths for murdering a six-year-old girl and her eight-year-old brother because they had seen him stealing a clock to sell to buy alcohol. Griffiths protested his innocence to clergy and his cell-mate, and when his wife visited him in the condemned cell he said, 'Well, I am to suffer for what I am not guilty of. As to murdering those dear children, God bless them, I couldn't murder them, my heart would not let me! I love children, and used to play marbles with them, I am so fond of children.' He might have played marbles with them and the evidence was circumstantial, but he was convicted.

He told his wife, 'Never mind, my girl, we shall meet in heaven.'

She gave him her handkerchief, and Griffiths affectionately kissed her before she left. Griffiths wrote that 'I am going to my last home' for a crime he was not guilty of, and prayed the Lord would help him through 'the valley of death'. He gave clergy the names of six former companions 'in vice', whom he asked to be ministered to.

A weeping Griffiths clutched his wife's handkerchief on the scaffold, placing it on his breast near to his heart. It was buried with him in the Campbell Street burial ground.

The *Chronicle* said it was the first time a criminal walking to the gallows had cried so bitterly as this man, and because of his denials 'people began to wonder whether it were in any way possible for his statement to be true'.

Griffiths was born Anglican but died a Catholic on his 27th birthday, hoping the Catholic clergy would be proven correct that confessing his earthly sins with the 'neck verse' of Psalm 51 would save him from future punishment.

Whether there would be a welcome of 10,000 angels, as some clergy promised, was unknown, but there was no farewell of angels. The *Chronicle* said it would scarcely be credited that for Griffiths' departure 'about 50 shoeless urchins and an equal number of grownups were stationed opposite the gaol, eagerly endeavouring to catch a glimpse of the murderer, which unless they had been gifted with the power of seeing through brick walls was quite impossible'.

In 1870, Blay and his wife absorbed the story of how John Regan, 46, drove his 16-year-old wife Emma and her 11-year-old sister Ellen in a chaise cart from Westbury to Launceston for some shopping. He bought his young wife a set of earrings and a mantle jacket. At Carrick on the way home they stopped for a drink and left 'singing and quite sociable and merry'.

But soon after, Regan gave the reins to Ellen and stepped into the cart to quarrel with Emma for spending money on a dress for her mother. 'What odds?' the girl said, apparently the only provocation, whereupon Regan, known as an inoffensive man, stood up and struck his wife in the face, put a thumb to her throat and pulled a knife out of his pocket, opening it with his teeth.

'Oh Johnny, what are you going to do?' Emma said.

'You b----, I'll kill you,' Regan said. When young Ellen grabbed his arm and said, 'Oh Johnny don't,' he told her: 'If you speak, I'll kill you too.'

Regan stabbed his wife in the neck, then behind the ear and twisted the knife around.

'A more terrible murder, with scarcely any provocation, has, perhaps, never been perpetrated,' the *Cornwall Chronicle* said.

Regan surrendered to a Catholic priest after a week in hiding, and was now on the scaffold dressed, at his request, in all-white shirt, vest and trousers. At the foot of the ladder, Regan kicked off his untied boots and ascended bare-footed.

When Blay pulled the bolt, 'the wretched man struggled for a long time, a full 12 minutes'.

Regan's family arranged for a hearse to collect his body. A crowd gathered at the front of the gaol, but finding the hearse was at the rear of the gaol they 'rushed helter skelter ... after the hearse, and seldom has so singular a funeral procession been seen as that which chased the hearse bearing Regan's remains to their last home'.

In 1878, Blay was called on to hang a teenager for killing his girlfriend, just his second hanging in Hobart Town in more than a decade.

Richard Copping, 19, was keen on Susannah Stacey, 18, and visited her at the family home at Bream Creek, near the Eaglehawk Neck isthmus. He was seen kissing Susannah by her father, Robert Stacey, but only 20 minutes later another daughter told him Copping was killing Susannah with an axe. Susannah had apparently told the young man, who came from a respected family, she had found someone else. He rushed to find an axe and killed her instantly.

The girl's father had called out, 'You wretch, you have murdered my daughter,' telling the inquest that when he confronted Copping 'he was sitting on the fence, and clapped his hands and said, "Yes, I know that I have. He then jumped off the fence, and said, "She deceived me, and I'll be hung for her like a man."'

Copping then ran off and attempted suicide. Unable to find any shot for his gun, he loaded three nails and shot himself in the face.

Copping was in a poor state in the days leading up to his execution, with gaol officials wondering if he would 'sink under the weight of his fearful forebodings' as he 'cried like a child'.

Lawyer Andrew Clark, who went on to become a principal architect of the Australian Constitution, argued for a plea of insanity. The court heard Copping had sought treatment just six months prior, and while the assessment was that while 'softening of his brain was the result of drinking and immoral habits', he was sane enough to be held responsible for the murder.

A young gaol chaplain, Reverend John Gray, dealing with his first hanging, gave Copping communion before he was led, sobbing, from his condemned cell. The teenager's 'cries were soul harrowing', the *Mercury* said, and the chaplain, 'much affected' by the sight, was unable to complete the concluding prayer.

After the hanging, one of only a handful Blay performed on someone born in the colony, Copping's brain was examined by four doctors. They found it weighed 54 ounces (1.5 kilograms), was well developed, and 'not the slightest trace of disease could be detected'.

Two months after the Copping execution, the *Mercury* joined its northern rivals in a push to end capital punishment, adopting the argument of English statesman John Stuart Mill on the contradiction for the condemned: 'You have the hangman, and you have the chaplain. The hangman to the condemned says "you are not worthy to live among mankind, I blot you out from the fellowship of men and the catalogue of the living". But the chaplain says "I pass you on penitent into the presence of God, and to take your place amongst the fellowship of the just."'

Blay must have wondered if his hanging business was going the way of the horse-drawn carts and coaches, now replaced by rail. Either through the decline of capital sentences, in part because of what the *Mercury* observed as 'the difficulty of getting the typical 12 to convict on a capital charge, though the evidence be as clear as day', or because the authorities might simply deem him too advanced in years.

But after a three-year silence the familiar call came once more, and 66-year-old Blay retrieved his hangbag to take the new steam train to Launceston, now just a seven-hour journey.

A fellow relic of the convict era, George Braxton, 61, was well known around Launceston as 'towney', doing bill-postering and odd jobs around the town hall, theatre and Club Hotel. He was seen as a 'quiet and inoffensive man', but this changed one Saturday night in April.

According to the *Examiner*, Braxton entered 'a house of ill-fame' kept by Ellen Sneezewell, a 34-year-old shoemaker's daughter paralysed on one side of her body, and demanded at the entrance to see her. It seemed Braxton had been intimate with the disabled prostitute for some time, but lately she 'appeared not to care about his company' and ordered him to stay away.

Told Sneezewell was asleep and to leave, Braxton went to the rear and entered the woman's bedroom, and was heard to say, 'Ellen, get up, or else I'll blow your brains out', before two shots were heard. One missed the target, but the other struck the woman in the breast, causing almost instant death. Braxton fled but was quickly apprehended.

While the jury deliberated, a nervous Braxton paced in the dock of the court, at times leaning uneasily against the rail. When the verdict was given, and before constables had time to remove him to his cell, Braxton put his hand to his throat.

'Look, he's cutting his throat!' someone called. A constable jumped into the dock and wrested from Braxton's hands a new razor. With an ugly wound across his throat, Braxton calmly waited for a doctor to arrive to stitch his severed windpipe. Sipping water, Braxton admitted he had kept the hidden razor in his boot since being apprehended.

What his razor didn't do to his throat, Blay's rope was about to.

On the scaffold, Braxton's final request was for Reverend William Hogg of the Trinity Church, to 'shake hands with me sir'. He then said, 'Lord have mercy on me,' several times as Blay placed the cap over his head and adjusted the noose. His last words were, 'I'm going go to see Jesus,' and just four minutes after walking to the gallows, the old man fell through the trapdoor.

The *Examiner* reported a feeling of relief as the

> anticipation of this terrible doom weighed heavily on the whole community ... this perhaps partly owing to the fact that the deceased was very generally known, but we would regard it as indicating a more humane and elevated public sentiment.
>
> There was a time when executions were so frequent, and were witnessed by hundreds of both sexes and all ages, that they had come to be regarded almost with indifference. Happily that condition of things has passed away, and the long intervals that now elapse between these events enable the community to realise their solemn and dreadful character.

The *Examiner* hoped it would be a 'long, very long' time before a similar event occurred again.

After not being called to hang anyone in Hobart for five years, Blay was given the call in 1883 after James Sutherland, 18, and James Ogden, 20, known as the Epping desperadoes, were convicted of murdering a telegraph linesman and the driver of a lemonade cart in the space of three days.

On the way into the inquest, some in the crowd threatened to do Blay's job for him by lynching the killers. One lashed out at Sutherland, who unperturbedly said they were cowards who wouldn't come after him in the forest, and he would glory in being let loose in the crowd.

'Let them tear [me] to pieces, for it's no use keeping me for three months and giving Solomon Blay a fiver,' Sutherland said. And at the trial, he also couldn't understand why the jury had to retire to consider their verdict. 'What do those ---- fools want to consider about? I've shot the man, isn't that enough?'

At their sentencing, the two men were handcuffed together. A subdued Ogden said, 'If they hang me they hang me innocently.' Sutherland, younger but continuing to show bravado, told his accomplice: 'You ---- cowardly hound, I've a great mind to smash you over the face with the irons.'

The demeanour and appearance of criminality was of great interest as doctors, newspapers, clergy and the public sought any explanation, physical or mental, to better understand it.

The *Examiner* correspondent put considerable effort into describing the two young men, particularly Sutherland, who seemed to possess not 'the smallest atom of humanity', with a very dark complexion, large eyes, low forehead, and 'the worst feature is the mouth with the expression of which appears cruel and determined'.

Sutherland's hands were 'more like the claws of a wild beast'. Ogden by contrast had 'a regular criminal head and face', but lacked the determination characteristic of his younger accomplice, and evidenced some conscience.

The physical appearance was deemed to provide 'clues', and doctors did dissections to look for evidence of brain disease. Hobart librarian Alfred Taylor, who pursued the pseudo-science of phrenology — based on the concept that the brain is the organ of the mind and that certain brain areas have localised and specific functions — gained permission to take death masks of Ogden and Sutherland. Many held to the 'convict look' theory, suggesting the criminal class had a physical look 'characteristic of natural dishonesty and cunning' evolved from the primitive physiques of early man and apes, a differentiation between the good and the bad.

On the night before their execution neither of the two

bushrangers slept, saying they wanted to see as much as they could of the world they would soon be leaving.

Now more subdued, Sutherland asked the Reverend John Mace to visit the widows of the two murdered men and seek their forgiveness. He also spoke bitterly of his life, 'saying the world had not been a pleasant one to him, that he had had no parents to look after him, but had been kicked about by those who got as much work as possible out of him without caring in the least about him,' the *Examiner* reported.

Ogden's mother said the boys were strongly influenced by reading the exploits in Victoria of the gang led by Edward 'Ned' Kelly, whose father John 'Red' Kelly left Launceston in 1848 after serving a seven-year sentence for stealing two pigs in Ireland. The younger Kelly was in trouble with police throughout his teenage years, his gang pursued as outlaws after the death of three policemen, before a violent confrontation at Glenrowan.

Three years after Kelly's execution in 1880, Odgen and Sutherland embarked on their own criminal path. But unlike their hero they didn't attract the same public following, prompt 30,000 signatures on a petition of mercy, or memorably say, 'Such is life,' when told the time of execution had been fixed. Although when asked if he had any regrets, Sutherland did succinctly reply: 'It's no use feeling sorry now.'

As Blay escorted them across the wooden bridge-way to the scaffold, Ogden carried in his right hand a bunch of flowers sent by a young girl attending Trinity Church Sunday School. He 'trembled violently', but neither he nor Sutherland flinched when Blay put the noose around their necks.

Looking 'more boyish than ever' with white caps shutting out the world, Blay drew the bolt. After their bodies were cut down after an hour, the little bouquet was found with Odgen, 'tightly clenched in his hand'.

Asked by one reporter if he had any aversion to hanging men as young as 18 and 20, Blay replied: 'No sir, somebody must do it, and it's my business.'

He was now nearing 70, white of hair and beard, gaunt, in the autumn of his life but still strong of spirit. In January 1884 in Campbell Street, Hobart, a young carriage driver left two horses tethered to a lamp, but they became startled and bolted. Opposite the Good Woman Hotel, 'Solomon Blay, the public executioner, saw the runaways and stood in the middle of the road, and held up his hands to try to stop them'.

In the spring there was another 'job' in Hobart, one which would provide unfavourable scrutiny.

Henry Stock, 22, had been married to Elizabeth, 17, who had a daughter from a previous relationship with a police constable. This was a source of constant friction, and they separated several times. When Stock was imprisoned for forgery, Elizabeth obtained a maintenance order against him. They were living apart until April 1884, when Stock was seen walking about 10 kilometres to a hut where Elizabeth and child were living. They were later found dead, with the shot in their bodies corresponding to what Stock carried in his pouch.

Stock protested his innocence, claiming not to have seen them, and at his first trial the jury could not reach a verdict. He was found guilty at a second trial, and unsuccessful efforts were made to commute his sentence to life imprisonment on the basis the evidence was circumstantial.

Stock evidenced a stoic indifference to his fate, save for the time he was visited in his cell by his mother, father, brother and grandfather, where he 'completely gave way at the sight of his relatives, and throwing himself on the floor of his cell was for a long time unable to control himself'.

The *Sydney Evening News* correspondent said that on the day of his execution Stock ate 'a hearty breakfast', and was found to have written on his cell wall: 'I hope to see the two Jenkins girls [two witnesses whose evidence went against him] here before long. I warn all young men, if they would keep out of this fatal cell, to keep from women.'

Asked on the scaffold if he had anything to say, Stock quietly stated, 'I swear by Heaven that I am innocent,' before 'the unhappy man stood face to face with The Great Unknown'.

But while Stock was to come face to face with the great unknown, it was not a quick meeting. Newspapers reported Stock's sufferings were 'apparently prolonged … he struggled violently at first, and his arms and hands twitched for nearly five minutes'. There was more uproar when a doctor examined the body and said death had not been by dislocation of the neck but rather by suffocation.

The attorney-general's revelations about how long Blay had persisted with a subsequent short drop even beyond its abandonment in England and despite advice from the Colonial Office, and his difficulty even when making the apparent 'exception' of an eight-foot drop for Stock, only cast a darker shadow over Blay's public service.

How many Blay executed was never well recorded, let alone how well he did so. The attorney-general gave inaccurate numbers to Parliament and some newspapers reported the number as low as 100, and Blay himself told anyone who asked that it 'is mine to know'. In fact he had despatched some 200 condemned men and women and, he maintained, always 'in a decent manner'.

Blay's lot had clearly worsened since his ill-fated return to England: his salary had been cut, hangings were in decline, and now, after a lifetime of loyal service, he was paying the price of parliamentary scrutiny and public condemnation. This wasn't a quiet and dignified finish as Her Majesty's finisher.

24

THE EXCLUSIVE CLUB

The colony's newspapers had an understandable interest in executions and executioners since the first convicts arrived. For most of his life Blay could read of executions elsewhere in the colony and the Empire, and in France and the United States. There were reports of peers being attacked, harassed, killed or driven to escape into demon drink, suicide, or asylum.

He was the newspapers' only reader with inside knowledge of Her Majesty's exclusive club, one that few wanted to join and one that most members, including himself, hadn't been able or willing to discuss. But the veil was beginning to be lifted as local papers were more openly reporting him and his work, and some of his peers were openly talking of their experiences.

Blay had managed to survive behind the veil, and had never

been of a mind to tempt fate by writing or talking openly of his experiences. But he would hear echoes of his thoughts in what was now being said by other hangmen.

In September 1883, Blay read of the death of William Marwood, the common hangman of England. Marwood, who had taken up hanging only in 1871, initially kept his role secret, even from his neighbours in the small town of Horncastle. When it did become known he was initially hooted and hissed, and was the subject of a popular rhyme, 'If Pa killed Ma who'd kill Pa — Marwood'.

When not on the 'circuit', as he called it, hanging 179 people in his 11 years, Marwood worked as a cobbler in a small shop. Blay would have been astonished to read he had the words 'Marwood, Crown Office' in large letters over the door and carried business cards stating 'William Marwood, Public Executioner, Horncastle, Lincolnshire'.

Among the tools of a country cobbler he had some coils of rope hanging from the roof. One was a rope used by William Calcraft, also a cobbler and the most famous English hangman, who despatched 450 victims in a 45-year career.

Marwood objected to the crude Calcraft technique, which 'choked' men to death on the end of a very short drop, not much more than two feet (0.6 metres), many victims taking extended periods to die. To speed things along, Calcraft sometimes resorted to pulling on their legs, or even climbing on their shoulders, adding to the gallows 'entertainment' for crowds of as many as 30,000.

Marwood was proud of his efforts to improve the hanging process, including the enhanced drop calculations and noose knot, and removing the steps up the gallows platform to make life easier for everyone. But things still went awry even for him. Even at his last hanging, just a few weeks before his death, a man's pinioned arm got caught up in the free rope hanging down his back, and the unfortunate victim had to be hanged twice.

Like Blay, Marwood refused persistent attempts to be

photographed. The English executioner even refused a £50 sitting offer, generous given he received only a £20 retainer and a £10 fee for each execution. In Hobart, everyone else in the chain of law and order — the governors, sheriffs, judges, police and convicts — sat for early photographers, but not Blay. This was despite inducements, and the promise of one that thought a photograph framed by the knots of ropes he had used would be an interesting exhibit at the Royal Society.

In early 1886, Blay would have been particularly taken with a report in the *Mercury*, reprinted from the *Pall Mall Gazette*, headlined 'Hanging and Hangmen. A Chat with an Expert'. The article was based on a conversation with an unidentified 'expert', who said he had seen 1000 men sentenced to death and about 300 executed.

An intense debate about capital punishment was underway in England, and the lengthy article aroused considerable interest, particularly as it came soon after a hanging scandal when a condemned man, weighing 15 stone (95 kilograms) was decapitated by the force of the drop. This execution was undertaken by Marwood's successor James Berry, a former boot salesman and policeman, who also carried a black-bordered business card. This followed another mishap earlier the same year when he pulled the lever and nothing happened. Even his stomping on the trapdoor was to no avail, and the man was eventually reprieved as 'the man they couldn't hang'.

Blay could have easily seen his name in the place of Calcraft, Marwood and Berry. But, notwithstanding some grim incidents where he literally had blood on his hands, it had never been said that he decapitated anyone or that he had met a man he couldn't hang.

The unidentified 'expert' said the task of hanging was understood best by a hangman, who 'does it in the way he thinks best'.

'It appears to me there is too much fuss made about hangings,' he said. 'The work is done very well. It has to be done, as so far as my experience goes, it is generally done very mercifully and very skilfully. There have been a few exceptions, but I never saw a really bad bungle.'

Blay would have taken some comfort that the expert said the longer drop had become a 'fancy', and as to the merits of short or long drops the English expert didn't see much difference between death by suffocation or neck-breaking. Ultimately, it was best left to 'the hangman who undertakes the work'.

'Which is the most merciful? Well with the long drop it is all over before you can say Jack Ketch, the short drop the man struggles for a minute or two, and then all is still. I should say the short drop is best.'

The essential quality for a hangman, he felt, was 'nerve'. He had seen 300 executed, 'but bless you, I forget 'em. It's part of my work, and I suppose I've got hard', but he didn't see himself as a hard man. He said:

> I cannot say that a hanging ever upset me. I am pretty imperturbable. I have been reproached for eating my breakfast half an hour afterwards, but after all what does it amount to? One man slays another, he in turn must be slain. And as long as the slaying is merciful, why should one be squeamish? Not that I am a hard man. A [medical] student may sicken over his first body, he may quiver when the knife draws the gush of blood, but he soon accustoms himself to the knife and to the gush. So do I with my hangings. Tremble? Not I.

Blay had become hardened, too. He may have quivered at his first hangings, but he had become accustomed to it. 'Somebody must do it,' he said more than once.

The Englishman proffered other views that probably resonated.

'Nor do I altogether hold with this privacy of execution,' he said. 'It is part of this terrible secrecy system ... I hold that the public execution ... drove home a great lesson. Men and women held their orgies and their saturnalia before the gallows, they jeered and flung about their rude jests and brutal jibes, but at heart they were struck with horror, and their mirth turned to melancholy when they were alone in their own chambers. Whatever they may say to the contrary, public executions were great examples.'

The issue was not hangings but that capital punishment was so subjective and 'absurdly out of keeping with a scientific age'. He was no advocate for the abolition of capital punishment, but the unequal punishments meted out to criminals was a weakness in the criminal system.

> The humane judge construes a murder as a manslaughter, the severe judge turns a manslaughter into murder. A judge may think six months hard labour a fit punishment for what another may deem 10 years penal servitude a fitting equivalent. Then our Home Secretary may see fit to reprieve where another lets the man hang. I would have degrees of sentence, as murders are of different degrees.

The expert believed poverty was the most common denominator. 'Poverty is the beginning of all crime, and all murders. There are murderers for revenge, murderers for jealousy, murderers for property — those the three exceptions — and murderers from poverty. Eradicate poverty and the hangman may put his rope in his pocket and go back to his old trade.'

In the winter of 1892, the *Mercury* carried an advertisement for *My Experiences as an Executioner*, with illustrations and portraits. The author was James Berry, the first English hangman to openly write and talk freely about his seven years in the trade.

Like Blay and most hangmen, Berry considered himself merely the last link in what he called the 'chain of legal retribution', his role as honourable as that of the policeman, prosecutor and judge. But he felt 'the law of capital punishment falls with terrible weight upon the hangman and that to allow a man to follow such an occupation is doing him a deadly wrong'.

Berry felt that because the demon power was in the men he had to execute, for a time he had been possessed by a legion of demons. He became so affected he planned to jump out of a train into the path of another. He was seen by a young man, who talked to the dejected hangman about his soul and took him to a Christian mission where, according to the preacher Simon Wigglesworth, 'he came under a mighty conviction of sin. For 2 1/2 hours he was literally sweating under conviction and you could see a vapour rising up from him. At the end of 2 1/2 hours he was graciously saved.'

Berry, like Blay, became a hangman out of expediency. Before selling boots, he had been a policeman on the beat. He happened to meet William Marwood, and a few days later spent an evening in the hangman's company.

Marwood, he wrote,

> keenly felt the odium with which his office was regarded by the public, and aimed, by performing his duties in a satisfactory manner, and by conducting his private life in a satisfactory manner, at removing the stigma which he felt was undeserved. I well remember one time … at the supper table that he remarked to a gentleman present, 'my position is not a pleasant one … no! It is NOT a pleasant one.'

Despite the stigma and unpleasantness, Berry applied for the job upon Marwood's death:

> I was simply driven to it by the poverty-stricken condition of my family, which I was unable to keep in reasonable comfort upon my earnings … engaged as a boot salesman on a small salary. I knew that I was a man of no extraordinary ability, so that my chances of rising were few, and I looked upon the vacancy of the executioner's post as being probably my one chance in life, my 'tide in the affairs of men'.

Berry said he had a great distaste for the work, and even his own family petitioned the Home Secretary to dismiss his application. But he convinced himself this was his chance to improve his life, 'my tide in the affairs of men'; he could do the job as well as anyone while 'somewhat improving the lot of those appointed to die'.

And just as Blay started his career in 1842 with a double hanging, doubts and nerves, so too did Berry with his first 'job', also a double-header, in 1884.

'I filled my time walking about the prison grounds, and thinking of the poor men who were nearing their end, full of life, and knowing the fatal hour, which made me quite ill to think about,' he said. He had no appetite for the meals provided him in the gaol, and barely slept.

> I fancied the ropes breaking, I fancied I was trembling and could not do it, I fancied I felt sick at the last push. I was nearly frantic in my mind, but I never let them know. I wished I had never undertaken such an awful calling. I regretted for awhile, and then I thought the public would only think I had not the pluck, and I would not allow my feelings to overthrow me, so I never gave way to such thoughts again.

Afterward, although he was 'so much affected by the sad sight I had witnessed', he willed himself not to fall victim to his own nerves, and developed a resolve that there was a job that had to be done, somebody had to do it, and he would do it as best he could.

His nerve, which he often sought to manage by taking a rod and basket — as well as his noose — to get in some fishing before or after an execution, was given its severest test the following year at the hanging of Robert Goodale, a wife murderer. Berry studied Marwood's 'table of drops', which suggested a drop of 7 feet 8 inches, (2.3 metres) for a man weighing 15 stone (95 kilograms) but was uneasy about such a long drop and decided to reduce it by two feet (0.6 metres).

After repeated testing of weight and length, on execution day a confident Berry pulled the lever, the drop fell, and the prisoner dropped out of sight.

> We were horrified however to see that the rope jerked upwards and for an instant I thought the noose had slipped from the culprit's head or that the rope had broken. But it was worse than that for the jerk had severed the head entirely from the body and both had fallen into the bottom of the pit. Of course death was instantaneous so that the poor fellow had not suffered in any way, but it was terrible to think that such a revolting thing should have occurred. We were all unnerved and shocked. The Governor, whose efforts to prevent any accident had kept his nerves at full strain, fairly broke down and wept.

Berry's nerve was fully tested, but he determinedly reviewed his table of drops and went about his business.

He said most people thought a murderer was a murderer and nothing else, just a fiend or monster different from the rest of humanity who by law, divine and national, had to die like a dog. But for him it wasn't so simple. A man who committed an ill deed, 'may or may not be naturally vicious, may or may not be really responsible for his actions, may or may not be devoutly penitent'.

He believed, from long study and 'some unique opportunities of judging', that for some low-class human brutes 'the fear of death is the only check that can in any way curb their lusts and passions. But … amongst those whom I have executed … there were men … who had not premeditated murder, who had taken no pleasure in it and expected no profit from it, and who, if they could by any means have been set at liberty, had within them the making of model citizens.'

Like most other former executioners, Berry was not in favour of abolishing capital punishment altogether, putting weight on the scriptural injunction 'whose sheddeth man's blood, by man shall his blood be shed'. But he felt attitudes towards murderers was based too much on sentiment and not enough on reason: 'Many people pity all murderers, whether they deserve it or not, many others condemn them body, soul and spirit, without considering to what extent they are the result of circumstances.'

Berry argued for more conditions under which capital punishment was imposed, suggesting juries have five classes of verdict: not guilty, not proven, and murder in the first, second or third degrees. Only in first degree murders in which both intent and result was murder would a judge have no options but to impose the death penalty.

Berry liked to know if the condemned had confessed to clergy, and if they had not he privately asked them so he was as certain as possible that he was 'not hanging an innocent person'.

Blay gave few signs of giving such deep thought to matters of innocence, justice or technique as he walked the same exclusive path as Ketch, Calcraft, Marwood and Berry. Asked about the task being difficult, he told the *Southern Star* in 1883: 'No sir, somebody must do it, and it's my business.' This reporter concluded Blay wasn't a cruel man, but one who regarded himself as merely an equal part of the integral machinery for the administration of justice, proud of his position and happy to receive the benefits.

Not a cruel man, perhaps, but detached. 'There is no harm in swinging a man if he deserves it,' Blay said, and a *Sydney Evening News* correspondent said Blay's view of the scaffold was that 'it's nothing when you get used to it'.

A hangman had to find his own way of doing the 'business', dealing with dreads and demons by developing a moral detachment, denial and rationalisation to emotionally distance themselves, or harnessing a resolute sense of duty. But Blay knew well that many executioners found the task one they never got used to, ending their days in drunken stupors, contemplating suicide or living in an asylum. His Victorian peer Michael Gately was once stoned and booed by a crowd of 500 in the streets of Melbourne, and another time fled to the watch-house for protection and tried to cut his own throat. And his New South Wales peer Alexander Green spent his final 25 years in a mental asylum.

In 1895, the *Examiner* published an extract from the newly published diary of a man who was more familiar with executions than anyone, and who didn't get used to it. Charles-Henri Sanson, who administered capital punishment in Paris for 40 years as the Royal Executioner for King Louis XVI and High Executioner in the First French Republic, dropped the guillotine blade 2918 times, including on the King himself, and revolutionaries like Robespierre, Danton, Saint-Just, Heber and Desmoulins.

Blay had done his share of multiple hangings, but he couldn't imagine Sanson's most terrible day's work:

The guillotine devoured 54 victims. My strength is at an end, and I almost fainted away. I have seen too much blood not to be callous. For some time I have been troubled with terrible visions. My hands tremble so that I have been compelled to give up cutting the hair of the doomed prisoners. I cannot convince myself of the reality of these weeping and praying victims ... I leave the scaffold to weep, though I cannot shed a tear.

Sanson had a mental breakdown from executing so many, including young boys and girls, and later wrote he had

seen the suffering and death of my fellow men too often and too closely to be moved easily. If what I feel is not pity, it must be the result of a malady of my nerves; perhaps it is the hand of God punishing me for my cowardly obedience to that which so little resembles the justice I was born to serve? For some time now, every day, when the hour [to collect condemned prisoners] comes, a vertigo seizes me that holds me in its grip and cruelly tortures me ... I feel a redoubling of the fever that night and day devours me; it is like a fire flowing under my skin.

Blay had never executed as many as Sanson, but he had done what few could bring themselves to do: look into the eyes of men and women, young and old, terminate their lives and then pay the law-finisher's price of being condemned for the law-maker's decision. And done so 200 times in a much smaller population, which meant he had perhaps the highest death rate in the world.

Society asked hangmen to be a functionary cog in a much larger wheel of law and order, but then denied them any respect and treated them as pariahs. As one newspaper put it, while capital punishment was 'a necessity in our system ... he [the hangman] should be treated as if he is the hole in the floor of the gallows'.

Soldiers were also authorised killers, but their work was away from public scrutiny, and was respected and generally celebrated. But the foot soldier on gallows duty in Her Majesty's service was despised. Governors, judges, magistrates, police and juries were all spokes in the same wheel of capital justice, but only the hangman was the 'butcher'.

A *Cornwall Chronicle* writer captured the duplicity in 1845:

On the scaffold stood two men, the one a murderer, the other the executioner of the law. I ask you which of these two ... was the object of sympathy with the spectators, and which of disgust and revulsion? Why, while the just and venerable judge in his ermine is an object, and justly, of reverence and honour, why is he who carries out the sentence of the judge to be a man forbidden ... the object of repulsion and disgust? Because the law itself shrinks, conscience-stricken, before the fulfilment of its own ordinances. I know of no clearer moral conduct than this — never command what you would be ashamed to do.

Hangmen like Blay were not ashamed, but must have wondered why 'the makers of law have honour and wealth, but I who finish what they begin can only creep among men by stealth?'

Blay might also have uniquely understood one English hangman who wrote in his memoirs that while he generally slept soundly, and was generally untroubled about those he had despatched, he did confess to one nightmare:

In the dream it is execution morning — and I am the condemned man! The cell doors open ... two figures come towards me, my arms are strapped ... I see the noose in front of me ... they start dragging me towards the gallows ... I am screaming for it to stop ... and I have woken in a cold sweat!

I have had the nightmare twice. The first time they got me as far as the door leading into the execution chamber before I woke up. The second time they actually got me on to the trap.

I am hoping that they do not come a third time ...

25

THE FINAL EXECUTION

Solomon Blay was now nearing 70. He wasn't called to the scaffold so often, but he was still the public hangman and still in the public eye.

In 1880, a Victorian newspaper described Blay as 'the Tasmanian Gately', referencing Melbourne hangman Michael Gately, who in turn was referred to as the Victorian Calcraft.

> He is nearly 70 years of age, and has put to death more criminals than perhaps any other man in the world ... he has occupied his present position for 45 years, and is still fit for duty. In the old times he had frequently to hang up seven or eight men in the morning. He is a man of some property, and we hope a reputable and better behaved member of the Civil Service than his Victorian contemporary.

Despite the government saying he had been 'worn out' when he resigned more than a decade ago, the grizzled hangman felt he was still fit for duty. Blay probably had the same view as New South Wales peer Robert 'Nosey' Howard, who said, 'You say I am getting old ... well of course I ain't getting younger, but there's many a good job in me yet.'

But there was little evidence to support the paper's claim of Blay being a man of property, having lost savings and income after his attempted escape back to the Mother Country, and returning to a pay cut and fewer hanging fees.

There just wasn't as much money for old rope as in the 'good old hanging days'. He was a pensioner hangman, but mostly just a pensioner. In 1883, the *Examiner* carried a report from a *Southern Star* reporter:

> The hangman, or as he prefers to be called, 'the public executioner', Solomon Blay is a quiet, inoffensive man who keeps a little dealer's shop in Argyle Street, near Brisbane Street. His home is neat and clean, in a word 'home like'.
>
> Blay is not sure as to his age, but considers himself and probably is, 70. His first duty as a hangman was performed just 40 years ago, since which time he has 'operated on', that is his own expression, over a hundred persons. 'Why bless you, sir,' he said to me yesterday, 'in the old days we used to put them through in batches of seven or eight.'

Despite, or perhaps because of, the demise of hanging, in the winter of 1883 Blay sought an increase in his salary, arguing that since his appointment in 1841 he had 'given satisfaction in his important office' without any increase despite the 'increase of business'. Sheriff John Swan supported him:

> This officer has served in an arduous and responsible position for nearly half a century. He has performed his duty with great care and unspoken nerve ... he has therefore performed many executions ... and [given] practically his service has been continuous, he would now have been entitled to a pension of nearly £50 per annum, but for his (brief) retirement. I have the honour to recommend that his

salary be raised to £80, which is less than he was receiving when he was pensioned. It may be argued that there is fortunately less frequent occasions for his service now than formerly, but such appointments should be held by trained and reliable officers, to ensure that the retaining fee should be sufficient. I think it would be very difficult to find a successor who would be equal in efficiency to Blay.

Blay's increase was duly approved, and he kept his modest pension. The *Examiner* had reported in August 1882 two 'curiosities' of the pension list: Blay, 'the Tasmanian Calcraft', receiving a pension of £23 15s 4d, and the other, 'Fanny Cochrane Smith, aboriginal woman, £24, is the only item in the list to remind us of the people we have displaced, and even she is not a pure aboriginal.'

In fact, Cochrane Smith was a 'full-blooded' Aboriginal person, and considered the last fluent speaker of a native Tasmanian language, with a wax cylinder recording of her singing being the only audio recording of any of the island's indigenous languages. Fanny Cochrane was among the Aboriginal people settled on Flinders Island during the Black War, her Indigenous name not known because the so-called Protector issued European names as part of the cultural suppression. After marrying an English sawyer and former convict, William Smith, she received a government pension and a 40-hectare land grant at Oyster Cove. She outlived Truganini, widely regarded as the last 'full-blooded' Tasmanian Aboriginal, by 30 years.

Cochrane and Blay, the 'curiosities' to the *Examiner*, were two extreme and final symbols of the unique and violent story of convictism in Van Diemen's Land, one black and one white, both living out their final days with the help of a government pension.

In the winter of 1884, Blay became a pensioner and widower, losing his wife Mary in a bronchitis outbreak. It had been 35 years since she deliberately committed arson in Ireland just to be transported to a better life in Van Diemen's Land, to a life of 31 years with a hangman.

The death notice in the *Mercury* recorded her name as 'Blaey', probably a printing error of the true Bleay name. Solomon's name was not spelled out, probably out of sensitivity to his identity: 'Blaey. On July 17 Mary, the beloved wife of S. Blaey, in the 54th year of her age, leaving no family. The funeral will leave her late residence, in Argyle Street, tomorrow (Saturday 19th) at half-past 2 o'clock, when friends are respectfully invited to attend. May she rest in peace.'

After being laid out at home she was taken in an ornate hearse, followed by five coaches, to be buried in an unmarked grave in the Catholic section of Cornelian Bay Cemetery, the ceremony conducted by a young priest from St Mary's Cathedral, which she had attended.

Blay was now alone, nearing the end of the line as an empire's *ultimum judicium*. But there would be one final dance on the end of the rope.

In 1887, virtually the entire 29,000 population of Hobart gathered on the Domain to celebrate Queen Victoria's Golden Jubilee. In the same year, the longest serving monarch's longest serving hangman had to 'operate on' another relic of convictism, Timothy Walker, 76, poor of sight and hearing.

On an early summer's day Walker, who had previously lived with Elizabeth Woods, met her on a street in Deloraine, near Launceston, outside the house where Elizabeth was now living with her aunt Harriett and 53-year-old partner Benjamin Hampton. With a double-barrel gun in his hands Walker asked her: 'Are you and me good friends?' The woman responded, 'No, and never will be.'

Walker said, 'You ---- cow, I will shoot you and blow your ---- brains out.'

When Hampton came out and asked Walker to move on, the old convict lifted his gun as if to strike Hampton, but instead it went off at close-range, hitting the man in the right arm. He then instantly shot him again in the left side, whereupon Hampton fell on the gun, his waistcoat and shirt burning from the gunshots.

'I said I would do it,' Walker said as he lifted the bleeding man to retrieve his gun, put it over his shoulder and left as Hampton declared with his final breath, 'I am done.'

Walker went to his daughter's house, gave her the gun and asked her to take care of a six-year-old boy he was 'keeping', as he was about to be arrested.

He told police that while going past the house the woman made faces and put her tongue out at him. He said, 'You hussy, you want shooting, and then Ben rushed out and tried to take the gun from me, when it went off.'

The *Examiner* listed the matters to come before the Supreme Court on 21 December: Frank Reilly, criminal assault; William Morgan, unnatural offence; Thomas Price, attempted bestiality; Lawrence Ryan, larceny; James Kennedy, indecent assault; John Jansen, unlawfully wounding; Clara Cleaver, concealment of birth; and 'the case of Timothy Walker, for murder, will probably be added to this list — one of the blackest ever placed before our courts.'

Walker continued to argue that the gun had gone off in a struggle, and family and friends attending him in gaol became convinced the murder was not as coldly premeditated as the court found. The attorney-general took the unusual step of ordering several witnesses to be re-interviewed before the Executive Council reaffirmed the death sentence. Hearing the news, Walker was reported in the *Mercury* to have accepted it 'with quiet resignation, and prepared himself for his awful end'.

Blay also had to prepare for what had once been such a familiar and frequent task. According to the *Examiner*, he 'has been under careful surveillance for the last few days so that he may not be absent when wanted tomorrow, and that his nerves may be strong for the performance of the dread task'.

At the first stroke of 8 o'clock on his final morning, Monday 10

January, Walker could see a guard of 12 policemen line up at the scaffold, and gaol officials and the hangman approaching his cell.

'He stepped to the door of his cell and with a cheery smile wished all good morning. It was an affecting sight,' the *Mercury* said.

Asked if he had anything to say, Walker replied: 'No, I have nothing. I leave myself in the hands of my Maker.'

Blay tied his hands behind his back and the two old men walked to the scaffold, Blay once more treading a path he had chosen, determinedly resolving to perform his duty, Walker treading a path he had not chosen, determinedly resolving not to succumb in a sobbing heap.

Both had been in the colony since arriving as convicts when they were both barely in their twenties. Now, more than half a century on, the oldest hangman in the Empire was standing alongside the oldest man he'd ever had to hang.

The white-haired executioner put his noose around the neck of the old condemned man, who tried to listen and respond to the prayers of the clergy, but was said in one newspaper report to be 'passed the allotted time of human life, and was so deaf as to be unable to hear the ministrations of the attendant clergyman, and he could only mumble as he looked round on the preparations for his death'.

Walker did exclaim, 'Lord bless my soul! God bless my poor, poor children.' They were his final words.

One newspaper said 'the execution was not an edifying spectacle', and a visiting pressman from interstate endeavoured to interview Blay after the execution, 'but he preserved a strict silence'.

Again he was asked: 'How many people have you hanged in your day?'

Again Blay replied: 'That is best known to myself.'

As had become the case towards the end of his career, newspapers now routinely identified Solomon Blay as the hangman. He didn't enjoy this, but at least this time the reporting might have given him some quiet satisfaction.

'The hangman, it was allowed, performed the painful ceremony in a skilful manner,' the *Mercury* said. 'There was a twitching of the muscles, caused, apparently, by muscular contraction, but the general belief was that the prisoner died easily.'

It said a doctor later verified that the old man's neck was dislocated and death 'must have been instantaneous'.

The *Examiner* also said the hangman 'evidently did it well'.

It was unusual for Blay to get any positive recognition for performing his duty 'well' and with 'skill', allowing a man to die 'easily', rather than criticism for a perceived coldness, brutishness or grim enjoyment, or reports of men and women taking too long to die. Perhaps it was unusual because Blay had, under orders, finally taken up a longer eight-foot (2.4-metre) drop.

Whether he died easy or hard, Timothy Walker would be the last ex-convict to hang in the colony and the last neck that Solomon Blay was to put a noose around. But it would not be his last time on the scaffold.

26

LETTING GO OF
THE ROPE

White of hair and beard and now a widower, Solomon Blay spent his final years alone in rented cottages and rooms. He was located mostly around the North Hobart area where he and Mary had lived, never far from Campbell Street Gaol and execution yard.

After 'operating on' the aged Timothy Walker some four years before, Blay now had the final task of passing the noose into the hands of a successor. The Sheriff's Department was endeavouring to maintain a code of silence, but newspapers became aware that Blay had resigned, this time for the last time, feeling truly that he and the gallows were 'worn out'.

In May 1891 the *Mercury* ran a headline, 'Wanted A Hangman', stating that Blay, who 'has "turned off" some 200 malefactors, has resigned his appointment on account of bodily weakness.'

The *Examiner* said he had 'worked off' 200 malefactors just like the hangman Ned Dennis in Charles Dickens' *Tale of Two Cities*, and that his 'bodily infirmity would preclude his continuance in the profession'. The *Examiner* referred to him falling into the 'sear and yellow leaf', from Shakespeare's *Macbeth*, evoking a tiredness of life and contemplation of old age without honour.

> I have lived long enough: my way of life
> Is fallen into the sear, the yellow leaf,
> And that which should accompany old age,
> As honour, love, obedience, troops of friends,
> I must not look to have; but, in their stead,
> Curses not loud but deep, mouth-honour, breath,
> Which the poor heart would fain deny, and dare not.

The *Examiner* said it understood the sheriff would respect Blay's retirement wishes, 'and that he will be allowed to enjoy his *elium clum dignitate* [battle for dignity in heaven] with the proud consciousness of having done the state some service'.

Blay was spared the judgement he had read just after his return from England. After William Calcraft had bungled a hanging in London, *The Telegraph* said he was a doddering old man whose 'frame is decrepit, his eye has lost its keenness and his head its cunning ... the dead tell no tales and we shall never know the agonies which some poor wretches have suffered in Calcraft's uncertain age. The executioner has outlived his hideous capacity.' It was time to recognise he was unable to accomplish his horrible task, so it was best he be given 'a decent pittance on which to end his days and let us be rid of him'.

Blay's own age and 'bodily weakness' was referred to, but he was said to maintain 'the zeal of an enthusiast', willing to supervise any future 'jobs' to ensure 'they are carried out in an artistic and thoroughly effectual manner'.

The *Mercury* hoped there would not be as much interest in the vacancy as had been recently evidenced in Melbourne, where 200 men applied to be an assistant hangman.

Just four men were considered, and the *Examiner* said:

> It is not at all probable that when the appointment is made the name of Solomon Blay's successor will be disclosed. The grounds urged for the secrecy is that the publication of the name would seriously injure the person appointed in the estimation of his fellow men, should he wish to turn his hand to other pursuits.
>
> It has been suggested to the department that the best possible way to conceal his identity will be for the executioner to wear a mask. This of course will beyond doubt be adopted.
>
> This, which is a new departure in the annals of public executions in Tasmania, has led to no end of small talk amongst those whose morbid tastes run in this direction.
>
> Blay, who will supervise the operations on the scaffold has, I am informed, given out that he is perfectly willing to discharge the duty, giving it as his reason that 'there is no harm in swinging a man if he deserves it'.

The old hangman was now 75, in his own mind willing to oversee a 'swinging', but his capacity was as questionable as that of the wooden bridge-way leading from the condemned cell to the scaffold. Its exposure to the elements had left it in a shaky condition, and urgent repairs had to be made so that once again someone could walk their final steps.

That someone was 19-year-old Arthur Cooley, convicted of killing Mary Ogilvie of Richmond while she was in a field gathering mushrooms. Her head was partially blown off and her body thrown into the river. The supposed motive, based largely on circumstantial evidence, was that the woman's well-known husband was a magistrate subpoenaed as a witness in a pending criminal case against Cooley for assaulting a woman.

The national *Bulletin* noted a new hangman had 'taken over the business so long and ably conducted by Mr Solomon Blay, and hopes by punctuality and strict attention to the obliteration of customers to merit a continuance'.

But it said times had changed in Hobart, which

has fallen off a lot of late years, and whereas eggs was undoubtedly eggs down there in the golden days, they aren't always eggs now. The System is dead, and the hangman doesn't shine in society as he once did, neither does the gaol-flogger move in the best circles, as the men of past years used to.

It was always thus. The hangman witherith, and the flogger fadeth, and all things pass away.

The year 1891, when Blay's role would 'witherith', saw an International Exhibition held in Launceston. Forty years before, Van Diemen's Land had exhibits at the first international exhibition at London's Crystal Palace, and again in Paris in 1889.

Now Launceston joined in showcasing revolution and advancement in industry, science and the arts in the global economy. It was also the year for a visit by General William Booth, founder and first general of the Salvation Army, whose corps had worked gaols and courts in Launceston and Hobart since 1883 despite a larrikin element throwing flour, mud and beer at them whenever they marched with their rousing music through town streets.

Blay wasn't of a mind to travel north for the exhibition, and unlike his wife had never marched to any Christian drum. For him, it was all about ordaining a new hangman. Arthur Cooley was apparently of the same mind, with the identity of the man to carry out his death sentence his 'sole anxiety', according to one report.

But no one was to know. Officials refused to disclose the new hangman's name, and when he arrived to perform his first hanging, under the watchful eye of Blay, the new hangman 'shrinks from recognition'.

Blay's anonymous successor was, the *Bulletin* said, 'disguised in false hair and red paint … why he was disguised Heaven only knows, but most likely it was because he was ashamed of himself.'

The *Mercury* recalled 'a touch of grim burlesque', the new hangman 'with his face besmeared with raddle [red pigment] and burnt cork … seeking thus to hide his identity'.

Describing him as being disguised 'like a hideous scarecrow', the *Mercury* sarcastically said the authorities should have studied stage effect more closely. It suggested

> a velvet mask, a doublet [jacket] of inky hue, scarlet hose, and skull and crossbones emblazoned on the breast. The attendant priest should have appeared with tonsured [shaved] skull and clad in robes incarnadine. The scaffold should have been draped in black, and a hidden orchestra should have played weird and woeful pianissimo strains, with a sudden fortissimo crash as the bolt was drawn, and a crescendo Jubilate as a finale.

More seriously, the *Mercury* said the attempt to disguise the identity of the hangman was an excess of caution. It said:

> Either this, or the public are getting ashamed of executions by the rude method of dislocating the neck. If this is so, science should be utilised. Our American cousins rid the world of undesirable lives by electricity. Why cannot we do it here? A touch on a button by an unseen operator and the offending one is launched into eternity. Anything would be better than a grim harlequinade which amid the awful solemnity of the occasion suggests the pranks of a mountebank. Happily the spectators yesterday were few.

The *Evening News* in Sydney also opined that the 'new hand' was ashamed of his role, and that Blay himself had 'probably become disgusted with his hideous office'. But the paper said the novice appeared to be no 'bungler' and had managed to 'work his man off in a way that would excite the admiration of Mr Dennis himself', referring to Ned Dennis, an executioner who carried out 201 hangings at Tyburn and Newgate in London and Middlesex in the late 1700s.

Charles Dickens later portrayed Dennis as an executioner who was himself executed in *Barnaby Rudge*, the author's character perhaps foreshadowing what Blay thought about due gratitude for his own long service to the Empire:

> When he remembered the great estimation in which his office was

held, and the constant demand for his services; when he bethought himself, how the Statute Book regarded him as a kind of Universal Medicine applicable to men, women, and children, of every age and variety of criminal constitution; and how high he stood, in his official capacity, in the favour of the Crown, and both Houses of Parliament, the Mint, and Bank of England, and the Judges of the land; when he recollected that whatever Ministry was in or out, he remained their peculiar pet and panacea, and that for his sake England stood single and conspicuous among the civilized nations of the earth: when he called these things to mind and dwelt upon them, he felt certain that the national gratitude must relieve him from the consequences of his late proceedings, and would certainly restore him to his old place in the happy social system.

Blay had applied his 'universal medicine' to men and women of all ages, and served as a 'panacea' for the Crown, numerous governors, judges and a line of colonial officials, but he wasn't leaving his place in the colony's social system with any farewell salutes or gratitude.

Gone were the days recalled by the *Bulletin* when the hangman would 'shine in society', the days when the *Mercury* said the executioner was 'a man of note, his "perks" were many, his personality known to all, and he hobnobbed convivially with the horny handed'. They were the days when he frequently had to call for 'ropes, soap and bags for seven', the days when he would perform in front of a thousand people or more.

Now the sheriff's 'veteran aide' was merely required to make the preliminary arrangements for what was a rare execution, this time by a hangman heavy in disguise. While he 'fondly lingered o'er the task' the fact was that 'his hand has lost its cunning for the final coup'.

The status, identity and omnipresence of the hangman had changed, but those judged to have stepped outside the law, even those in their teens like Cooley, could still feel a piece of soaped rope around their neck.

To the clergy, however, Cooley was also a victim, evidence that while some brutality had eased, and the colony had made great progress in its first 100 years, it had not made much progress in criminal punishment and rehabilitation.

Reverend Herbert Finnis said Cooley showed how someone with 'the making of a great and splendid man' had instead got to the point where, aged just 19, he 'had reached a stage of brutality at which all the higher and nobler instincts of his nature had almost entirely ceased to act ... a wild savage of the primeval forest ... he was ready for any act of lust or cruelty'.

Reverend Finnis said that when he asked Cooley how his life had come to this, the young man said it was primarily due to drink, but the clergyman felt there were other reasons which ought to be understood by lawmakers and society. He said Cooley had shown a hard and unkind temperament even at the age of nine or 10, but just when a father or Sunday School pastor might have had some useful counsel he was sent away from home, living without restraint and learning to drink. He was then convicted of an offence while still 'almost a boy', barely 16, and put in Hobart Gaol for 18 months.

Here he was

compelled to associate with hardened scoundrels, who certainly influenced him in any way but the right one ... if the sentence had been reformatory instead of merely retributive and vindictive, he might have here had the higher and yet almost dormant qualities of his nature called out, but as it was the third great downward influence of his life was here brought to bear upon him.

The companionship of one criminal in particular had a terrible remit and bore a fearful fruit after the expiration of his term of imprisonment. 'He has learnt a thing or two here,' they roughly said, as his mother received him at the prison doors.

For three months after his return home, he went on fairly well, and that brings him almost to his 18th year. The work of neglect has been all but completed by a beneficent and shall we say Christian Government ... rabbit shooting and its cruelties, drinking, and standing and dawdling in the public house, all go to prepare him for his two last acts, which bring him into conflict with the authorities.

The end of his life we know too well. Once more the Government authorities deliver him to his relatives, this time a corpse.

This boy of 19 was not a monster of vice; he was not a hardened criminal; but one who could love and worship, pray and feel like any other man, and the very qualities which from want of proper training, and under the wicked system of prison discipline here in vogue, ripened into brutal vices, would, under suitable conditions, have made him a very king of men.

Who is to be the next victim of our national blindness? If it is not one or other of the juvenile offenders now in H.M. gaol it is not our fault. We may not be able to do away with the other evil influences which marred Cooley's life, but we may, aye we must, classify our prisoners. Roads, bridges, ornamental public buildings, what are they if we are making criminals of our people?

Even to the end Cooley was under the influence of hardened criminals. As was the custom for condemned men, gaol officials nominated a 'suitable' prisoner to spend their last night with them. The young man's final company was William Morgan, sentenced to death for committing 'an unnatural act' and 'outraging' a young girl before his sentence was commuted.

On execution day, a typically cool August morning, young Cooley took his final steps to the scaffold, a bunch of violets in his hand. Blay stood by, closely watching someone else do for the first time what he had been doing for half a century.

He would walk the gallows no more, having hanged more than 200 men and women. He handed his rope to a successor who would have to wait 21 years before performing his first unsupervised job at Campbell Street Gaol, then perform only two more before the last hanging in 1946.

Blay had been Her Majesty's hangman for 50 of the colony's first 88 years, the leading man in a long-running theatre of public justice and spectacle. His final performance was as an aged assistant hidden behind gaol walls amid disguise and distaste. His life as the 'finisher' was over.

27

DEATH OF A
HANGMAN

Having trod the scaffold for the final time as *eminent carnificem*, 75-year-old Solomon Blay had well outlived the average lifespan of his fellow convicts of the early 19th century. He was now gaunt and grizzled, wearing the arthritic legacy of too many days and nights in cold stone gaol cells.

'Old Sol' was free of the noose, but not free of memory, trouble, or alcohol.

In pubs and shops he would still be confronted by some who wouldn't let him forget, and there might be a 'warfare of words', as one newspaper reported, with taunts about those who had 'escaped' him.

Some people were curious about executions, and now that he was finished, Blay didn't always shy away from what he had done.

Some said he sometimes took 'a particular delight in recalling the hangings he had performed', and that speaking of one double hanging he said it 'was with the greatest of delight that I hanged those two chaps'.

But he wasn't interested in any more notoriety than he already had. He had only a few brief exchanges with pressmen, and did not, as the *Mercury* reported, 'like English executioners, glory in his shame', a reference to James Berry, who even before his retirement as England's executioner lectured on crime and criminals, producing relics and mementoes.

Like most hangmen doing their best to hide their true identity, Blay maintained a 'mortal horror' of being photographed, according to *The Clipper*:

> All kinds of inducements were offered him to attend and be seated before the camera, but the softest blandishments failed in this matter. This, it was alleged, was due to the eccentricities of a certain person whose taste for the gruesome apparently overcame his natural discretion and who suggested that an enlargement of the old man with a frame formed of the gilded knots of the ropes which had hanged the wretches he had officiated upon would have formed an interesting exhibit for the Royal Society.

Blay himself was finishing as he had started his hanging life; with alcohol his sole companion. His frequent interjections of 'amen' caused laughter at a political meeting in North Hobart in 1886. In 1889, he pleaded not guilty to using obscene language in Brisbane Street, and was fined 10 shillings 6 pence or 14 days imprisonment. In 1890 he was given the same sentence for disturbing the peace, and close to Christmas in 1891 he admitted to being drunk in Liverpool Street and was fined five shillings, or seven days imprisonment.

More seriously, he narrowly escaped death in early 1893, after falling asleep with a candle left burning on a chair in his rented room. Around midnight two constables on street patrol saw the reflection of fire in the window, and managed to put it out.

Later that year the colony as one bought 300,000 raffle tickets at £1 each in the first lottery in the colony, with the Bank of Van Diemen's Land major assets, its own building and Hadley's Orient Hotel, being raffled by liquidators through George Adams, the genesis of the famous Tattersall's empire.

Blay's raffle number didn't come up, but in the lottery of life in the colony he had outlived many.

He had not succumbed, like most colonial hangmen, to depression or suicide. He might have drunk his own silent toast in 1894 on reading how Victorian peer William Perrins, known as 'Jones the hangman', had tired of 'contemptuous leers and persecutions of neighbours' and drank to excess before cutting his own throat.

Blay, too, had been subjected to leers and persecution, used sedatives to calm his nerves and sometimes drank to excess, but he was not in an asylum or a grave.

In June 1987, the *Clipper* cheered:

Set the bells a ringing,
And let the trumpets play,
We cannot raise a man to scrag;
And we've pensioned off old Blay,
The gallows beams have got dry rot,
Gone mouldy in the sun,
And we couldn't raise the elbow grease
Of rope and soap for one!

And a week later, in a satirical piece about a celebratory jubilee procession, it suggested that 'Solomon Blay and the dog snaveller [be] mounted on triumphal car. Implements of their respective trades to be portrayed in flowers and evergreens'.

Eight weeks later there was not only no more calls for 'rope and soap'. There was no more Solomon Blay to call on.

His hometown *Mercury* reported in its 'epitome of news' on Thursday 19 August: 'Solomon Blay, late public executioner, died in Hobart hospital yesterday morning.' Further down, it expanded:

> Death of Solomon Blay — The well-known character Solomon Blay, formerly public executioner, died yesterday at the General Hospital after a short illness. He entered the hospital on Thursday last suffering from dropsy. There is a peculiarity in his record in regard to the number 7. He was sent out from Oxford in 1837, appointed public executioner in 1847 [sic], received a free pardon in 1857, hanged Timothy Walker, the last man he operated on, in 1887, and has now died in 1897.

On the same day, the *Examiner*, under the simple headline 'Solomon Blay' reported:

> This morning Solomon Blay, formerly public executioner, died at the General Hospital, after a short but painful illness. He entered the hospital on Thursday last suffering from dropsy, and succumbed as stated above. He was sent out from Oxford in 1837, and was appointed public executioner in 1847 [sic]. He received a free pardon in 1857. The last man he hanged was Timothy Walker, in 1887.

Dropsy was the term at the time for the swelling of soft tissues due to the accumulation of excess water. Today he might have been said to have suffered oedema, or swelling due to excess fluid, a condition usually caused by heart failure, cirrhosis of the liver and kidney disease. Blay's long life, replete with rope and rum, had taken its toll.

Two days later, in its summary of the week's news, the *Mercury* repeated that 'Solomon Bleay, or Blay, for many years public hangman of the colony, is dead, after spending his last days as a marine store dealer in a small way at the capital. Bleay was at the last a quiet, reserved man, who did not, like English executioners, "glory in his shame" … and of late years he persistently refused to perform the duties of the office.'

It was the first time the hangman's original name of 'Bleay' had been positively used since he first set foot in the colony.

His death was reported throughout Australia and throughout England, including the Manchester *Evening News*, Birmingham

Daily Post and London *Morning Post*.

From the bigger towns of Sydney, Melbourne, Perth, Adelaide and Brisbane, to the smaller townships like Albury, Bathurst, Dubbo, Broken Hill, Maitland, Kalgoorlie and Barcaldine, the nation was told of the passing of the public executioner, with many referencing the peculiarity of the number seven, and that he had retired on a pension.

For some, like the *Zeehan and Dundas Herald*, who regarded him as 'the government man butcher', he needed no introduction or fond farewell. All that needed to be said in its 'concise column' was: 'Solomon Blay is dead.'

The most fulsome report was in the *Clipper*. Under the headline 'Exit Solomon Blay. An Old Time Identity Gone', the Hobart newspaper recognised the significance: 'One of the connecting links between Vandemonia and Tasmania was severed on Wednesday last when old Solomon Blay, erstwhile hangman, shuffled.'

The *Clipper* said it had been suggested 'Old Sol' had never seen a man hanged: 'He would officiate in all the wretched details to the letter, and when the sheriff's signal warned him the lever working the bolt was to be removed, he invariably turned his back upon the victim.'

It also claimed that among Blay's effects was a box 'containing about 200 pieces of knotted rope. These are the knots cut off the ropes of every man he has hanged. They are labelled and ticketed, and form a most interesting collection of relics for those who are that way inclined.'

Whether this was true — and many years later someone claimed an ancestor had talked of discovering a box of his ropes under a bed — infusing facts with fictional embellishment was a familiar and continuing literary technique.

Several newspapers in New South Wales reported that Blay 'was the original' of a famous story, 'Absalom Day's Promotion' by Price Warung, published in 1890 in the *Bulletin*. Warung was the pseudonym of William Astley, a well-known journalist and short story writer, who spent much of his life collecting firsthand testimony of Australian history. He lived and married in Tasmania, and would certainly have been familiar with Solomon Blay.

In Astley's account, a young 'Absalom Day' had broken into a house and been capitally sentenced, and put on the scaffold with 11 others, but after the then-hangman stormed off, saying it was 'a wholesale butcherin'', the sheriff began promising each of the condemned life and a free pardon 'if you will hang the rest'.

Down the line the sheriff continued, being refused each time, until he came to the second-last man, Absalom Day, who gasped: 'I'll do it Mr Sheriff; I'll hang 'em sir — only life sir, only life!'

The *Bulletin* article said after being 'found guilty and sentenced to death on Saturday morning, he [Absalom Day] had won promotion on the Monday'.

After leaving the 11 dangling men, prison chaplain Parson Ford was introduced to a young naturalist from aboard the visiting *Beagle*, and said, 'Proud to know you sir. I only hope we shall be able to show you a thing or two in the colony before you leave.'

'I don't doubt it,' said Charles Darwin, who, the story continued, had just witnessed the execution. 'I have already got some new light on a subject on which I am theorising — the kinship of man with the lower orders of animal life.'

Astley had bastardised Solomon Blay's name and elements of his life, such as his re-appointment as executioner to avoid being sentenced to transportation for life, and used the names of some real convicts among the 12 on the scaffold. But it was a meshing of fact and fiction, for example Charles Darwin visited Hobart in 1836, before Blay had even arrived in the colony.

But Astley had a reputation for convict storytelling akin to Marcus Clarke, and the *Bulletin* was well read, forming some of the popular imagery about Blay.

On his death, most newspapers cited the frequency of 'seven' in his life: while he hadn't been made a hangman in 1847 as most newspapers said, he was sent to the colony in 1837, pardoned in 1857, hanged his last man in 1887 and died in 1897. Others said he had 'seven letters in his Jewish-Christian name', claimed that when hazard, an old dice game and forerunner of craps, was being played he would remark, 'Seven's the main, we'll all throw it some day', and noted he spent seven days in hospital before he 'threw a seven himself and handed in his record to his maker'.

The papers were not sure how many he had hanged. The *Mercury* said he 'used to say he had hanged 99 people, but would never complete the century', but the paper itself reported 13 years before that his toll was then 196, and in 1891 that a replacement was needed for Blay 'who has in his time "turned off" some 200 malefactors'.

The *Northern Argus* in South Australia said he had 'slung about 210 souls into the next world', and some, such as the *Otago Witness* in New Zealand, claimed 'Solomon Blay put to death more criminals than perhaps any other man in the world'.

On the question Blay himself had only ever said, as he did again after his final hanging, 'That is best known to myself'.

He didn't hang more criminals than anyone in the world — another former convict, Alexander Green, despatched 470 in New South Wales — but Blay probably had the highest hang rate per capita and was the Empire's youngest and longest serving hangmen. Through his noose passed an estimated 206 people, who were the human face of an empire's banishment and condemnation of its unwanted — men and women, old and young, white and coloured. Whether they were rightly or wrongly condemned for murder, assault, rape, bushranging, robbery or sodomy, Blay's was the last face they saw.

He heard many curse the cruel lottery of life that saw them become victims of poverty, punishment and alcohol. He heard many apologise to their victims, seek forgiveness and pray for God's mercy, while others proclaimed their innocence and remained fiercely defiant to their last breath.

Blay had seen some men and women walk boldly to the scaffold, while others sobbed and trembled and had to be physically held up. Some waved goodbye to everyone and said some farewell words, others stayed silent and still. Some held hands or kissed a fellow condemned man, some carried a bouquet of flowers, a handkerchief or plait of hair of a loved one. What they had in common was to be hanged by him until they were dead, some quickly from a broken neck, others by agonising strangulation.

The finisher's own finish was alone in a hospital bed. Did he dream the hangman's nightmare of screaming as another led him to the scaffold? Or, like James Berry, did he have a sleepless night 'wishing as I had so often wished that I had never taken on the grim, heartrending and mind-torturing work of the public executioner'? The answer went with him to the Cornelian Bay Cemetery on 21 August 1897. On the Derwent waterfront where he had arrived 60 years before, his body was quietly dropped by an undertaker's rope into his own eternity, not beside his wife Mary but in the pauper section.

In the capital chain of Her Majesty's justice — the various governors, attorney-generals, Supreme Court judges, sheriffs, bishops and clergy — Blay was not publicly farewelled, respected, lauded or rewarded.

While others in this judicial chain played their role with public endorsement, many even knighted, Blay was the only one who personally delivered their decisions, conferring what Marcus Clarke described as 'the Order of the Halter'. While others could afford discretion, he could not. As the under-sheriff's 'operator', Blay's lot was to play the grimmest hand in the grimmest system.

It had been his choice to become and remain an executioner for the term of his natural life, out of expediency to minimise his own punishment and maximise his prospects.

Reflecting King Solomon's words that 'your own soul is nourished when you are kind, destroyed when you are cruel', he had to live with demons and demonisation. That was the price of having an occupation, reputation and status as a merchant of death.

And there was no peace for a hangman, even in death.

In 1904, British soldier Isaac Tyrell recalled in his book *From England to the Antipodes and India, with Startling Revelations* an evening walk with his brother in Hobart in the late 1840s and how 'we met a fine stalwart well-dressed man who accosted my brother in a familiar tone', only to be told this respectable-looking man was 'Solomon Blay, the hangman'.

One of Tyrell's 'startling revelations' was that Blay had once badly misjudged the length of the rope when hanging a tall man called Happy Jack. 'Solomon Blay allowed too much rope with the result that the unfortunate man came down on the lid of his coffin which was in accordance with the then practice kept below the drop, and smashed it. As life was not extinct, Happy Jack had to be finished off by Solomon Blay clinging to his body and strangling him. It was a most revolting sight.'

More than half a century later, in 1960, under the headline 'Hanging lag broke Aust. neck record. The grisly life of Solomon Blay', the *Tasmanian Truth* said his record was 'never likely to be broken ... in the course of his long life he executed 312 [*sic*] of his fellowmen'. The *Truth* said

> even those callous times produced few men less troubled by scruples than Solomon Blay ... no job could have better suited Blay's temperament ... [he had] a sinister geniality ... sent many an unfortunate victim to his doom with a taunt ringing in his ears ... Utterly without human feelings, except where the safety of his own skin was concerned, he entered on his ghastly duties with the greatest enthusiasm ... nothing pleased him better than to be congratulated by the Sheriff on a neat piece of work.

And nearly a century later in 1985, in a full-page feature headlined

'Famed Tasmanian executioner even topped own father', the *Daily Mirror* said Blay was 'the ideal hangman ... apparently, completely without emotions or scruples ... he might as well have been hanging the weekly washing as fellow humans'.

Both newspapers claimed Blay had been called on to hang his own father and two of his brothers. 'To his credit Blay was a little irritated that the authorities had not provided a substitute on that occasion, but when they pointed out that it was impossible to find a stand-in at a moment's notice, he went on with the business with his usual nonchalance,' the papers said. 'The old gentleman protested that it was scarcely the sort of behaviour one expected in a dutiful son, but Solomon merely told him he was lucky not to be in the hands of a novice, and advised him to step quickly on the trap and keep his mouth shut if he wanted a nice clean job.' And as his brothers were of the same height and weight, the same rope would easily do for both.

The facts of Blay's life were remarkable enough without fictional embellishment.

His story was that of a poor Oxford child who resorted to petty crime to survive, was banished as common convict #2598, and became the 'common hangman' by choice. He had lived through the worst and best, as an ancient civilisation's land transitioned to Van Diemen's Land, the place of exile on the edge of an empire, which became Tasmania, a centrepiece in the evolution of *Terra Australis Incognita* to nationhood.

He was referenced in parliaments, pulpits, books, poetry and newspapers because he held the noose, the potent symbol of an empire's cruelty to men, women and children; its corruption, hypocrisy and greed; the lottery of impoverishment and justice; the desperation and brutality of humankind.

But, notwithstanding the hellish birth of Van Diemen's Land, Blay had seen the other side of the coin, the pursuit of a better world: understanding the evolution of life; exploring Antarctica; founding

Melbourne; establishing the first Royal Society branch outside England; championing the earliest national pastimes of regattas, circuses, live theatre, horse-racing, pubs, wood-chopping, golf, cricket and football; introducing apples and salmon; starting major wool and food exports; producing singers who travelled the world; having a governor's wife adopt an Aboriginal child; being open to the social activism of Quakers, Jews, Catholics, Presbyterians, Protestants and Masons; producing the genesis of federation and a constitution; creating the country's first Jewish synagogue, chamber of commerce, commercial power station, electric tramway, port authority, compulsory state education, telephone call, anaesthetic operation and, perhaps most appropriately, the national lottery.

A new world had emerged from the old.

Around the time of Blay's death, Oscar Wilde was penning *The Ballad of Reading Gaol* after his incarceration for 'homosexual offences', juxtaposing the life of an executed man and his own with the line 'each man kills the thing he loves'.

Solomon Blay likely killed something of himself each time he killed another. But the final judgement of Solomon was that in a unique time and place, he had done the job of surviving.

SELECT BIBLIOGRAPHY
AND SOURCES

Abbott, Geoffrey. *Ultimate True Stories of Female Executions*. Wakefield Press, 2007.

Adams, Simon. *The Unforgiving Rope: Murder and Hanging on Australia's Western Frontier*. University of Western Australia, 2009.

Aldrich, Robert. *Colonialism and Homosexuality*. Routledge, 2002.

Alexander, Alison. *Tasmania's Convicts: How Felons Built a Society*. Allen and Unwin, 2010.

Alexander, Alison. *The Ambitions of Jane Franklin, Victorian Lady Adventurer*. Allen and Unwin, 2013.

Alexander, Alison. *The Southern Midlands: A History*. Southern Midlands Council, 2012.

Alleyn, Susan. *An Unsuitable Job for a Gentleman*. www.susannealleyn.com, 2013.

Andrews, Barry (ed). *Tales of the Convict System*. University of Queensland, 1975.

Ballyn, Susan. *Brutality versus Common Sense: The 'Mutiny Ships'*, in Haebich, Anna and Offord, Baden (eds). *Landscapes of Exile: Once Perilous, Now Safe*. Peter Lang, 2008.

Barnard, Edwin. *Exiled: The Port Arthur Convict Photographs*. National Library, 2010.

Bateson, Charles. *The Convict Ships, 1787–1868*. Brown, Son and Ferguson, 1959.

Beckett, Ray and Richard. *Hangman: The Life and Times of Alexander Green*. Nelson, 1980.

Bennett, John Michael. *Sir John Pedder: First Chief Justice of Tasmania 1824–1854*. Federation Press, 2003.

Berry, James. *My Experiences as an Executioner*. H. Snowden Ward (ed). Percy Lund and Co, 1913.

Bolt, Frank. *Old Hobart Town*. Waratah Publications, 1981.

Boxall, George E. *History of Australian Bushrangers*. T. Fisher Unwin, 1899.

Boyce, James. *Van Diemen's Land*. Black Inc., 2009.

Brand, Ian and Stainworth, Mark. *Care and Control: Female Convict Transportation Voyages to VDL 1818–1853*. Flinders University, 1994.

Brand, Ian. *Executions at Campbell Street Gaol, 1857–1946*, Penitentiary Chapel.

Brown, George; Button, David; Mercer, Elizabeth; Mercer, Peter and Rieusset, Brian. *The Penitentiary Chapel Historic Site*. National Trust, 2007.

Button, Henry. *Flotsam and Jetsam*. A. W. Birchall & Sons, 1909.

Causer, Tim. *Anti-transportation: 'Unnatural Crime' and the 'Horrors' of Norfolk Island*. University College, 2012.

Clarke, Marcus. *For The Term of His Natural Life*. Penguin, 2000.

Clune, Frank. *Martin Cash*. Angus and Robertson, 1955.

Cox, Robert. *A Compulsion to Kill*. Glass House Books, 2014.

Crowley, Trudy. *A Drift of Derwent Ducks: Lives of the 200 Irish Convicts Transported Per 'Australasia' from Dublin to Hobart 1849*. Research Tasmania, 2005.

Crowley, Trudy. *Convict Lives in Cascades Female Factory*. Convict Women's Press, 2012.

Davis, Richard P. *The Tasmanian Gallows: A Study of Capital Punishment*. Cat & Fiddle Press, 1974.

Dernley, Syd with Newman, David. *The Hangman's Tale: Memoirs of a Public Executioner*. Pan, 1989.

Desmond, Adrian and Moore, James. *Darwin*. Michael Joseph, 1991.

Donohoe, James Hugh. *Stories and Tales of the Transported Convicts*. J. Donohoe, 1990.

Ellis, John. *Diary of a Hangman*. True Crime Library, 1996.

Emberg, Buck Thor and Emberg, Joan Dehle (eds). *The Uncensored Story of Martin Cash, As Told to Lester Burke*. Regal, 1991.

Emmett, E .T. *Tasmania, by Road and Track*. Melbourne University Press, 1953.

Evans, Stewart P. *Executioner: The Chronicles of James Berry, Victorian Hangman*. Sutton Publishing, 2004.

Forsyth, W. D. *Governor Arthur's Convict System 1824–1836*. Sydney University Press, 1970.

Frost, Lucy and Downes, Christopher. *Footsteps and Voices: A Historical look into the Cascades Female Factory*. Female Factory Historic Site, 2004.

Frost, Lucy and Hamish, Maxwell-Stuart. *Chain Letters: Narrating Convict Lives*. Melbourne University Press, 2002.

Gilchrist, Catie. 'Space, Sexuality and Convict Resistance in Van Diemen's Land'. *Eras Journal*. Monash University, 2006.

Goc, Nicola. *Women, Infanticide and the Press*. Farnham, 2013.

Goodrick, Joan. *Life in Old Van Diemen's Land*. Rigby, 1977.

Harman, Kristyn. *Aboriginal Convicts in Australia, Khoisan, and Maori Exiles*. University of New South Wales Press, 2012.

Hill, David. *1788: The Brutal Truth of the First Fleet*. Random House, 2008.

Hill, David. *The Making of Australia*. Random House, 2014.

Hirst, Warwick. *Great Convict Escapes in Colonial Australia*. Simon & Shuster, 2003.

Howard, Patrick. *To Hell or Hobart*. Kangaroo Press, 1993.

Huett, Sandra. *Only in Tasmania*. Striped Wolf Publishing, 1971.

Hughes, Robert. *Fatal Shore: The epic of Australia's founding*. Vintage Books, 1986.

Jones, Barry. *Dictionary of World Biography*. Information Australia, 1998.

Laurence, John. *A History of Capital Punishment*. Citadel Press, 1960.

Macdougall, J. C. *Thoughts on Convict Management, Captain Maconochie*. John W. Parker, 1839.

Mclean, Ian. *Why Australia Prospered*. Princeton University Press, 2003.

McMahon, Anne. *Convicts at Sea: The Voyages of the Irish Convict Transports to VDL 1840-1853*. Anne McMahon, 2011.

Midgley, Graham. *University Life in 18th century Oxford*. Yale University Press, 1996.

Moore, James. *Convicts of Van Diemen's Land 1840-1853*. Cat & Fiddle Press, 1976.

Newton, John. *A Savage History: Whaling in the Pacific and Southern Ocean*. University of New South Wales Press, 2013.

Oliver, Stephen. *Intercolonial*. Puriri Press, 2013.

O'Neill, Judith. *Transported to Van Diemen's Land: The Story of Two Convicts*. Cambridge University Press, 1977.

Parkhill, Trevor and Kineally, Christine. *Famine in Ulster*. Ulster Historic Foundation, 1997.

Petrow, Stefan. *After Arthur: Policing in Van Diemen's Land 1817-1846*, University of Tasmania, 1999.

Petrow, Stefan. *Military Outrage: the riot of the 96th regiment in Launceston 1845*. Tasmanian Historical Research Association, 2008.

Porter, James. Autobiography. *Hobart Town Almanack and VDL Annual*. William Gore Elliston, 1838.

Porter, Trevor J. *Executions in the Colony and State of Victoria 1842-1967*. The Wednesday Press, 1999.

Pridmore, Walter. *Oatlands, a Colonial Treasure*. Forty Degrees South, 2010.

Reece, Bob (ed). *Irish Convict Lives*. Crossing Press, 1993.

Rees, Sian. *The Floating Brothel*. Hodder, 2001.

Rees, Sian. *The Ship Thieves*. Aurum Press, 2006.

Richmond, Carol. *Banished! Sentences of Transportation from Oxfordshire Courts 1787-1867*. Oxfordshire Black Sheep, 2007.

Rieusset, Brian. *Campbell Street Gaol History*. Brian Rieusset, 2006.

Rieusset, Brian. *Hobart Town 1831*. Brian Rieusset, 1997.

Rieusset, Brian. *The Trial of Margaret Coghlin*. Brian Rieusset, 1997.

Roe, Michael. *Civilisation in Van Diemen's Land? Darwin's Problematic 'Yes'*. Royal Society of Tasmania, 2009.

Shakespeare, Nicholas. *In Tasmania: Adventures At the End of the World*. Random House, 2010.

Sierp, Allan. *Colonial Life in Tasmania: 50 years of photography 1855–1905*. Rigby, 1976.

Sly, Nicola. *Oxfordshire Murders*. The History Press, 2012.

Smith, Coultman. *Shadow Over Tasmania*. Coultman Smith, 1941.

Snow, Samuel. *The Exile's Return*. Cleveland, 1846.

Snowden, Dianne. *A White Flag Burning: Irish Women who Committed Arson*. University of Tasmania, 2005.

Stancombe, G. H. *Highway in Van Diemen's Land*. G. Hawley Stancombe, 1969.

Starck, Nigel. *The First Celebrity: Anthony Trollope's Australasian Odyssey*. Lansdown Media 2014.

Sweeney, Christopher. *Transported: In Place of Death: Convicts in Australia*. Macmillan, 1981.

Swiss, Deborah. *The Tin Ticket: The Heroic Journey of Australia's Convict Women*. Berkley Books, 2010.

Syme, J. *Nine Years in Van Diemen's Land*, J. Syme, 1848.

Tardif, Phillip. *Notorious Strumpets and Dangerous Girls: Convict Women Van Diemen's Land 1803–1829*. Angus and Robertson, 1990.

Von Stieglitz, K. R. *A History of Oatlands and Jericho*. Telegraph Printery, 1960.

Walker, James Backhouse. *Early Tasmania*. Royal Society of Tasmania, 1888.

Webb, Simon. *Executions: A History of Capital Punishment in Britain*. The History Press, 2012.

Weeding, J. S. *A History of Oatlands, Tasmania*. Derwent Printery; I. D. Simpson, 1988.

Weeding, J. S. *A History of the Southern Midlands of Tasmania*. Regal Publications, 1973.

Welsh, Frank. *Australia: A new history of the great Southern Land*. Overlook, 2006.

White, Charles. *Early Australian History: Convict Life in NSW and VDL*. C. and G. S. White, 1889.

Whites, Charles. *History of Australian Bushranging*. Angus and Robertson, 1900.

Wilkie, Douglas. *'Take the Times as They Go, and the Men as They Are': The Stories of John Perez De Castanos, Piedro Caligani and Louisa La Grange*. Melbourne University Press, 2012.

Wylie, Paul R. *The Irish general: Thomas Francis Meagher*. University of Oklahoma Press, 2011.

USEFUL WEBSITES

Australian Dictionary of Biography, *www.adb.anuedu.au*

British Newspapers, *www.britishnewspaperarchive.co.uk*

Companion to Tasmanian History, *www.tas.edu.au*

Convict records, *www.convictrecords.com.au*

Dictionary of Sydney, *www.dictionaryofsydney.org*

Founders and Survivors, *www.foundersandsurvivors.org*

Free Settler or Felon?, *www.jenwilletts.com*

Heaven and Hell Together, *www.heavenandhelltogether.com*, archived at *www.pandora.nla.gov.au/tep/136421*

Macquarie Law School, *www.law.mq.edu.au*

National Archives, *www.nationalarchives.gov.uk*

National Library of Australia, *www.nla.gov.au/trove*

On The Convict Trail, *www.ontheconvicttrail.blogspot.com.au*

Oxfordshire History, *www.oxfordshire.gov.uk*

Parliament of Tasmania, *www.parliament.tas.gov.au*

Penitentiary Chapel Historic Site, *www.penitentiarychapel.com*

Port Arthur Historic Site, Tasmania, *www.portarthur.org.au*

Project Gutenberg Australia, *www.gutenberg.net.au*

Queen Victoria Museum and Art Gallery, *www.qvmag.tas.gov.au*

Southern Midlands Tasmania, *www.southernmidlands.tas.gov.au*

Tasmanian Archives and Heritage Office, *www.linc.tas.gov.au*

Tasmanian Museum and Art Gallery, *www.tmag.tas.gov.au*

The James Gammell Chronicles, *www.jamesgammellchronicles.blogspot.com.au*

ACKNOWLEDGMENTS

Thanks to all those, past and present, whose efforts to write, preserve, understand and share our history have helped influence and sustain this book.

Thanks especially to the mostly anonymous editors and correspondents of early newspapers in Van Diemen's Land, and in turn the mostly anonymous efforts of editors and contributors to Trove, the National Library's rich digital materials resource.

Thanks to all the authors, academics, historians, historic societies, genealogists and family tree compilers who in their own way are continuously revisiting and revealing personal and national stories. I specifically acknowledge the often under-resourced State Libraries of Tasmania and Victoria; Tasmanian Archive and Heritage Office; National Archives; staff and volunteers at the Campbell Street Gaol, especially curator Brian Rieusset and the earlier work of the late

Ian Brand; the Female Convicts Research Centre; Female Factory Research Group; and all those who underpin various convict, shipping and cemetery databases. The collective work, and its democratic access, is a national asset.

I was fortified by the almost immediate interest of Melbourne Books in the first draft manuscript, and then the collaboration of its team, led by publisher David Tenenbaum and editor Chloe Brien, to bring the book to life.

Thanks also to friends and family who helped sustain the project and myself, through timely injections of confidence, criticism and caffeine. I am particularly grateful to Michael Gawenda for his long-standing personal and professional support, and Andrew Rule for his interest and valued advice.

Personal thanks to my ancestors for what they forged. My parents for all they have provided, especially my mother Pat for showing me the windows into Tasmanian history. My late brother Martin for showing courage and grace. Last but not least, Maureen for being so supportive of such an indulgent and time-consuming journey.

THE AUTHOR

Steve Harris is a fourth-generation Tasmanian. Recent research into his own family history, which includes convicts, policemen and settlers, re-ignited a broad interest in aspects of Australia's national story largely forgotten or untold.

He has long been engaged with words and outcomes as publisher and editor-in-chief of *The Age*; editor-in-chief of the *Herald and Weekly Times*; founding editor of *The Sunday Age*; founder of *Melbourne Magazine*; CEO of Melbourne Football Club; and founding director of the Centre for Leadership and Public Interest at Swinburne University. He is a John S. Knight Fellow at Stanford University, a life member of the Melbourne Press Club, and was awarded an Australian Centenary Medal in 2001 for services to the profession and community. This is his first book.

www.ingramcontent.com/pod-product-compliance
Lightning Source LLC
Chambersburg PA
CBHW031042110426
42740CB00048B/787